Guy Hull is the bestselling author of *The Dogs that Made Australia*. He is a qualified and experienced dog behaviourist possessed of an encyclopaedic knowledge of dog breeds, cross-breeds and types, their histories and traits, with a passion for the historic and current role of the dog and other domestic animals in Australian society. Based in the Northern Rivers region of New South Wales, Guy is the editor of *Kelpie Quarterly* online magazine and an editorial partner in and behavioural consultant for Perfect Pets – The Ethical Pet Directory.

# The Ferals that Ate Australia

# Guy Hull

ABC
BOOKS

The ABC 'Wave' device is a trademark of the Australian Broadcasting Corporation and is used under licence by HarperCollins*Publishers* Australia.

**HarperCollins*Publishers***
Australia • Brazil • Canada • France • Germany • Holland • India
Italy • Japan • Mexico • New Zealand • Poland • Spain • Sweden
Switzerland • United Kingdom • United States of America

First published in Australia in 2021
by HarperCollins*Publishers* Australia Pty Limited
Level 13, 201 Elizabeth Street, Sydney NSW 2000
ABN 36 009 913 517
harpercollins.com.au

A catalogue record for this book is available from the National Library of Australia

ISBN 978 0 7333 4176 2 (paperback)
ISBN 978 1 4607 1324 2 (ebook)

Cover design by Darren Holt, HarperCollins Design Studio
Cover images: Rabbit, rat and camel by istockphoto.com; Cat by shutterstock.com; Hat by Smith Archive / Alamy Stock Photo; Hair by Chronicle / Alamy Stock Photo; Horse by Florilegius / Alamy Stock Photo; Boar by Albatross / Alamy Stock Photo; Cane Toad by Album / Alamy Stock Photo; Fox courtesy freevintageillustrations.com; Seascape by Atkins, Samuel, 'HMS *Endeavour* off the coast of New Holland' (1794) courtesy National Library of Australia; Landscape by Joseph Lycett, 'Burwood Villa, New South Wales, the property of Alexander Riley Esqr.' courtesy La Trobe Library, State Library of Victoria; 'Kangaroo dog owned by Mr Dunn of Castlereagh Street, Sydney' (1853), painted by Thomas Tyrwhitt Balcombe courtesy Mitchell Library, State Library of New South Wales; The red kangaroo (*Macropus rufus*) illustrated by Charles Dessalines D'Orbigny (1806–1876) courtesy rawpixel.com; European Starling (*Sturnus vulgaris*) illustrated by the von Wright brothers courtesy rawpixel.com
Author photograph by Adam Klumper
Typeset in Bembo Std by HarperCollins Design Studio
Printed and bound by CPI Group (UK) Ltd, Croydon, CR0 4YY

Dedicated with love to my funny,
darling Kirsty.

# Contents

# Introduction

One sheep station morning was much like another in the last decades of the nineteenth century. It was typically dry, magpies carolled at dawn and sheep were on the move as they got about their day. Galahs cackled and glink-glinked and hung upside down from uppermost branches or flew madcap sorties through the treetops, while just this side of the barbed-wire boundary appeared little excavations: the newly mined overnight earthworks that marked frontline trenches of a remorseless invasion.

Later, when the sun hoisted itself high overhead, the little invaders slept in the appropriated subterranean real estate of giant scrub worms, bilbies, wombats and marsupial moles. Above them, the bewildered grazier sought the shade and stared at his discovery. The diggings presented a benign façade that didn't deceive his whining sheep dogs, who poked questing noses into each new burrow entrance as their master, wrestling with the gravity of the situation and wondering if a few holes were all that much to worry about, rolled a cigarette and scratched his head.

A few holes had none of the drama of the ear-piercing arrival of thousands of corellas, or the hopping anarchy of a hundred thousand mice, or the whirring, roiling maelstrom of a locust swarm. This was something altogether different –

a silent nocturnal incursion; a rapid, capillary-like seeping that won its territory by feet and by yards. The invaders gained ground by expanding their population then scampering forward again and digging in, while the homesteads and towns all slumbered.

This was how the rabbits of earth's greatest ever plague did business. Billions of rabbits sought to occupy every last piece of habitable land and devour every last bit of edible anything. They laid waste to over five million square kilometres of the largest island on earth. They even swam rivers and climbed trees to do it.

*

The animals that feral-bombed Australia are like the uninvited visitors who saw the light on, dropped in, made themselves at home, cleaned out the fridge and never left. That's the way bio-invasion works and, unfortunately for Australia, it's nothing new.

No matter where or when they made themselves at home, the non-native blow-ins tipped the natural order on its head and, in all but one instance, the consequence has been catastrophic environmental imbalance.

The ferals of south-eastern Australia have always played some part in my life. I'm one of Australia's post-war baby boomers, the myxomatosis generation, the first in a hundred years not to live under the thrall of the rabbit. We of the post-World War II generation grew up hearing all about life under the rabbit's regime from our parents and grandparents, who in some cases lived on little else. As a boy, my father had trapped and shot rabbits on the Brewarrina town common to help his mother keep food on the table for a large, ravenous, and impoverished family. The skins of those rabbits earned him a few bob a week, which he gave his mother for housekeeping.

So entrenched was our rabbit culture that even Australia's most successful rugby league team took its moniker from some of their rabbit-merchant players, who trapped their quarry in the sandy, rabbit-infested Botany region and peddled them around South Sydney calling out, 'Rabbitoh! Come and get your fresh rabbits! Rabbitoh!'

Bush-bred family and friends were no help in my early attempts at feral-origin divining. For all my father's bush stories, he had no idea. My knowledge of Australian history ensured I was wryly amused when one of my uncles told me that, 'Wild pigs and rabbits and foxes came out with Captain Cook when he brought out the convicts!'

Oh dear. I found it remarkable that even people who grew up surrounded by ferals had no idea about their origins.

Eventually I got the good oil on Australia's feral story – not out west under the shade of a coolabah tree, but from a book in my local library in Sydney's leafy Hills district. Eric Rolls was a New South Wales grazier and environmentalist. His book *They All Ran Wild*, published in 1969, first revealed the feral story to me and many others. However, now in 2020, the feral situation is much altered. The introduction of new bio-invaders and more recent developments in the war against the long-term ferals has dated that masterful work.

I got my feral animal education from *They All Ran Wild*, though I didn't find it until about ten years after its publication. I often cite the late Mr Rolls and do so with the greatest admiration for his commitment to the tortuous years of painstaking research needed to construct his detailed and entertaining narrative. I'm almost embarrassed that researching *The Ferals that Ate Australia* was easy by comparison.

Then there is the vexing use of the terms 'domestic', 'wild' and 'feral'. Your genuine feral is the domestic animal or livestock gone wild, or the escaped wild farmed animal, like deer. Wild creatures commonly referred to as ferals are the game species: rabbits, hares and foxes. Uncontrolled or free-ranging domestic animals have the same environmental impact as ferals or wild species. Feral cat or domestic? To the devoured bandicoot, what's the difference? Likewise, vegetation is stripped bare alike by domestic livestock, feral livestock and rabbits.

The environment doesn't differentiate between domestic, feral and wild animals. If it's not native, it's damaging, and that'll do me. I've taken that lead and tarred the lot with the one feral brush. Of course, that fundamental simplification is not technically correct, but such trifles should not get within cooee of a good yarn.

So henceforth, 'the ferals that ate Australia' include the vermin stowaways, the poorly controlled pets and domestic stock, the domestic or wild livestock escapees and deliberate releases, the 'seemed like a good idea at the time' approaches and sporting releases, the failed biological controllers, and the illegally imported and released pets.

The truth is that Australia's ferals have had no choice but to obey instinct's irresistible drive to survive amid the unnatural circumstances and turmoil created for them by humans. It's nothing personal, though humans have understandably seen the battles against the 'feral peril' as a war. When you are fighting a creature that threatens your survival, it is difficult to see the conflict in any other light.

It's quite the paradox that Australia, a land so harsh, so dry, so alien, and so unwelcoming, should prove to be vulnerable to bio-invasion. Over the last two hundred years, introduced heritage bio-thieves have dominated and displaced our unique fauna, diluted our faunal identity, and degraded the very essence of Australia.

The bush was once a sparsely populated place. Prehistoric Australia was a lean land, a well-oiled but sparse machine that got by on very little and asked for even less. Before 1788, every terrestrial creature in Australia walked, climbed, dug or hopped on padded mammalian feet, or avian or reptilian feet, or wriggled about on its abdomen. The hoofed ungulates were entirely absent from Australia.

It is hard to imagine, but the western division of New South Wales was originally a pristine environment that required little rain to thrive. It easily coped with the vagaries of El Niño. Its inhabitants placed minimal demand on the land and its resources. Drought was a rare occurrence in naturally dryish prehistoric Australia. The pioneers of western New South Wales agreed that, before livestock overran the region, just one inch of rain was sufficient to spruce the land up and provide luxuriant, long-lasting feed. Yet such was its gross mismanagement that the region averaging 30 centimetres of rainfall a year collapsed under the weight of its invaders.

Apart from the hordes of domestic livestock, outlaw rabbits, foxes, cats, dogs, hares, pigs, deer and goats are more widespread than ever. They often outnumber native herbivores, particularly the most vulnerable little ones. Then there are feral horses, donkeys, cattle, camels and water buffalo; the cane toads, house geckoes, squirrels, tilapia, and gambusia. What a mess!

Prehistoric Australia was an ark shielded from the outside world for millions of years by the protecting hand of isolation. Its unique fauna evolved free from the influences that shaped evolution in other parts of the world, and Australia became the land of the marsupial. Placental mammals dominated the rest of the world but in Australia the only endemic placental mammals were the mostly inconspicuous native bats and small rodents.

Time and technology eventually opened the gates for foreign people and their foreign animals. Prior to the British invasion of Australia – for an invasion it was – Australia's environmental stewards had done a tidy job of keeping everything in balance for around 60,000 years.

British colonisation was the beginning of the end for natural Australia. Since 1788, around ten per cent of Australia's endemic terrestrial mammalian species have become extinct. Compare that to just one extinction since the settlement of continental North America in 1607. Australia's native animal extinctions are the world's worst.[1]

Modern Australia emerged united and prosperous chiefly because of wool. Livestock, principally the merino, was colonial Australia's industrial flagship. But the millions of hard-hoofed sheep that enriched Australians kicked the life out of Australia. From the very outset, conventional farming in New South Wales found itself on the back foot. The poor soil and irregular rainfall was unsuited to intensive agriculture. Ungulates such as the merino are almost all herbivores that consume large amounts of feed and drink vast amounts of water. Australia could have coped with a reasonable number of them, but millions eroded the land and sucked the environment dry. The graziers naïvely expected what appeared to be indestructible grazing land to sustain intensive pastoralism like Britain did, but on a grander scale. But by simply conducting their daily economy, the ungulates trampled the fragile interior. They destroyed pristine vegetation and habitat, displaced millions of native creatures, and drove some species to extinction.

Struggling crops and livestock suffered constant predation by native animals and imported pests, which were unable to resist instinct's powerful urge to make an easier living. Our pastoral pioneers were only able to put down roots by taking war to nature and eliminating the competition.

Their hit list was as long as your arm. Some of their targets were just native creatures that drank water and ate grass. Others, such as the dingo, fox and feral dog, drank water and admittedly ate sheep or crops. All instinctively appreciated the easier living agriculture offered them. Others just got in the way. But as much as pastoralism did its best to exterminate anything that looked sideways at its tempting primary productions, the industry often had a harder job keeping that product happy and at home.

In wool-mad nineteenth century rural Australia, strychnine poison was the pastoralist's attack dog and kingmaker. The dingoes are now gone from most of the sheep lands, and they didn't move out because the new neighbours had noisy parties. Their new neighbours poisoned them out of existence because the dingoes developed an addiction to mutton and lamb. As we shall see, millions of foxes have replaced the dingoes, and laugh at the half-hearted attempts to eliminate them.

Avarice for wool foolishly rolled out the rabbit's red carpet. With native predators such as the dingo, quoll and wedge-tailed eagle virtually eradicated, there was nothing to keep tabs on the little floppy-eared terrors. Wool's reward for all that destruction was to find itself flat on its back in the choking red dust with a rabbit's foot planted firmly on its throat.

Today, fragile Australia is still dealing with the damage caused by all those hard-hoofed animals, domestic and feral. Yet the even bigger feral story is the ravages of 'acclimatisation' and the deliberate release of foreign wild animals. Acclimatisation became the obsession of affluent (usually homesick) British-born gentlemen with more money than sense. They felt it was their patriotic duty to convert Australia into something much more 'British' and far less 'Australian'. The acclimatisers – self-funded individuals or acclimatisation societies – were certainly successful in some of their acclimatisation ventures, and unsuccessful in others. We have them to thank for the rabbit, the fox, the hare, common mynas, starlings, sparrows, redfin perch and other invasive species that proliferate at the expense of Australian native fauna and livestock.

*The Ferals that Ate Australia* is chiefly the story of how these concurrent acts of nineteenth century environmental recklessness – agriculture and acclimatisation – converged to start a feral war that devastated the environment and stunted modern Australia's agricultural, economic and social development.

One hundred and fifty years on, and at incalculable cost, that inconclusive conflict rages yet. Just imagine how much healthier, wealthier and happier Australia would be if that pointless, totally avoidable ravaging never happened in the first place.

# Australia's First Feral

All feral species in Australia are native wannabes – square pegs in round holes that deplete and destroy the environments that support them. The carnivorous ferals – the foxes, cats and dogs – plus the omnivorous pig and cane toad indiscriminately exploit anything and everything that moves or doesn't.

Only one invasive species has ever possessed the wherewithal to morph itself into a round peg, capable of working with Australia's natural grain rather than against it. That animal was so influential that it not only got in step with the natural order but rearranged it and established a bio-invasion precedent and blueprint that has so far proven impossible to replicate.

The dingo was once a companion dog that became Australia's first feral. It dominated the continent, quickly establishing its niche at the top of the ecosystem. By that time, the people of Australia accepted it as part of the natural order and their culture. When they enshrined it in their folklore, it was a feral dog no longer. How long all that took is anyone's guess – several hundred years at least. Even if it took thousands, that's some achievement. But the prehistoric feral dog that commandeered Australia was no ordinary dog.

Human agency is the cause of most bio-invasion. Someone made it happen. The generic South-east Asian dog arrived in

Australia's tropical north somewhere between 3500 and 5000 years ago as the shipmate of the Lapita people, who colonised Melanesia and Polynesia, and sometimes visited northern Australia in their seagoing canoes. These dogs were companions, pets valued for many of the same reasons we value our dogs today. Researchers believe that the visiting Lapita gave as few as one pair to Aboriginal people as a gift. It is possible, however, that the dogs that arrived may have escaped a Lapita staging camp or even survived shipwreck, or some other similar circumstance. If Aboriginal people did receive puppies as gifts, they were certainly a foreign placental novelty for the world's most isolated people.

The Asian dog was, and still is, quite dingo-like. It was a stranger, a large placental mammal, a barking, howling anomaly in the land of the mostly silent marsupial. The only placental mammals in Australia were the bats and native rodents.

By today's fur-baby standards, the Asian dog of 5000 years ago was hardly domesticated. In South-east Asia today, those same breeds are more naturally suited to life on the fringes of human society than as beloved, devoted family pets. As such, the dog's questing, adventurous spirit may have been too much for its new owners, and it was only a matter of time before it gained its independence from Australia's humans. In fact, the process of independence probably happened within the first generation of Asian dogs to arrive.

Only skinny dogs turn wild. Hunger can create a powerful bond between humans and dogs but, unmanaged, a dog's hunger can weaken and destroy that bond. Just as domestic dogs turn feral today by having too much hunger and too much freedom, the Asian dogs in northern Australia would have roamed further and further to feed themselves ... and then just kept on going.

The dog is the second-most adaptable creature on earth. It can live just about anywhere. It is far more adaptable than the wolf, way more than any of the big cats, and almost as adaptable as its sometimes best mate, the human. That flexibility makes for a successful invader and, in its complete continental conquest, it set the standard for feral invasion of Australia. It went forth in numbers, but it did not overpopulate or harass humans. In fact it appears the new dog mostly kept on the humans' right side.

Australia's prehistoric feral dog proved to be an exceptional coloniser. It was flexible in its hunting habits, and not at all fussy about what it ate. It changed the predatory hierarchy on mainland Australia and its accessible islands, eliminating the carnivorous opposition and filling the vacant niches, colonising every habitable corner of the continent without destroying it.

Because the Asian dog invaded thousands of years ago, it is easy to completely miss the ugly side of the conquest. It was no bloodless coup. The Asian dog drove at least two native species into extinction – three if you include the flightless bird we know as the Tasmanian native hen, which was once common on the mainland. That's a lot of killing, and things got messy. How the dog fully changed the ecosystem we shall never know.

The emerging dingo outcompeted the marsupial thylacine by being bigger, smarter, and better built to kill large prey.[1] The thylacine had a greater bite force than the dingo, but it was less capable of holding onto struggling prey, and therefore restricted to preying on smaller marsupials. Dogs have a smaller energy requirement than that of the thylacine and, coupled with their instinct to make the easiest, safest living possible, they would have also preferred smaller prey that was easier and safer to kill, and easier to drag back to the den for puppies to feed on when they were hunting alone. This put them on a collision course with the thylacine.

The dog enjoyed distinct advantages over the thylacine in size, brains and numbers. Bergmann's Rule is a biological law that states that, within a broadly distributed population of a species, individuals grow larger in colder environments. The mainland thylacines were much smaller than those found in Tasmania, and much smaller than the feral dogs. The female thylacines were hardly larger than a fox terrier.

Large predators hate smaller predators. The big cats kill the smaller cats at every opportunity and wolves will not tolerate smaller canines like dogs and coyotes. Dogs hate foxes and cats, and there is no doubt the feral dog had it in for the thylacine. The thylacine brain was also only half the size of a dingo's, so it is probable they were severely handicapped when it came to matching wits with the dog (like a lot of people).

In competition with dogs, the thylacines were severely outnumbered. The feral dog could fight its battles as a family group whereas the thylacine was strictly a loner. Against the highly mobile, organised canines, the thylacine stood no chance. The natives had no effective defensive strategies against the sudden appearance and attack of alien invaders. That's why invasive species are so successful.

Science attributes the thylacine's extinction on the mainland mostly to climate change and a shift in Aboriginal land-use patterns. However, there's no question that the arrival of the Asian dog exerted its own pressure on the native mammal – the relentless dogs conquered all before them in short order.

*

The dog's ability to become attached to humans no doubt made it a much more likeable creature than the reclusive thylacine or the cranky little Tasmanian devil. The Asian dog endeared itself to the people who saw human-like characteristics in it and realistically viewed it for what it was – an efficient and necessary part of the workings of life, and in some cases, something of a valued, renewable domestic resource: a part-time pet.

But even though there was a regular consorting between the species, the dingo remained a wild creature that only tolerated human control while it was young and totally dependent. As soon as it got big enough to care for itself, the dingo nicked off before it was kicked out.

The dingo eats anything, and the easier the meal, the better. Unlike its feral dog ancestor, it often hunts alone, sometimes in pairs, but rarely as an entire family except when exploiting carrion or tackling large dangerous game like kangaroos. Harassing little rodents or lizards out of their burrows, digging up turtle eggs, or taking young birds from ground nests is an easy, one-dingo job that spreads the predation around and doesn't over-harvest any one prey species. Dingoes have large territories which provide them with enough opportunities for survival.

The dingo may have been a genuine feral animal when it arrived in this country during the Neolithic age, but it had a couple of thousand years in which to establish itself as a genuine wolf subspecies and a naturalised Aussie to boot. It has long been an integral component of the Australian ecosystem and, as a native, it is itself now threatened by the new feral dog breeds that have arrived since British invasion.

Does the Australian ecosystem have the wherewithal to adjust to the presence of other ferals and eventually integrate them into the ecosystem as it did the dingo? Could the fox, for example, one day qualify as a native? Or the rabbit? One shudders at the thought that creatures such as the cane toad might one day become natural components.

The dog that became the dingo was the advance party of further feral invasions. Time finally arrived for the southern land when Lieutenant James Cook stepped ashore in Botany Bay in 1770. Australia couldn't conceive it or hear it, but the clock had begun ticking. And the modern feral destruction of native Australia would leave nothing to the imagination.

# PART ONE

# Phillip's Ferals

The First Fleet sailed into Port Jackson on 26 January 1788, carrying all the common farm animals that one might expect from European travellers seeking to establish a prison colony that might one day be self-sufficient. The livestock consisted of six black Cape cattle, provisioned on the journey from a resupply in the Cape of Good Hope in South Africa; six horses; forty-four sheep; thirty-two hogs; and nineteen goats. Of the six common barnyard species, only the donkey didn't make the trip, which was odd because beasts of burden would have been handy in New South Wales. Among the poultry were over a hundred fowl, eighty-seven chickens, thirty-five ducks, twenty-nine geese, eighteen turkeys, and five rabbits (the Royal Navy considered rabbits to be poultry). Then there were the companion animals: Governor Phillip's greyhounds and 'puppies', and Reverend Johnson's cats and some kittens.[1]

Other than the harmless, temporary poultry, every one of the above species would one day contribute to the destruction of Australia. Not that Englishmen then or later had any inkling that their stock, so benign at home, could run wild and destroy this harsh, hostile place they all feared and hated. That sort of thing didn't happen in England, where one's livestock behaved as one's livestock should. But this wasn't England.

Governor Arthur Phillip arrived with an ill-placed confidence in New South Wales. James Cook and Joseph Banks, who had written New South Wales a glowing report card, had chanced upon the country lush and verdant, and the weather on its best behaviour during a balmy 1770 autumn. The First Fleet arrived in high summer, when the weather was at its blistering worst and the land, other than drenchings from terrifying summer electrical storms around Sydney, was parched.

At least they had made it. They had just survived an eight-month journey around the world without losing a ship. The people disembarked, yards for the stock were built, and the livestock were brought ashore on 29 January. Everyone was happy to have survived the journey, but no one was happy to be in foreign, frightening New South Wales except the governor.

CHAPTER 1

# Cattle Head for Greener Pastures

T hree months before arriving in Sydney Harbour, the eleven ships of the First Fleet had made it safely to Table Bay at the Cape of Good Hope to refit, repair, reprovision and embark all the livestock they could carry before they cast off for the last and most perilous leg of their journey.

As John Hunter, the captain of the *Sirius*, Arthur's second in command and private artist and journalist, recorded:

> The officers on board the transports, who were to compose the garrison, had each provided themselves with such livestock as they could find room for, not merely for the purpose of living upon during the passage, but with a view of stocking their little farms in the country to which we were going; every person in the fleet was with that view determined to live wholly on salt provisions, in order that as much live stock as possible might be landed on our arrival.[1]

The colony's future judge advocate, David Collins, was impressed with the cattle. 'The meat of the Cape cattle was excellent,' he wrote. 'The black cattle were large, strong and remarkable for the great space between their horns.'[2]

The wait for the approval of the provisions kept convicts chained in the holds and unnecessarily extended the misery of their nine months' voyage, but it also caused the fleet to sail into appallingly bad late-season weather and furious seas in the Southern Ocean. Captain Hunter recorded the stresses this placed on the unfortunate cattle:

> The poor animals were frequently thrown with much violence off their legs, and exceedingly bruised by their falls, although every method, which could be contrived for their ease and comfort, was practised; the ship was very ill fitted for such a cargo; and the very lumbered condition she had constantly been in rendered it impossible to do more for them, except by putting slings under them; a method which, when proposed, was rejected by those to whose care and management they were intrusted; from an idea, that they would entirely lose the use of their legs by such means, although it were only practised in bad weather.[3]

At the beginning of May 1788, just three months after their arrival, the stock brought on the fleet was doing alright, except the fat-tailed sheep, which were rapidly dying. The entry in Governor Phillip's journal suggests the cause was poisonous grass:

> The rank grass under the trees, unfortunately proved fatal to all the sheep purchased by Governor Phillip, on his own and on the public account. Those which private individuals kept close to their own tents, and fed entirely there, were preserved. Hogs and poultry not only thrive but increase fast.[4]

We now know it was sheep scab that made the poor beasts suffer so, and those kept close to their humans (and away from the contagious, scab-infected sheep) were saved from the worst of it. At least the pigs and chooks were breeding up. But then Governor Phillip, in an act of unfathomable flippancy – or worse, blatant disdain of the indisputable scientific fact that it's very bad luck to tempt fate – imprudently wrote, 'the black cattle will doubtless succeed as well, and it will be easy in future to secure them from straying.'[5]

Oh dear! No sooner had he dangled that irresistible morsel before fate's drooling maw than the supposedly 'easy to secure' cattle, left momentarily unattended by a convict named Corbett, strolled out of Sydney and disappeared into the bush. Goneski!

It was a big deal for Sydney. They were short on rations and couldn't afford the loss of two bulls and four heifers. The colony's judge advocate, David Collins, stated that Corbett, despite warnings that he'd forfeit his life if any harm befell the cattle, was in the habit of leaving them alone.[6] Seeing which way the wind was blowing, Corbett likewise made off into the bush.

The authorities fruitlessly searched for Corbett and the cattle for a month. Eventually the governor thought they must have fallen prey to the local Aboriginal people. Poor old Edward Corbett staggered back into the colony weeks later, emaciated and worn out by the privations he suffered while hiding in the bush. Marine Captain and journalist Watkin Tench reported that during repeated examinations it was plain that Corbett was clueless as to where the cattle might be and was in no way involved in having driven them off, as originally assumed. The privations he endured in the bush did not save him from the scaffold.

The cattle making off was always going to happen. It's what unrestrained cattle in Australia do. This lot were the first, and they certainly wouldn't be the last. Besides, after the horrific ship-borne ordeal endured by these unlucky creatures, it's hardly surprising they developed an aversion to humans.

Phillip should have slaughtered the lot on arrival and salted the beef. It would not have lasted long with so many hungry mouths to feed, but at least they would have gained some benefit from the cattle. Now it was too late.

For seven years, no one gave the black cattle much of a second thought. But in October 1795, two trusted, but unnamed, convict kangaroo hunters, armed with muskets, butchery equipment and kangaroo dogs set out from Sydney, and there, in the little-known country to the south-west in the vicinity of the Nepean River, they saw a large herd of black cattle.

They hurried back to Sydney and reported their find, but Governor Hunter, who had succeeded Phillip, was preoccupied with administrative matters and could not leave his duties, so he sent Henry Hacking, a sailor with a colourful but dependable reputation, to investigate. Hacking and the two convict hunters found the cattle in the same place. They returned and led Hunter and a party of other officers on a two-day ride to view the cattle. Crossing the Nepean towards the end of the second day they found the herd, which they estimated to number around sixty.

Hunter and his party camped for the night but there was discussion about whether the cattle found were the lost Cape cattle or another herd that might have been endemic to the region for some time. Hunter thought they should shoot a calf and examine it. Hacking and the two convict hunters hid in wait for the mob to pass so that they might take a clean shot at a youngster, but a bull caught their scent and came up behind them so furiously that it was either him or them. They shot the bull, which had the build of the Cape cattle, including the widespread horns, the moderate hump between shoulders, and a short thin tail, similar in type to the Drakensberger cattle of today, though no doubt not as well-bred or conditioned.[7]

Hunter now had the self-propagating beef resource the colony needed. The loss of the cattle in the first instance might have cost Edward Corbett his life, but in the fullness of time it demonstrated that beef cattle could survive wild New South Wales. The dingoes, the Aboriginal peoples, the environment and climate had not managed to exterminate them. And, happily, the icing on the cake was the discovery of a large tract of superior grazing land, which became known as the Cowpastures (near modern-day Camden).

After that close brush with the belligerent bull, and after shooting and partly consuming a large calf that noisily adopted them and could not be convinced to return to the herd, Hunter's party headed back to Sydney. They had to dodge a bushfire to the west of Sydney at Prospect to do so, and naval surgeon (and later explorer) George Bass wrote that the weather was so oppressively hot that a small terrier that accompanied the party died of heat exhaustion.

The governor took another ride out to check on the cattle in June's cool weather of 1796. He found them again easily, and surveyed what he described as the finest country yet discovered in New South Wales from the top of the highest hill in the area, which he named Mount Hunter. During this excursion Hunter's party counted ninety-four head. But since the government's own livestock had received a resupply in the intervening years, Hunter decided to leave the herd undisturbed and to prohibit the crossing of the Nepean River so that they could multiply in peace. The threat of starvation no longer haunted the colony and there was no urgent need to cull the cattle of the Cowpastures.

In 1801, the wild cattle at the Cowpastures numbered around 600 head and Governor King, Hunter's successor, had a hut built for an overseer to ensure there was no poaching there. In December 1803, Governor King went to look over the cattle himself, and the herd's size was estimated to be between 3000 and 5000. It appears there had been more than the one mob of escaped cattle in Sydney's south-west and they had combined.[8]

Governor Lachlan Macquarie visited the Cowpastures in 1810 and estimated the wild cattle to number between 4000 and 5000. Always one for capital improvements, Macquarie had stockyards built at the Cowpastures to tame or slaughter the beasts. Over the next few years, he set up other stockyards around the region.

Protecting the cattle was extremely difficult to enforce. Local settlers were illegally catching or shooting them, and stealing horses to run down the wild cattle became commonplace. In 1816, three men arrested and charged for poaching the feral cattle suffered the death penalty as an example and deterrent to others.[9]

Around 900 wild cattle were sold or incorporated into the government's domestic herds by the early 1820s. They were the lucky ones. Cowpastures became the centre of John Macarthur's growing wool industry, and the animals had become a liability that the government could no longer bear. They were dangerous and destructive to local farming infrastructure and to the local merino sheep. Five thousand sets of hoofs stomping around the place would have drastically changed the nature of even the most fertile downs of what we now call the Macarthur region. One Sydney newspaper said that the wild herd was 'dangerous and a nuisance and demoralizing to cattle of quieter education and better breeding'.[10] Governor Major–General Sir Thomas Brisbane ordered their destruction in 1824. The feral cattle of the Cowpastures had run their course and were all gone by 1824. No one mourned their extinction.

\*

The chief by-product of nineteenth century beef-cattle farming was feral cattle. No matter how well managed unfenced cattle were, there were always escapes. Without fencing, stockmen had to keep in regular contact with their stock and keep them used to human control. That is easier said than done. The difference between domestic and wild cattle was as little as a week or two and, over the years, wild cattle were a common and at times dangerous fact of life in rural Australia.

Cattle usually become feral because they're missed in musters. In the mid-twentieth-century, experienced cattlemen estimated that on the huge cattle runs in the Northern Territory anything up to twenty-five per cent of a station's herd lived and died as feral creatures in the scrub.[11]

Cattle also made off when being walked to markets or other holdings. This may have occurred when they 'rushed' or stampeded in large numbers. In 1959, drovers lost almost 600 head, which rushed from a mob walking from the Kimberleys in Western Australia to Queensland.[12] In the 1800s, it was also common for individual recalcitrants to break away from a moving mob and make off into the bush. Cattle dogs were an enthusiastic and mostly effective remedy for that problem.

Beef cattle would play a secondary role to wool in Australia's development, but in the early days cattle got a good head start. Large private producers continually imported better stock and selected large runs to raise their beef. It was difficult work with little in the way of fencing to keep cattle quiet and contained.

The Hall family were one of the largest of several large-scale beef producers in colonial Australia. In all they eventually controlled over a million acres (405ha) that stretched from the Hawkesbury River northwards through New South Wales and into central Queensland at Surat. The Halls also owned their own holding and sale yards in Sydney at Liberty Plains, now Auburn.[13] They had plenty of cattle and they had plenty of trouble with them.

Historian Bert Howard believes the Hall brothers lost a mob of around 200 head in particularly rough country early in the 1800s. If 200 head of cattle decide they are no longer going to play the game, then there is little a couple of blokes on horses can do about it. It appears the loss of these cattle was the impetus for Thomas Hall to develop his Hall's heelers, the direct ancestor of Australia's cattle dogs.

For around a century cattle, domestic and feral, were damaging the native bush everywhere they went. Hundreds of cattle would have inflicted an enormous amount of damage on the once-pristine environment. Cattle are hard on thin-soiled country such as the interior of Australia. In hilly country they do damage dislodging ground cover in scrambling up and down slopes. They trample river and creek beds, and wallow, defecate and urinate in water holes and waterways.

Anywhere there was free-ranging beef farming, feral cattle established themselves. They survive best where the country is most dense, rugged, or inaccessible, but they're not a feral that tends to have long-lived populations. Wild cattle are either too troublesome or too valuable to be allowed to live independently for long, and these days the only remaining herds are in the most remote country across Australia's north.

The cattle of early New South Wales were pretty darn rough. Thousands of unmanaged cattle would make a life for themselves in the scrub. These feral beasts, like the cattle of the Cowpastures, developed a reputation for independence and resenting outside interference.

Wild cattle roamed throughout unfenced pastoral Australia, and typically became a dangerous nuisance wherever they established themselves. It wasn't until the late nineteenth century, when wire fencing became commonplace, and rail or road transport superseded droving, that their toll on the environment diminished.

# CHAPTER 2

# Brumby's Hawkesbury Horses

Two stallions and four mares embarked at the Cape of Good Hope and arrived with the First Fleet in 1788. Shipments of saddles and working farm horses followed, and horses escaping into the bush would have happened as a matter of course. In the early days in Australia, when horses were in short supply, most people, including pastoralists, rode Shanks's pony (they walked). Pedestrian pioneering inevitably resulted in stock losses. Much the same as with the feralisation of cattle, early Australian pastoralism inadvertently offered excellent opportunities for horses to run wild. New country came without paddock fences, so escape was common.

Horses first turned feral on the fringes of expanding Sydney. Even though there was a great shortage of horses in New South Wales in the formative years, by the 1830s it was reported that 'bush horses' abounded in the hills around the town.[1] That was to be expected. People lose stock. James Brumby certainly did.

James Brumby was born at Scotton, Lincolnshire in 1771.[2] As a private in the New South Wales Corps he is known to have been in Sydney from around 1794. Around this time, the governor granted him 25 acres (10ha) at Hunter's Hill but later revoked this grant. In 1797, Brumby received a grant of 100 acres (40ha) at Mulgrave near Windsor on the Hawkesbury

River. There he bred horses, which were still in short supply in the colony.

In 1804, and promoted to the rank of sergeant, Brumby left New South Wales with a group led by Colonel William Paterson to establish the northern Van Diemen's Land settlement at Port Dalrymple. He left behind his horses, which somehow became feral and subsequently known as 'Brumby's horses'. Before long, all feral horses became known as 'brumbies' and they'd do alright in the bush because they were way too fast and way too big for dingoes to bother with.

Australia's feral horse problem arose wherever horses went. Before the railway or the motor car, the horse was your means of transport if you could afford it, as well as an important draught animal. Horses transported people and goods on their backs, pulled carriages and coaches, worked in mines, on farms and stations, and had to be tied up, hobbled or fenced to keep them from roaming.

Like cattle, they escaped from properties or were lost by drovers. Escaping muster was, and remains, a major cause of station horses turning feral. Droving plants always travelled with a mob of spare mounts and it was the horse tailer's job to hobble them at night. If the horses made off, the drovers had to keep moving; there was no time to chase after the runaways. Drovers lost hundreds of horses over the years, many of which joined or formed feral mobs.

Feral horses proved a terrifying problem for the environment, for farmers and for travellers, as an 1867 article in *Illustrated Australian News for Home* described:

The incident occurred last summer on the Lachlan plains, N.S.W., to two well-known squatters of Riverina. They

27

were travelling in a light-four-wheeled buggy, with a pair of Cobb and Co.'s coach horses, and when well out on the plain a large herd of wild horses were startled by their approach. one mob bore down towards them headed by a large black stallion, and this animal charged madly to within a hundred yards of the vehicle, when he brought up suddenly, raising his head and rearing savagely as only such creatures can rear, the mob meanwhile thundering round in wild career.

The buggy horses, much startled, were difficult to control. one of the gentlemen alighted, and with a branch of stunted scrub kept the brute at bay. Fortunately a wire fence which runs across the plain was within a quarter of a mile, and towards it the party retreated until the gate was gained, when it was hastily passed and banged in the face of the wild horse which was attempting to follow, and so perplexed him that he retired to the mob. His object seemed to be to attack the harness horses, and to the travellers the position was one of extreme danger.

These wild horses on the plains of the Lachlan and Murrumbidgee are becoming a perfect scourge, and though naturally shy, are at a certain season of the year, dangerous to approach. The squatters lose many stock horses and brood mares by these joining the mobs of wild animals, which come down at night to the streams and waterholes.[3]

It wasn't only coach travellers or squatters who had to be wary, as this warning in the *Riverina Recorder* indicates:

In brumby country, the passing traveller must needs tend his horses closely; for the young brumby stallions, constantly driven from their haunts by the older sires, wander in search of companions, and show marvellous intelligence and tact in taking these, when found, into seclusion. It is always a difficult matter to recover stray stock from the brumby mobs. The term 'with the brumbies' is a common one throughout bush in Australia to signify hopelessly lost. Portions of western New South Wales and southern Queensland were some years ago almost devastated by brumbies; and all sorts of devices were resorted to by squatters to rid themselves of the pests. Many sheep owners fenced in their waterholes with barbed wire in such a way that, nothing larger than a sheep could enter to drink.[4]

For farmers and graziers, wild horses were a constant enemy, competing for food and water with other stock, damaging infrastructure and luring domestic horses, especially mares, away to join the mob, and/or inseminating brood mares with inferior seed. People who live with feral horses lose their sense of humour because they are such a bad influence on their domestic horses.

The same problems were seen across the country. In 1927 the behaviour of wild horses became an issue around Wanneroo, 40 kilometres north Perth:

Wanneroo is well watered by natural springs, and all the year-round feed in plenty abounds there. It has, therefore, become the natural home for generations of unclaimed horses, who, freed from the bondage of men, have established a colony of their own. Most of these horses run on legs which incline towards each other at the knees.

Hardly any are vigorous enough to pull a goat cart. Their lack of physical charm is a minor detail when compared with their evil tendencies.

The settlers affirm that the wild horses frequently lure the tame ones into the bush, where it is exceedingly difficult to discover their whereabouts: and, further, that when people are driving along the roads the wild horses dash out upon them and frighten both man and beast. The settlers have been advised that they have the remedy in their own hands, and that with powder and shot they can rid themselves of the nuisance.[5]

*

In 1901, an article on feral horses in the *Albury Banner and Wodonga Express* noted that wild horses were getting rare in New South Wales. One subscriber wrote to say that forty years ago he saw mobs of brumbies within fifteen miles of West Maitland, and they were everywhere in the country from there to Queensland.[6]

But there were places where brumbies would never relinquish their territories, including the Snowy Mountains of New South Wales and Victoria. The brumbies of the Snowy Mountains were made famous throughout Australia thanks to the poems of Banjo Paterson, and obviously considered stock of some worth, if this report from the *Snowy River Mail* is anything to go by:

On the Dargo High Plains, for instance, those horses are, perhaps 100 strong. When the snow season arrives, they move down from the 5000 feet altitudes to the unoccupied valleys. occasionally the stockmen employed by the cattlemen who hold grazing rights to the mountain pastures try to catch and break them in. only an expert country rider would essay the task. The going is almost precipitous and covered with basaltic boulders, snow gums and other timber.

The mount of the stockman is fed on oats and chaff. It easily outlasts the horses subsisting on the watery grasses of the heights. The wild horses are run to a standstill, roped and then taken to the homestead. Some valuable stock horses are thus obtained. Among the cattlemen are riders, hardy, alert, wiry and tireless. They take a joy in wild-horse hunting, finding in it plenty of adventure.[7]

If there was any decline in brumby numbers, that was about to change. By the turn of the century, the motor vehicle, with its internal combustion engine, was about to put thousands of horses out of their jobs. Its first casualties were the beasts of burden: camels and donkeys, which serviced the interior and north-west, then horses, which worked everywhere else and had superseded bullocks. It wasn't only draught animals. Horses bred as remounts for the British army in India and Egypt were made redundant and turned off properties as mechanisation took over defence forces. Across the country, motorised transport displaced the working and saddle horse. Some redundant horses retired into secure paddocks to live their lives out generally forgotten. Those released off property formed feral mobs that bred up to troublesome numbers.

Everywhere around Australia people were turning horses loose as soon as they cranked over their new lorries. And brumby mobs were forming in all shapes and sizes. In the

Pilliga Scrub in western New South Wales, a large population, faced with dwindling fodder in the scrubland, resorted to feeding on the feral prickly pear that infested the region and large portions of eastern Australia country. These brumbies descended from excellent domestic stock and had taken to invading the town of Gwabegar and creating a dangerous nuisance of themselves.[8]

In 1948, the rugged Wolgan and Newnes districts north of Lithgow, New South Wales, were home to hundreds of wild Shetland ponies that defied all attempts at capture by professional trappers and circus promoters. The ponies, which allegedly had the agility of mountain goats, thrived in steep mountains, canyons and thick scrub.

The ponies had worked in the shale-oil mine at Newnes. Their average height was around a metre and they had hauled rail trucks through the tunnels in the mine. After the works closed, the ponies somehow found their way into the bush. The king of the ponies was a wily old dapple-grey stallion with a flowing silver mane. He was only 12 hands (120 centimetres). Scores of people set traps for the ponies, but the animals were invariably too cunning for capture. Their eventual fate is unknown.[9]

During the late nineteenth and early twentieth centuries, feral horses were everywhere apart from the driest and wettest regions. Now they remain only in pockets around Australia. While the brumbies of the Snowy Mountains are Australia's highest profile feral horses, the largest concentrations remain in the northern half of the continent wherever large-scale cattle stations have traditionally relied on horses for stock work. They are absent from the Kimberly region of north-west Western Australia primarily because of their susceptibility to walkabout — otherwise known as Kimberley disease — a virulent condition caused by eating rattlepod plants.

Whether to allow the continued presence of feral horses in several national parks is an ongoing debate, with passionate arguments for and against. There's no question they're degrading the alpine environment, and conservationists want them eliminated, but brumbies have a strong emotional hold over a great many Australians, who have no stomach for brumby culling. That hasn't stopped the grim work of feral-horse destruction for over a century by the folks at pastoralism's sharp end.

# CHAPTER 3

# Goats Take Over Sydney Town

The goat is a creature that loves the dark side. A goat only tolerates domestication because it hasn't yet worked out a way to escape it. Like the cat, the goat is born with an independent nature.

Nineteen goats arrived in New South Wales on the First Fleet in 1788. Also like cats, goats are keen sailors. They are tailor-made for sea travel: small, clean, good doers on short rations, outgoing and extroverted, and have incredible balance, which holds them in good stead during a nasty blow. Additionally, they make excellent eating, provide fresh milk in conditions that would have long killed a milking cow, and they are not shy at reproducing while at sea.

Every home in the Sydney colony needed fresh milk, and goats were far cheaper and easier to maintain on small allotments than a milking cow. As they were small and hardy, ate a range of plants and provided milk and meat, they were convenient livestock for early Sydneysiders. The problem was that goats will be goats and are extremely difficult to contain.

Goats laugh at conventional fencing and move around their localities at will. The grazing or browsing is always better on the other side of the fence. As goat numbers increased, hundreds escaped their yards and mixed in large loose mobs, which destroyed gardens and vegetable plots, causing a great civic nuisance. An 1801 proclamation from Governor Philip Gidley King regarding cur dogs also included wandering goats. Their owners had to contain their goats or face fines.

Out on the settlement's farming periphery, the dingo was still king and any smallish livestock turning feral was making a temporary lifestyle choice. In 1794, before agricultural pioneer and colonial contrarian John Macarthur got into merinos, he wrote to his brother James in England claiming that he owned 250 acres (100 ha) of land, three horses, two cows, a hundred and thirty goats and one hundred hogs.[1] There is no way you could keep that many goats and pigs contained and managed without letting them free range to forage during the day. They'd all be doing their fair share of environmental damage, but they, like all medium-sized stock of the time, were also at great risk.

Goats are particularly vulnerable to dingo predation and have never been able to coexist with them. Medium- and small-sized livestock were easy kills, so dingoes kept the smaller ferals like goats under control in grazing country. It wasn't until the dingo was a memory in the open grazing lands that feral goats began to flourish.

When Sydney became more urbanised, the settlement's goat problem started to abate. Sydney's goats went with its pioneers, who took them on their journeys seeking grazing lands or other fortunes beyond the once-impenetrable Great Dividing Range.

Just as they had been on the First Fleet, goats were ideally suited to meet the self-sufficiency needs of the pioneering homestead. Along with the dog, goats accompanied pioneers no matter where they ventured. Henry Lamond was a Queensland-based bushman and a popular writer during the early to mid-1900s. He succinctly summed up the worth of the goat to Australia's outback pioneers:

> Goats follow civilization; in many instances they march ahead of it and mark its advance. No outback town could possibly exist without its mobs of goats; no railway camp would be complete without them; how many outback babies in the north are alive to-day because the trusty old nanny supplied the milk to support their young lives? Goats were indispensable.[2]

The few individuals who owned the large mobs usually yarded them at night for protection but left them to their own devices during the day to feed. Roaming at large, these goats found plenty of means to walk off the job, run the dingo gauntlet and try to form viable feral populations. Little by little, here and there, someone got lazy, or distracted, or left a gate open, or didn't build an adequate fence, and their goats wandered off and took their chances in the bush. In England, if one's house goat wandered off, it'd end up on the farm next door. In Australia, a short wander in the wrong direction and there was a fair chance the goat might be gone for good.

Semi-feral town goat herds were a fact of country life throughout Australia during the nineteenth and early- to mid-twentieth centuries. Part-time feral goat herds first formed on the fringes of communities when house milkers and their kids made off and joined their fellows. But these mobs were such a problem overgrazing the town surrounds and raiding gardens that townfolk became seriously fed up with them. Towns like Collie and Warren in central western New South Wales declared war was on goats in 1921. Townsfolk shot semi-feral town goats in their thousands as they did at Quambone, New South Wales which, overrun by over a thousand goats, became known as Goat Town.[3]

As people and town dogs pressured them, goats would decamp for the relative safety of the bush. Australia's interior is well suited to goats, though they'd prefer their habitat to be a little more precipitous; if they can't have hilly country, they always favour thick scrub. They are everywhere the browsing's good, except the tropics, the deserts, swampy country, and dingo or feral dog country. Being intensive browsers and grazers, they do damage disproportionate to their numbers. They have no problems climbing suitable trees to reach low branches they can't reach by standing on their hind legs.

Town and homestead goats were the source of large feral mobs that found the living in the interior grazing country easy going once the dingoes were gone. Failed commercial ventures, abandoned settlements and the coming of the motor vehicle in outback Australia led to the mass feralisation of goats. The easier availability of fresh cow's milk and other dairy products resulted in domestic goats being freed to fend for themselves.

In the mountainous Great Dividing Range, goats usually inhabited poor country that was not good grazing land, so they were more tolerable. But in the sheep- and rabbit-ravaged western division of New South Wales they made enemies because of their contempt of fences, their heavy consumption of water, and their propensity to graze and outcompete sheep. There was absolutely no money to be made in them and they were unpopular guests on any property. Graziers in the worst-infested areas were offering hunters a shilling for each goat scalp.[4]

Unlike most of New South Wales, where the dingo had been eradicated, in central and western Queensland goats found it difficult to survive dingo predation. They are not a particularly swift animal, certainly not able to outrun a dingo. Stations reported losses of homestead goats to dingoes and this letter to the *Sydney Mail* in 1937 gives an interesting insight into the rarely witnessed life and death struggles in the bush:

> Another youth and I were out looking for a steer to kill on Cardigan [station], where we were employed ... While hunting for a beast we came across a goat standing in water up to its neck and disturbed a dingo that had worn a pad around this small hole, approximately six yards across. I rescued the goat and laid it on the sand, but it took truly little notice, for it had evidently been in the hole for a long time.
>
> By the time I put it down at the homestead it was dead. The dingo must have cut it out from the rest, and the goat, realising that there was no other escape, had made for the water, and remained there for days and nights on end, with the dog walking round and round. There were thousands upon thousands of footprints.[5]

Feral goat numbers increased again during the Second World War. A plague of wild goats added to the troubles of pastoralists in the flogged, drought-stricken far west of New South Wales in the mid-1940s. Great herds of goats were ranging station properties eating the last vestiges of fodder. Because they can live on much less than sheep and need less water, they thrived, where sheep starved.

In 1948, Mr J W Swift, a Perth wholesale butcher, planned to export live feral goats from the Murchison and north-west to Singapore for food for native plantation workers. He said that he had orders for as many as he could get.[6] He didn't end up establishing that export trade, but at least someone could see value in feral goats.

# CHAPTER 4

# Pigs Dig their Snouts into the Environmental Trough

T he feral pig's reputation happily wallows in exaggeration and rural myth. Much of the feral pig nonsense started with fictitious stories pedalled in the early twentieth-century media by so-called 'adventure writers', and people believed what they read and embellished it when propagating such information. The most popular myth claims they occupied Australia before British colonisation because James Cook liberated them on Cape York in 1770. This ridiculous 1943 excerpt is from the usually reliable *Walkabout* magazine:

> Captain Cook is held responsible for the introduction of wild pigs into North Queensland. The famous explorer was noted for his experiments in acclimatisation; he was continually experimenting with the introduction of plants and animals to the various countries and islands which he discovered and visited.
>
> When the intrepid navigator came to Australia in 1770, he made one of these experiments. In August of that year he had to beach his ship, the *Endeavour*, for repairs, which were carried out at the mouth of a river, which he named the Endeavour, and on the banks of which the North

Queensland port of Cooktown now stands. Whilst waiting for his ship to be overhauled, Cook, who had several semi-domesticated pigs from the South Seas on board, decided to release some of the animals, probably believing that future settlers would profit by the introduction.

Those pigs were the progenitors of countless thousands of wild pigs which now swarm throughout the far north of Queensland, where for many years they have been an unmitigated curse. Prolific breeders, they were kept partly in check in the early days by the aborigines, who speared them for food. But gradually the pigs gained the upper hand, and to-day they are more plentiful than ever.

It is impossible to imagine the damage caused by the ravenous hordes of pigs. The animals usually congregate in great herds; it is by no means unusual to see a herd of fifty or a hundred, led by some monster boar as lord and master.

Many human beings have also been mutilated by the animals, and some have even been killed by the razor-sharp tusks of the savage boars ... They have a remarkable speed for such heavy creatures; they thunder along over rough ground and should their wickedly tusked head meet with anything short of a steam-roller or a rock there is generally trouble.[1]

Cook's journal contains no mention of his releasing pigs anywhere during his 1770 visit. He certainly landed a sow with suckers at the Endeavour River site. A fire the local Aboriginal peoples started killed one of the suckers, but none escaped, and Cook certainly didn't release any, though he did release pigs sourced from Tonga into Queen Charlotte Sound in New Zealand in 1773. Feral pigs are known as 'Captain

Cookers' in both New Zealand (for a good reason) and in northern Queensland (based on a myth).

The first pigs to set permanent trotters in Australia were the thirty-two that arrived in New South Wales fifteen years later, aboard the First Fleet in 1788. And for a couple of decades thereafter pigs, along with other livestock, arrived on nearly every supply ship that dropped anchor in Sydney Cove. It was common for Sydney Town households to keep a stied pig, though few kept them under control. Most pigs just roamed at large around the settlement and became a nuisance. There's your pig for you.

In February 1795, orders were issued that landholders could shoot trespassing pigs if they entered private property. Later, roaming nuisance pigs faced impoundment, but they continued to cause trouble for Sydneysiders for another ten years. By then they were causing all sorts of problems in Van Diemen's Land.

In the early 1800s, David Collins recorded the problems they were having with pigs roaming about the Hobart colony, sticking their snouts into everyone's business ... and gardens. Collins promulgated the first example of impractical and unworkable animal-management legislation that would be a hallmark of Australian government.

> It having been the practice for some time past to shoot such
> hogs (pursuant to an order which their destructive qualities
> had rendered necessary in the lieutenant-governor's time)
> as were found trespassing in gardens or cultivated grounds,
> and the loss of the animals being greatly felt by the owners,
> as well as detrimental to the increase of that kind of stock,
> the governor directed, that instead of firing at them when
> found trespassing, they should be taken to the provost-

marshal, by whom (if the damage done, which was to be
ascertained before a magistrate, was not paid for within
twenty-four hours) they were to be delivered to the
commissary as public property, and the damages paid as far
as the value of the animal would admit.[2]

About the only thing you can do with a marauding pig rooting
up your veggie patch, besides trying to shoo it away, is to shoot
it. Collins expected the offended citizen to capture the pig and
march it off to the provost-marshal. Good luck with that.

Sydney might have been where Australia's feral pig problem
began, but as with goats, increased urban density of the town
would eventually clean up the problem. And as with goats, the
people who ventured out to the interior took pigs with them,
and what was once a city problem became the bush's problem.

It is impossible to ascribe a certain event to the beginning
of the feral pig story in Australia. They were ferals just waiting
to happen because early pig-keeping practices in rural Australia
'managed' pigs in a semi-feral state. The botanist and explorer
Allan Cunningham noted this means of pig management: pigs
were kept in sties overnight, permitted to forage on their own
during the day, and lured by their keeper back to the sty of an
evening with a cob of corn. It was obvious even in 1827 that
they consumed anything they found. Cunningham observed
that they fed on grasses, herbs, wild roots and native yams,
particularly on the margins of rivers or marshy grounds, and
on virtually any small creatures which came their way.[3]

There were obviously occasions when free-ranging
domestic pigs found offers more appealing than a corn cob.
Pigs have a strong need for plenty of water, not just for
drinking but for wallowing, and they lie up during the day in

thick protective cover. They are not found very far from either water or mud. In Australia's eastern interior feral pigs quickly occupied the swampy lignum country found in the semi-arid regions of the Darling River system.

\*

The feral pig just can't keep out of trouble. Appallingly mannered, they're the true bogans of the feral community. Murder, vandalism, environmental destruction ... no Australian mammalian feral boasts anything approaching the feral pig's rap sheet. They eat virtually anything, will kill, and consume whatever they can – mammal, reptile, bird, amphibian, fish, mollusc, crustacean, all edible vegetation ... you name it, feral pigs are destroying it. And they're so voracious they leave nothing for even the blowflies. They destroy any environment, raid and destroy crops, degrade and pollute rivers, wetlands and dams, destroy irrigation, fencing and other infrastructure, and spread disease. They're the worst ungulate feral Australia must contend with, and when you consider the environmental damage done by buffalo, donkeys, goats and camels, that's saying something.

They've been a pain everywhere they set themselves up for over a hundred years, although they have had their supporters. Small local populations were a handy thing for isolated settlers. Some cattle graziers tolerated a few pigs because of their bizarre contribution to paddock hygiene – they keep blowflies under control by locating and eating the carrion that would become breeding grounds for flies. They also root out rabbit warrens and eat the rabbit kittens; and in the native rat plague of 1940 to 1943, they ate thousands of rats. Some districts have reported the virtual extinction of snakes by pig colonies; and, of course, people usually appreciated the pork as an alternative source of meat in cattle- and sheep-raising areas.[4] But they are not so welcome in sheep country, where they have a reputation for lamb killing and predation on weak sheep or those caught in bogs along riverbanks and earthen dams.

In 1918 and true to form, feral pigs in the Blackall district of central west Queensland caused as much trouble as the dingo. Just like everywhere else, they were a menace to sheep, as they drank and polluted the water, and when ewes heavy in lamb came in to drink, the pigs attacked and killed them. They were even more destructive in the lambing season, killing newborn lambs.[5]

Dead-sheep eating turned out to be a disaster for the wild pigs and everyone and everything else in the Nyngan district of western New South Wales in 1924. There was an anthrax outbreak on a sheep property there that caused serious concern. It was discovered in the local feral pigs, which had either spread it to sheep or contracted it from eating the carcase of an infected sheep.[6]

Pigs are the oddest livestock ungulate. Not only are they the only livestock omnivore, but they bear tusks, not horns or antlers, and are the most prolific of their tribe. Pigs are sexually mature at six months, have a short gestation of three and a half months, and bear up to ten young in a litter. Once they colonise an area, they rapidly populate it and are difficult to eliminate.

Feral pigs are pushy and aggressive by nature and can be quite pugnacious, but left to their own devices they pose little threat to people. Every second bloke who's been pig shooting claims an aggressive boar charged and treed them. Like most animals, pigs will flee in the face of danger, but if the pursuit persists, especially when chased and harassed by dogs, they will bail up and face their attacker. Adults of both sexes will charge if pressed – exhibiting behaviour exactly like that of the true wild boar of Europe and Asia.

Pigs are highly intelligent and resourceful and, being a highly destructive omnivore, do far more damage to their habitat than any other feral animal. Cats, foxes and feral dogs kill. Rabbits denude. Pigs kill, denude, and trash the place. From rooting up sea turtle nest sites to killing lizards, snakes and native birds (and destroying their nest sites), to killing lambs, or bulldozing acres of land searching for tubers, feral pigs really are Australia's worst feral nightmare.

In open country feral pigs could not thrive while dingoes still ruled the roost. Once dingoes disappeared from the sheep lands in the late 1800s, feral pigs became a real problem and assumed a role as apex predator in the absence of dingoes or wild dogs. In dense mountain or tropical wetlands and rainforest, pigs have abundant natural cover and thrive despite dingo predation.

*

Feral pigs were well and truly established in Queensland and western New South Wales by the twentieth century. Pig country means pig problems. In 1907, on Mount Cornish station, near Charleville in south-western Queensland, pigs were killing newborn lambs. Shooting parties were knocking over fifty to sixty a day. That scenario was playing out throughout sheep country in Queensland and New South Wales.[7]

Six years later and about 1000 kilometres north at Kynuna, feral pigs devoured one Frank O'Byrne who apparently died while wrapped up in his blankets camped out and working at Dagworth station. The pigs ate everything except his left-hand and 'certain bones'.[8]

Around the same time, the pig market in the Sydney saleyards was receiving consignments of trapped wild pigs from stations in the Moree region of New South Wales. The trip down had not taught them any manners and they kept charging people walking past their yards during the sales. Once sold, their hopeful buyers would head back to the bush to try to fatten them on corn, expecting that after six weeks to two months they'd be back in Sydney: plump, respectable stock, delighting buyers who cater for epicurean tastes. Sadly, wild-caught older feral pigs are difficult to quieten, highly strung and usually unhappy with confinement. Always nervy and on guard they can be hard to put condition on.[9]

Traditionally, the home of the feral pig in New South Wales has been the rivers of the Barwon–Darling system. These are actually the same river. It is the Barwon from Mungindi on the Queensland–New South Wales border until its confluence with the Culgoa River east of Bourke, where it becomes known as the Darling. There was another large colony around the junction of the Murrumbidgee and Lachlan rivers in south-western New South Wales, and feral pigs were thick around Balranald. In 1929 one station near Balranald poisoned over 2000 pigs in one season.[10] Huge numbers for sure, and this was happening all over pig country in eastern Australia.

The two world wars indirectly advanced the cause of the feral pig. While men were off getting themselves killed or permanently maimed or mentally damaged on behalf of Mother England, the weeds grew and the pests proliferated on the family farm. Manpower was missing from the land and severe restrictions on the sale of ammunition and firearms saw pest numbers greatly increase during the early- to mid-twentieth century. The Macquarie Marshes on the Macquarie River north of Warren in western New South Wales has been a wild pig enclave ever since they invaded and populated the region in the late 1800s. When the First World War ended in 1918, 10,000 pigs on two properties that bordered the marshes were destroyed in one year.[11] In 1939, shooting and poisoning dispatched 119,363 wild pigs in the Longreach Shire in Queensland alone. That's a lot of pigs and a lot of damage both caused and saved. Bounties paid on feral pigs in Queensland and New South Wales encouraged men to hunt them, but their numbers built up dramatically again during the war years, when the blokes who were supposed to be at war with the pigs were away fighting the Germans and Japanese instead.[12]

Wild pigs trampled wheat crops and killed sheep in north-west New South Wales all throughout the twentieth century. One Moree farmer reported that in 1948, he lost wheat worth £750 when a mob of pigs trashed his 300-hectare crop. Before the war, the Moree district was mainly a grazing area, but a vast wheat belt developed there during the war years. The pigs invaded properties within four miles of the town feasting on the crop.[13]

Feral pigs are Australia's most hunted large feral. Pig sticking – mounted hunters chasing and killing pigs with homemade lances constructed from long hickory rake handles tipped with single hand-shear blades – was popular in western Queensland and New South Wales around the late-nineteenth and early-twentieth centuries. Sporting firearms in large calibres soon became the favoured method of hunting and general pest extermination.

The feral pig's value as a game animal and as game meat have seen its range dramatically expanded as hunters established new populations. Catching young boars and castrating or 'marking' and releasing them was once a common practice. Emasculated boars, called barrows, grow larger than boars, make better eating, and do not exhibit 'boar taint', an offensive odour found in the meat of entire boars.

*

Not a whole lot was known about feral-pig biology until Dr EM Pullar of the Melbourne University Veterinary Research Institute published *The Wild (Feral) Pigs of Australia: Their Origin, Distribution and Economic Importance* in 1953. Dr Pullar sourced much of his information from the press, scientific and farming journals, government departments and individuals. Seven hundred copies of a questionnaire devised by him were distributed to individuals in 1947 and he received about an equal number of replies from all states and the Northern Territory.

Dr Pullar demolished the 'Captain Cookers' theory, but to ascertain when feral pigs first set trotters in Australia he studied the journals of several explorers and navigators from the period immediately prior to the expansion of the pastoral industry from 1830 to 1865 that described country known to be pig infested at the time of Pullar's study. Explorers' journals usually listed the game observed and shot each day and variously noted the existence of feral cattle, buffalo and stray horses. Yet Pullar found only two references to feral pigs and they weren't even on the mainland: Lieutenant John Lort Stokes of the Royal Navy, surveying uncharted parts of the Australian coastline in the HMS *Beagle* between 1837 and 1843, saw pigs that had been liberated on an island in Bass Strait; and Joseph Jukes, a naturalist aboard the HMS *Fly*, liberated a boar and a sow on an island near the Queensland coast in 1847 but shot them and their progeny a year later.

The earliest any old-timer from pig country anywhere in Australia could remember feral pigs being prevalent was around 1870, but by the time of the questionnaire, memories would have been foggy. Again, as with the feral goat, the proliferation of feral pigs seems to coincide with a decline in dingoes.

Dr Pullar was the first to use the term 'feral' pigs rather than the commonly used 'wild' pigs. He noted that there existed two types of feral pigs, which he designated as 'early' types and the 'recent' types. The early-type pigs, he wrote, were becoming increasing scarce, while the recent-types were becoming the predominant animal. The early-type pig is small, black or dark red in colour, with a large head and shoulders, narrow back and small hind legs. The recent type pig resembles a poorly developed modern domestic pig. They are relatively larger (about double the weight of the early-type pigs), and a high proportion are of lighter or mixed colours. Dr Pullar thought that the pigs of the early type are the direct descendants of those that escaped or were liberated early in the settlement of the continent, while the recent type pigs are the progeny of recent additions – perhaps released by graziers to improve the eating qualities of the local ferals or sty escapees.

Working on responses from his questionnaire, Pullar described the largest area distribution of feral pigs as most of

Queensland, except the far south-west and south-east, and the adjoining upper Darling region of New South Wales and the junction of the Lachlan and Murrumbidgee Rivers in the south-west of the state. Ferals were also on Flinders Island in Bass Strait, Kangaroo Island in South Australia, and isolated populations lived across coastal Western Australia and the western portion of the Top End of the Northern Territory.

Today feral pigs have expanded their range to occupy all of Queensland and almost all New South Wales. They are abundant now in parts of Western Australia, around Geraldton, Port Hedland and the Kimberley region. They are in direct contact with stock, grazing over the same areas, wallowing in the common waterholes, and eating any stock that may die. They have been responsible for the spread of anthrax and tuberculosis, and they likely assist in the spread of swine fever, rinderpest, and foot and mouth disease.

## CHAPTER 5

# Feral Dogs Rule

The First Fleeters and other subsequent colonists were hopeless dog managers. Dogs were given way too much freedom in the colony, in the vain hope that being at liberty they'd dutifully kill the rats that plagued Sydney. Alas, the dogs had other plans and making the easiest living they could, they took to scavenging and making a complete nuisance of themselves. It was easier to steal unattended food or get into the garbage than chase rats. When Sydney's dogs started consorting with the equally unrestrained wild dingoes and the young dingoes owned by the local folk, the Eora, that's when the trouble really began.

Governor Phillip, on his return from an exploratory boat journey north to Broken Bay and then along the Hawkesbury River, had the mortification to find that dogs had killed five ewes and a lamb very near his camp, and in the middle of the day. How this had been allowed to happen, no one knew, but it was conjectured that they must have been killed by dogs belonging to the Eora.

An attack during the middle of the day sounds more like the work of domestic dogs. For their part, the Eora were likely to have kept their adopted dingo puppies only until the dogs reached sexual maturity, when they would up and leave. The small terriers and spaniels the colonists brought with them, presumably the 'puppies' listed in the shipping manifests would have been much more attractive companions. The Eora must have loved the idea of a four-legged friend who hung around through thick and thin, for better or for worse, because there'd be lots of worse. These dogs were twice as cuddly and twice as faithful and having two seasons a year as opposed to the dingoes' one, proved to be twice as productive as well. They were also twice as troublesome.

The thing with urban feral dogs is that someone allows them to lapse into ferality. Dogs only make their own way when there is nothing to keep them at home – no companionship, no rope or chain, no pen, and certainly no food. The mechanisms that caused the Asian dog to turn feral 5000 years before remained the same in nineteenth-century Sydney. And they remain the same today. The offspring of the colonists' various dogs and the Eora's various dogs and dingoes formed the basis of one of New South Wales's most enduring pains in the neck – colonial Sydney's cur dog: a street-wise mongrel that no town needs. They were mongrels of every imaginable description and breeding.

Sydney's cur dogs became a real problem in the early nineteenth century. Just thirty years after colonisation, 10,000 cur dogs were living by their own means in the town. Uncontrolled, roaming pets formed packs with other uncontrolled dogs, all at different stages of their transition to ferality. Packs of threatening dogs hounded people everywhere, chasing saddle horses and horse-drawn vehicles, killing pets and stock, raiding homes and preying on the growing numbers of sheep, poultry, and urban feral goats and pigs that roamed at large in and around the town. It is always a rough old show when dogs rule the roost.

Sydneysiders had had enough by the turn of the nineteenth century. David Collins wrote that, 'Much mischief had been done by them among the hogs, sheep, goats, and fowls of individuals.'[1] In February 1801, Governor King issued this cur-clean-up proclamation:

Several individuals having complained of the great decrease of their sheep and lambs by the curs with which this colony abounds ... and as the breeding stock of sheep is of the greatest consequence to the welfare of this colony, no person is to suffer any cur dogs to follow them, or any cart, wheelbarrow, etc, the governor having given permission to those who have flocks of sheep to order their herdsmen to kill any dogs that approach them, and the owners will forfeit treble the value of any stock killed by them. Persons who keep cur dogs that are in the habit of flying at horses are to destroy them, otherwise they will be indicted as a nuisance. It is recommended to those who have more dogs than one (except Greyhounds or terriers) to kill them, as a tax will shortly be laid on all cur dogs.[2]

No one took any notice of the proclamation. Six years later, King's successor, Governor William Bligh, who had a fair bit of experience with mutiny, thought he'd do something about it:

Whereas a number of sheep and lambs, the property of Government and others, in and about Sydney, have been worried and killed by Dogs belonging to individuals in this Town and its Vicinity; It is hereby ordered, that every Dog, of every description be immediately destroyed,

except those of Officers and respectable Housekeepers.
Kangaroo Dogs and House Dogs, which are kept for the
defence of the Premises of such Officers or respectable
Housekeepers, are to be kept chained up; and the
Constables are hereby authorised to take every means in
their power to carry this Order into execution. Any
persons from the date hereof, who are known to keep
Dogs contrary to this Order, will on conviction before two
or more Magistrates forfeit the sum of Ten Pounds, to be
levied on their respective goods and chattels, half to the
Informer, and half to the Orphan Fund; and further to be
answerable for all damages incurred by the violation of
this Order.[3]

Bligh's order was big fat fail. There was tough talk in it, but
tough talk is cheap, and Sydneysiders proved to be about as
obedient as the crew of the *Bounty*. Sydney's feral dog problem
seemed like it was never going to go away. By 1830, the feral-
dog problem throughout New South Wales had become so
acute that a new Dog Act imposed a tax upon all owners of
dogs not gainfully employed. *The Australian* on 1 May of that
year reported:

To such as have never visited New South Wales – to such
as have never, been teased, attacked, worried, and put into
a fever by the multitudes of noisy mongrels which have,
infested the most, not less than the least populous of its
principal towns ... The annoyances from dogs in Sydney,
in Parramatta, in Liverpool, in Windsor, in short, in every,
town, village, and hamlet ... have most unquestionably
been great and mortifying; and the mode adopted for their

suppression, though perhaps the most effectual, is of itself a
nuisance ... The shepherd's dog, the grazier's dog, the
farmer's mastiff, all are exempted. Townspeople are the
victims; and few orderly well-disposed persons, we think,
will on a fair view of it, object to an Act which threatens
to exterminate that plague of plagues – the dog-plague.

No piece of legislation was ever going to clean up the
thousands of aggressive mongrels holding urban New South
Wales to ransom. Then, in the mid-nineteenth century, wool
growers stepped up their fight against the dingo and began
mass poisoning campaigns with strychnine and arsenic. The
readily sourced and easy to use poisons of the day took care of
the feral dogs just as easily, and dog baiting became the go-to
problem dog solver in Australia for a century or more.

CHAPTER 6

# No Place for Scabby Sheep

When the convict settlement plonked itself down at Port Jackson with forty-four fat-tailed sheep, wool production was the farthest thing from anyone's mind. Certainly, there was never any expectation of this huge, unknown landmass ever becoming the premier producer and exporter of the world's most valuable natural fibre. But sheep are a major player in this story. When it comes to the damage they have caused the land, they are neck and neck in a photo finish with the rabbit. Maybe beaten by a short half-nose.

When we look at the start that sheep got in New South Wales, it is remarkable anyone bothered to persist with them at all. The sheep that embarked at the Cape of Good Hope and arrived in Port Jackson were temporary visitors, promptly consumed or destroyed by nature, scab and local dogs. Another sixty-six sheep brought in on the HMS *Gorgon* in 1791 by Captain John Parker fared no better. The first merino sheep (only a few dozen) arrived at the penal colony at Sydney Cove on the HMS *Reliance* on 20 August 1797. Governor Hunter had dispatched its captain, Henry Waterhouse, to collect provisions from the Cape of Good Hope. The *Reliance* circumnavigated the bottom of the globe to reach the Cape and returned with more black cattle, three mares, and the nearly sixty merino sheep that would start the wool industry in New South Wales.

Merinos were found to revel in the dry conditions in New South Wales. Unlike the fat-tailed sheep that were brought out by the First Fleet, the merinos were scab free and thrived despite needing to be penned up of a night and protected from dingo attack.

John Macarthur, one of Australia's wool pioneers, began wool-growing at Elizabeth Farm, his property at Rose Hill, near Parramatta. He was the first to export merino wool in 1807 – 245 pounds (111 kilograms) from a subsequent land grant he called Camden Park, formerly the Cowpastures. It was the beginning of an industry that soon became the chief export and source of wealth for the country.

Sheep are one of the best things to happen to modern Australians and one of the worst things to happen to the Australian environment. There is no escaping the fact that Australia's countryside paid an enormous price as modern Australia rode to affluence on the back of the merino.

The sheep is the one ungulate in Australia that hasn't become a feral problem. It doesn't need to. Yet there isn't a sheep born that wouldn't prefer to break the bonds of domestication and make off into the bush to live independently as a wild rebel. That's why they instinctively run away when approached. Unfortunately, for the sheep, it's all about imagery. 'Wild and woolly' works for everything other than them, and they will only ever be a sheep in sheep's clothing.

The feral sheep does not impart the same emotional response as the mud-encrusted, tusk-clicking feral boar, or the rugged, ragged, stinking billy goat. Popular perceptions have pigeonholed them as intellectually challenged scaredy cats – hardly feral animal material. Still, over the years sheep have occasionally managed to evade the shepherd, the mounted ringer, or the ag bikes and kelpies, and made a semi-successful dash for freedom.

But alas, needing an annual shear seriously limits a sheep's tenure on the dark side. Eventually, usually a matter of around three or four years at best, their fleece becomes such an impediment it can almost incapacitate them. By then they're little more than a wool-blind, daggy, pissy, four-legged, stick-and-burr-infested wool ball.

The sheep's role in this timeline is one of industrialised environmental damage, giving with one hand and taking with the other, and little else. The sheep has nothing of the goat's initiative or adventurous spirit. It is far more dog-like in that it tolerates domestication and willingly suffers (and requires) someone else doing the thinking for it.

However, before the merino could establish true dominance over the emerging nation, their way needed paving and the natural order needed to be upended and driven into the ground. The dingoes and feral dogs had to go. Free-ranging large canines and sheep are a volatile mix, and while the dingoes had been making the life of sheep a misery since day dot, throughout sheep country, domestic dogs turned feral became more prevalent as the centuries wore on.

Uncontrolled town dogs were forming packs and venturing out at night to run down and kill sheep in sprees known as 'surplus killing'. Eventually those town dog packs became wilder and wilder until they ceased dependence on humans entirely and became first-generation feral dogs. Sheep farmers closest to town have always had to deal with nocturnal dog attacks, a habit so addictive that domestic or feral dogs that were engaged in surplus killing were every bit as damaging as dingoes − worse, because they were familiar with people. This excerpt from the *Sydney Mail* of 5 January 1921 gives a vivid account of the problem, and the 'sporting' solution:

A party of settlers on the outskirts of the Inverell district had a little experience of domestic dogs gone wild which showed them how difficult it would be to eradicate the real native-born Australian. There were known to be seven or eight dogs altogether, and they hunted in threes or fours. They held sway over an area of about 10,000 acres of improved country running sheep. They sought refuge during daylight, and when pursued made for a dense scrub, some four thousand acres in area, extending along the back of the improved country referred to.

These dogs showed all the native cunning of the dingo, with the added advantage of being more intelligent. They were mostly cattle-dog, with perhaps a dash of bulldog blood. It was well over twelve months from the time these dogs put in an appearance until the last one was disposed of. And this last one when caught was in the act of raising a family of ten. The settlers concerned lost hundreds of sheep. One returned soldier who was on the edge of the scrub had all his sheep destroyed. The settlers used to yard their flocks every night, which meant knocking them about terribly, and starving them as well, as this episode took place during the recent drought.

Some of the dogs in the early stages were shot in drives; others were shot by chance at watering-places, one or two were poisoned, and the last two were trapped. The hollow log where the puppies were found was in the thick of the scrub, but right in the line of the drives, which shows that the dogs quietly lay in their retreat while the drivers went past them. If such a thing as this can happen in a close-in part of New South Wales, where the average holding is about 2000 acres, and where there are always plenty of people to put in Sundays and holidays at the sport of dog-driving, how long is it going to take people in the far west, with their big areas and their sparse population, to eradicate dingoes without the aid of wire netting?

Yet methods to eradicate those 'dingoes' out west and closer to urban areas had been in place for decades. In 1848, a gentleman calling himself 'Innovator' was advocating an innovative method of disposing of the feral dog and dingo:

My plan of bringing strychnia to bear on the growth of wool, and the state of the market and pocket, is as follows. All round the boundaries of the run, let there be points chosen, easily to be recognized, about one or two miles apart; between these, at regular intervals of time, let a trail be drawn, and poison deposited at each. This can be dragged by a man on horseback, at a canter, and the baits be laid on the track without the bearer alighting from his horse.

The poison should be placed in a deep narrow slit, cut in a lump of meat as big as an apple or small orange, by means of a small penknife; this obviates the risk of the strychnia being shaken off by the dog, when first raising the meat from the ground ... In addition to thus protecting the boundary, a similar course should be pursued in directions across the run, more particularly along roads, cattle or splitters' tracks, paths of any kind, and in hot

weather by lonely waterholes, such being the localities
where signs of native dogs are most frequently met with.

The Innovator continued:

By this course, when carefully carried out, it has been
proved beyond a doubt that all dogs, at one time on a run
possessing much cover for them, have been destroyed, none
but dead ones having been seen for many weeks after even
a partial adoption of the above system.[1]

Another innovator, Mr HS Wills of Port Phillip, was of the
same mind. In a letter dated 18 December 1849, reprinted in
various newspapers, he said strychnine allowed him to run
much larger shepherded flocks on his property. His losses by
wild dogs were at one time incalculable, he said, but now wild
and tame dogs avoided his 'neighbourhood'. He claimed that
in the first fourteen days of May of that year he destroyed forty
wild dogs on his station.

One or two ounces of strychnine will clear any run in the
country. A bait taken from the flank of a sheep, set on
ramrod wire, out of reach of cats, and taken up at daylight
to avoid crows, will continue good two or three weeks, if
smeared with fresh fat occasionally. As wires are not always
at hand, twine fastened to a lateral branch, and secured by
a peg to the earth, will answer the purpose.

On this the bait can be secured at any reasonable
distance from the ground. Where a road offers, the trail
can be extended for miles by securing carrion to the axle
of a light cart or gig, and driving at the rate of six knots,

leaving a bait a mile at intervals. It is advisable to throw a few small pieces round about your wire to arrest a dog in his rapid run, or he may pass a bait or two.[2]

The District of Port Phillip became the colony of Victoria in 1851, and shortly thereafter sheep scab appeared among the colony's flock. There is no doubt it originated in New South Wales, but scab loves a cool climate, and it ran rampant through Victoria's flocks. It is a debilitating and highly infectious skin condition that causes severe skin abrasion and irritation and leads to wool shedding, weakened foraging and death. Lambs are particularly susceptible.

Yarding sheep at nights in folds – temporary pens – to hopefully keep them safe from nocturnal dingo predation also contributed to the spread of the disease, as sheep in close contact with their fellows is the surest method of transmission. Getting rid of the dingoes and feral dogs, and doing away with folding sheep at night was an important strategy in controlling scab.

Around this time, gold rushes began at different locations around the new colony. Victoria attracted people from all over the world and because of the wealth generated by wool and gold, Melbourne became Australia's leading city for a while.

Alongside the gold-rush influx of immigrants in the 1850s, canine distemper arrived in Sydney and found the thousands of feral dogs roaming the streets the perfect vector for spreading the contagion to domestic pets and the dingo:

If the distemper now raging so virulently amongst the dog tribe were to thin the city of a moiety of the useless yelping mongrels with which it is infested, it would be esteemed, but unfortunately the disease has hitherto principally developed itself in animals of superior breed, whose loss it will be difficult to replace. Some idea of the extent of the mortality may be gleaned from the circumstance of at least 57 carcasses having been removed from the streets and buried on Tuesday.[3]

It wouldn't take long for the awful disease to transmit to the dingoes of the Bathurst goldfields and throughout Victoria. The press reported the demise of the local dingoes with undisguised glee:

> We have just been informed that the distemper which has lately committed such fearful ravages amongst the canine species has extended its operations to the 'dingo tribe'. Our informant, a gentleman in whose veracity we have perfect confidence, tells us that not only have the wild dogs been found dead about the bush, but that several have been discovered in a state of helplessness from the prostration induced by the disease. This is glorious news for the shepherd as well as the sheep, and the stockholders will have little reason to complain if 100 per cent of their 'brushes' adorn the barn doors of their establishments from the fatality.[4]

Central and western Victoria, favoured by the geographical and apothecarial gods, had wide open country that supported the poisoning campaign. Strychnine, along with the canine distemper epidemic, exterminated the dingoes in short order. The area became the envy of the colonial anti-dingo legions. Newspapers celebrated it:

Oh, yes, the people of Geelong have nearly annihilated the wild dogs, and the men of Portland Bay are fast following so worthy an example. It now remains to be seen what will be done in Eastern Australia; something great, most likely, if not most wonderful.[5]

Without the dingo, central Victoria became a pastoral paradise, the envy of the other colonies, safer for sheep than even England, the greatest terrestrial threat to sheep being the odd delinquent domestic dog with a death-wish and a commensurately short life expectancy. Squatter and sheep prospered, and wool made many men great fortunes. True, the kangaroos proliferated in the dingo's absence, but those signs of serious imbalance were not apparent for a people oblivious to the dangerous predator vacuum they'd created.

Soon New South Wales, South Australia and Western Australia would emulate Victoria's folly and extirpate the dingo from their prime grazing regions. Queensland tried.

The widespread removal of the dingo in sheep country coincided with the introduction of wire boundary and paddock fencing. Eliminating the dingo was meant to provide the opportunity for a safe paddock environment for shepherd-less sheep charged with looking after themselves for a change. The passage of time has shown that things didn't quite work out that way, and before long agriculture would pay the price for eliminating the dingo.

*

As the First Fleet set anchor in Sydney Harbour, there was no indication that rabbits would prove to be the nation's greatest feral villain. Five rabbits were brought with Governor Phillip as 'poultry', but they wouldn't have lasted long when rations began to dwindle. That's providing they lasted *that* long. Every carnivore slinking about the little settlement (hungry marines and convicts included) would have been licking their lips at the mere sight of the justifiably nervous bunnies in their makeshift hutches.

The Reverend Samuel Marsden arrived on the Second Fleet and quickly became a prominent member of the small colony. He functioned as a magistrate, at variance with his clerical vocation, and was known for his severe treatment of criminals and Catholics (whom the flogging parson considered to be much the same creature).

At the turn of the nineteenth century, he kept an enclosure of domestic silver-grey rabbits at Parramatta and accused botanist and explorer George Caley, who was collecting specimens for Sir Joseph Banks, of allowing his dog to harass his rabbits.

The incident created a public, high-profile squabble. Caley hotly denied his dog was responsible. Yet if it wasn't Caley's dog, then what was killing the flogging parson's rabbits? If not a domestic, feral or wild canine, it may well have been the local quolls. Quolls have a reputation for fierce bloodthirstiness and are the very devil on small domestic stock like poultry ... and particularly love killing rabbits.

Indeed, introducing domestic rabbits to the colonies as free-ranging game proved to be spectacularly unsuccessful ... at least while quolls were abundant, as an article in the *Sydney Morning Herald* of 23 February 1926 suggested:

> Before these [wild rabbits], probably a hundred or more
> distinct efforts were made by as many of the first settlers to

breed rabbits in N.S.W., all of which failed owing to the
native cat [quoll]. For a while, they bred and prospered,
until native cats discovered and wiped them out. From
1820 to 1869 probably not a year passed but some
adventurous man or boy tried to turn them out and breed
them; but all met with the same fate – extermination by
the native cat.

In the nineteenth century quolls – known as native cats – were
commonplace. But the quoll was a victim of the widespread
dingo cull, by-kill along with goannas and eagles, of the
intensive poisoning campaign. Their destruction was a fact
many would regret.

There are two types of quoll. The largest is the tiger quoll
(or spotted tail quoll), often called the tiger cat. It is not only
*not* a cat but has spots instead of tiger stripes. The tiger quoll
can weigh up to 7 kilograms, while the eastern and western
quoll are smaller and weigh half that. The eastern quoll is
extinct on the mainland but, like the spotted tail quoll,
abundant in Tasmania.

Quolls were voracious and fearless predators, tackling game
much larger than themselves. Back in 1885, WW Richardson
of Moonagee Hall, Ashfield, knew it was a mistake to kill off
the quolls, and he wasn't backwards in telling the editor of the
*Sydney Morning Herald*:

> I think that the whole-sale destruction of wild cats, native
> and otherwise, has been a mistake, and the extension of the
> rabbit pest is in a great measure due to their attempted
> extermination by the wholesale use of poison all over the
> colonies since sheep have been turned loose in paddocks.

It might be as well to consider how far such animals might be protected from extinction, as being the best check, we can have against the increase of the rabbits. It is true that poultry-breeders suffer at times from their attacks, but it is a very simple matter to protect poultry-yards, and if ever driven to the straits of hunger native cats and their kindred will be compelled to fall back on the rabbit, which is just what we want them to do.

It is simply a question for consideration whether rabbits are the greatest nuisance or native cats, weasels, stoats, and other so-called vermin. Experience shows that the rabbits are, and to attack them, with any chance of success we must defend their natural foes.[6]

Tasmanian devils too preyed heavily on rabbits and assisted the quolls in keeping the numbers down in the island colony once rabbits had become an established pest:

For several miles out from the Western Tier the rabbits do not increase so rapidly as in other parts of Tasmania, and this has been attributed to the exertions of the devils, tiger cats, and native cats. This opinion has led to many of the landholders regarding the tiger cats as extremely useful animals, and whenever one of them is caught in a box-trap he is allowed to depart peaceably.[7]

The wild rabbit is actually a native to France, Spain, Portugal and North Africa. They are in fact ferals in Britain, introduced by either the Romans or the Normans, or possibly both. Rabbits have never overpopulated Britain because of constant predation by foxes, stoats, humans and birds of prey, and because the bitter winters take an annual toll on their population. The thick, rich soils of Britain don't suit rabbits as well as the thin sandy soils of mainland Australia, Tasmania and their offshore islands. The rabbit problem in Tasmania would eventually get bad, but due to its cold winters, quolls, devils and feral cats, it would never get as catastrophically bad as on the mainland.

On the mainland, where the dingo wars raged, and strychnine was king, every native carnivorous creature that would take a poison bait was virtually driven, if not to total extinction, then near to it. Removing the native predators just gave the rabbit, and the fox a decade after it, carte blanche.

> For years rabbits were turned loose in all parts of the
> colony, and many were the regrets that these efforts at
> acclimatisation were failures. The dingo and the native cat
> were too strong for the rabbits and devoured them as fast as
> they appeared in either the scrub or the open country. At
> last, as their natural enemies were destroyed by poison and
> other means, the rabbits began to flourish.[8]

There is no question that the dingo was a shocking sheep killer, and quolls were the devil on poultry, both species committed surplus killers. Their shocking depredations earned both terrible reputations and most farmers were not sorry to see their demise. But the biggest predatorial bum rap was the framing of the wedge-tailed eagle. A supposed lamb killer as bad as the dingo, clueless graziers shot or poisoned countless wedgies, and rabbiters – who accused them of preying on rabbits – killed just as many. Wedge-tailed eagles do hunt rabbits. And they may have taken the odd weak newborn lamb, but they're also happy carrion-eaters, so eagles seen feeding on fox-killed lambs likely copped the blame for the kills. Is it just me or is it odd that, since they became a protected species, wedgies suddenly stopped killing all those lambs? Just like that! Will miracles ever cease?

So, strychnine, ignorance, and indomitable industry eliminated a great swathe of Australia's native predators to protect the merino. But scratch that thin protective veneer and the reality was that the merinos were probably worse off. What the predator vacuum really did was lay pastoralism, and the broader environment, defenceless before the coming biological plagues which, unlike the native 'pests', could never be overcome.

# PART TWO

# Acclimatisation and Exploration

The nineteenth century was the century of European discovery in Australia. Inevitably explorers ventured into the unknown interior of the continent, first looking for grazing land and the mythical 'inland sea' into which they presumed the western-flowing rivers of New South Wales emptied. When Captain Charles Sturt put that theory to rest in 1830 by tracing the Murray River to Lake Alexandrina, near Adelaide, which then emptied into the Southern Ocean, the new unmapped horizon became what lay beyond the north and west of the Darling River.

It was a time of manpower, horsepower and bullockpower, leather, wood, chain and rope, blood, sweat and tears, and the constant battle against the traditional owners of the land and an unforgiving environment that also repelled the human intruders but had plenty of time for their escapees.

Nevertheless, the country opened up to pastoralists, who established profitable runs and produced great wealth. Some pastoralists became so rich they tried to re-create their own little piece of England in Australia. Acclimatisation societies sprang up in Victoria, New South Wales and the other colonies. Their members, and independent acclimatisers, imported and released rabbits, hares, deer, foxes, trout, salmon, mynas, starlings, sparrows, finches, and alpacas; doves and pigeons and a range of fish.

The Acclimatisation Society of Victoria had much bigger plans for many more exotic species, with no thought given to the consequences of such liberations. They even considered importing and releasing boa constrictors and monkeys. While acclimatisers cost Australia countless millions in damage caused by their totally unnecessary releases, we should be grateful that most of their more stupid ideas never got off the ground or failed.

CHAPTER 7

# Camels and Donkeys
# Open the Interior

The hardships experienced by European explorers of Australia's interior, and the heavy toll exploration took on horses and bullocks, led to sensible calls for the introduction and use of camels for exploring, settling and supplying the outback and desert areas of Australia.

*The Perth Gazette and the Western Australian Journal* led the charge in 1835:

> In this hilly country, and especially New Holland, so
> deficient in streams and lakes; an animal so patient of thirst,
> and so capable of transporting large burdens from
> considerable distances, could not fail to be most useful to the
> settler. Of all species of land carriage (excepting of course the
> steam carriage railway) the camel is the cheapest and most
> expeditious. Even in bringing wool from the most remote
> stock-runs, and returning with provisions for the shepherds,
> these animals would be a most valuable acquisition.
>
> They are extremely tame and domestic, and in the
> absence of rich pasture grass, would derive a large portion
> of their support from the branches of trees … They are not
> disposed, like our bullocks, to stray away from their

drivers, gathering as much food in an hour, after being relieved from their burden and let loose in the evening, as will serve them to ruminate for the whole night, and support them the next day. Perhaps some enterprising capitalist will be so good as to hazard a little of his money in conferring so great a benefit on the colony as the introduction of this animal from Asia would be.[1]

The government of the colony of New South Wales enquired into the possibility of importing camels from the Upper Ganges Valley. South Australia most appreciated the camel's value for exploration. Governor Gawler of that newly established colony also investigated the importation of camels in the 1830s, although nothing came of any of these early enquiries.

In early 1841, Sayyid Said bin Sultan, the Imam of Muscat, the capital of Oman, dispatched one male and two female camels to Sydney. The male camel died on the voyage, but the two females disembarked in good condition in May 1841. For a time, the Domain in Sydney was their home, and an 1845 painting by George Edwards Peacock shows the camels grazing there. It is doubtful the Domain camels received proper care and attention. They began to get irritable and were becoming an unacceptable risk to the spectators who flocked there to see them. Eventually the government decided to send them south to Eden where the pioneering Imlay brothers were known to have four camels of their own.[2]

In July 1852, the New South Wales Chief Commissioner of Crown Lands requested Mr AW Manning, the local Commissioner, to report on the condition of the government camels roaming the Bega district.

Manning reported that he had made two attempts to see

them, but had failed, and though he meant to renew the attempt, it would be difficult to succeed:

> As no horse would go near the creatures, and many narrow
> escapes had occurred from their chasing the horses
> employed to get a sight of them. I fear, it will be quite
> impossible to affix any distinctive mark on them, as was
> directed by the Government in March; for they cannot be
> run into any yard for the purpose of branding – or be kept
> there even if got in.

But in September 1852, Mr Manning, after much difficulty, did succeed in finding them. He wrote that the seven he sighted were in excellent condition, and quiet. The old ones allowed him to feed them with bread, and even to handle their feet; but the young ones, though quiet enough, were too timid to let him approach them closely.[3]

Nothing more was heard of the camels of the south coast of New South Wales until October 1869, and by 1883 the camels had all died, allegedly of tick infestation.[4]

\*

The first explorer to use a camel in Australia was John Ainsworth Horrocks and by the end he no doubt wished he hadn't. Horrocks arrived in South Australia from Britain in 1839 and decided, in 1846, to go big and investigate the unknown country in the colony's north around Lake Torrens. Accompanied by five others including ST Gill, the renowned artist, he set out on 29 July. With them went Horrocks's notoriously bad-natured camel, Harry.

The expedition proved to be a disaster. The party began by proceeding north into the Flinders Ranges, where Horrocks discovered a pass, which he named after himself, as you would. Harry regularly bit the men and the goats but, as ill-tempered as he was, he was able to carry heavy loads of up to 160 kilograms and travel days without water. He was useful enough providing you didn't get too close to him.

By 21 August they had reached Edward Eyre's old camp at Depot Creek. Then on 1 September, while skirting a salt lake, disaster struck:

> In going around this lake – which I named Lake Gill [Lake Dutton] – Kilroy who was walking ahead of the party stopped, saying he saw a beautiful bird, which he recommended me to shoot to add to the collection. My gun being loaded with slugs in one barrel and ball in the other, I stopped the camel to get at the shot belt which I could not get without his laying down. Whilst Mr Gill was unfastening it, I was screwing the ramrod into the wad over the slugs, standing close alongside of the camel. At this moment the camel gave a lurch to one side and caught his pack on the lock of my gun, which discharged the barrel I was unloading; the contents of which first took off the middle finger of my right hand between the second and third joints, and entered my left cheek by my lower jaw, knocking out a row of teeth from my upper jaw.[5]

They carried Horrocks home grievously wounded on 20 September. A doctor came from Adelaide but there was little he could do for the raging infection, and Horrocks survived but three more days. He courageously dictated a letter in which he described the failed expedition. He requested his workers shoot Harry to prevent him injuring anyone else. The straw that broke big bad Harry's back was his savagely biting an Aboriginal stockman on the head after the party returned home. The station hands, who'd had enough of his foul temper and dangerous behaviour, were happy to comply with Horrocks's instructions.[6]

The consequences of John Horrocks's experiment with camels did nothing to quell interest in them. During the late 1850s, prominent Australians continued to call for their use, including South Australian Governor Richard MacDonnell, who had previous camel experience:

> I despair of much being achieved even with horses; and I
> certainly think we have never given explorers fair play in
> not equipping them with camels or dromedaries and
> waterskins, which in Africa I found the best methods of
> carrying liquid.[7]

All this agitating for camels occurred at a time when little was known of the interior and when acclimatisation, discovery and showing off Victoria's newfound gold- and wool-derived wealth were all the rage. The Royal Society of Victoria enjoyed an over-active membership of gentlemen determined to address what they termed as the 'ghastly blank', the great mysterious emptiness that stared them in the face when they perused the map of the continent.[8] They hoped exploration would bring the light of civilisation to the hideous unknown in the centre of the continent.

An expedition party of gallant Victorian explorers imbued with the fervour of British patriotism and the exotic assistance of faithful camels seemed the perfect pairing to show the world Victoria's commitment to colouring-in the continent and blazing a trail from Melbourne to the Gulf of Carpentaria. The Royal Society had influential people within and without the membership, and the government was all too willing to assist in beating the South Australians to the punch and blazing a glorious trail from south to north.

Dr Thomas Embling, Member of the Legislative Council for Collingwood in Victoria, was influential in convincing the Victorian parliament to acquire camels. He addressed the Exploration Committee of the Royal Society of Victoria on 1 September 1858 and intimated, on behalf of the government, that they were willing to place a sum of money on the estimates adequate to the purchase and transport of twenty or thirty camels; and added that a military officer, George James Landells, who was about to proceed to India with horses, was willing to undertake the selection and shipment of the camels while he was there.

Landells was no mug. He was a horse trader who exported Walers from Australia to India as cavalry remounts. He arrived in Calcutta in December 1858 with a budget of around £300 and travelled extensively through what is now Pakistan to secure quality camels for the Royal Society. His instructions were to purchase both the Arabian dromedaries (one hump) and Mongolian bactrians (two humps), but as it turned out, Landells bought only dromedaries. It was a wise decision.

Landells and nine cameleers walked the eighteen camels he bought 1000 kilometres from Lahore to Karachi. En route, he met Englishman and soldier John King, who had spent sixteen months recovering from a serious illness at Rawalpindi. Landells offered King a role in managing the cameleers and the camels, so King secured a discharge from the army and joined Landells. Little did King know that he was about to sign up for colonial Australia's greatest exploratory fiasco: the Royal Society's Victorian Exploratory Expedition to the Gulf of Carpentaria, better known as the Burke and Wills expedition.

On 13 June 1860, all the camels George Landells had sourced in the subcontinent arrived at Port Melbourne aboard the *Chinsurah*. After proudly parading through the streets of Melbourne, they took up residence in improvised stables at Parliament House before moving on to Royal Park.

Landells, King, the cameleers and camels arrived just in time to join the Royal Society's proposed south-to-north crossing of the continent. Ill-planned, poorly staffed and pathetically managed, the expeditionary party that crawled out of Melbourne on 20 August 1860 is the most regrettable saga in the exploration of Australia. The entire party consisted of twenty-two men, twenty-three horses, eighteen wagon horses, and twenty-seven camels.[9]

From the outset, Landells, who had signed on as second in charge and camel master, encountered constant interference, meddling and bullying from the party's leader, Robert O'Hara Burke. By the time the group reached Menindee in western New South Wales, he'd had enough. Landells resigned, fearing that Burke in his rage was about to shoot him, and convinced that he could not execute his agreed duties under Burke's leadership. He was also convinced the expedition had no hope under Burke's mismanagement and that they'd probably all perish. He wasn't far wrong.

At Menindee, Burke divided the party, taking sixteen camels north to Cooper Creek. He lost four camels on the way and then took a party of just four men and six camels onwards.

With supplies perilously low, they made a dash for the Gulf of Carpentaria.

Along with William John Wills, John King and Charley Gray, and suffering enormous privation, the closest they got to their goal was tasting the salt water of a tidal stream just south of the Gulf of Carpentaria. Mangrove swamps blocked their access to the coast. Burke later wrote in his journal, 'At the conclusion of the report, it would be well to say that we reached the sea, but we could not obtain a view of the open ocean, although we made every endeavour to do so.'[10]

It was a disappointing way to end their quest for the shores of the Gulf. Worse was to come when they turned back again for Cooper Creek. Charlie Gray died on the way; Burke and Wills perished soon after making it to their old camp. John King was the only survivor. He lived several months with the local Aboriginal peoples before his rescuers returned him safely to Melbourne, a feted hero.

Camels, of course, can endure the toughest conditions. But under Burke's inexperienced, neglectful and often emotionally wrought leadership, only four of the sixteen taken north from Menindee survived. Two of the missing camels were later found at Truro Station, on the Murray River in South Australia later that year, and the third was spotted far to the north-east in western New South Wales. The three abandoned or lost camels were all bulls, so there was no wild reproduction.[11]

As it turned out the various relief expeditions and search parties that went in search of Burke and Wills added much more intelligence, detail and colour to the ghastly blank than the expedition proper.

*

A common myth credits Sir Thomas Elder, the South Australian rural entrepreneur, with the introduction of the camel into Australia. That honour, as we have seen, goes to Landells and King, and Imlay before them. Elder, however, was the most effectual and influential of the early camel importers and breeders. He was a firm supporter of camels for the inland:

> The exploration of the interior is a subject which has
> engaged my attention for a number of years, and I had
> partly the furtherance of this object in view when in 1865
> I imported camels from India, which have now become
> quite acclimatized in South Australia, and have increased
> in number from 110 to 500 or 600. Without camels, which
> can go a week or ten days without water on a pinch, the
> interior could never have been successfully explored, and
> the ships of the desert, as they are called, are the only
> animals that we know of fit for such an undertaking.[12]

Elder was the backer of a camel importation scheme that proved to be invaluable in the development of the interior, although it appears the idea was the work of his partner, Samuel Stuckey.

In 1860, Elder funded Stuckey to travel to northern India (now Pakistan) to research the breeding and care of camels, to purchase a breeding herd, and to engage experienced cameleers. Stuckey was unable to charter a suitable ship and had to return to Adelaide empty-handed.

In 1861, it was obvious the Burke and Wills expedition was in big trouble. Elder and Stuckey accompanied the explorer

John McKinlay, who led a South Australian-sanctioned expedition to rescue the ill-fated party. They made it to within 110 kilometres of Cooper Creek and Elder urged McKinlay to send a camel-mounted advance party to rescue any survivors. McKinlay refused to do so, preferring to continue with horses. Eventually their horses gave in and they had to turn back. Elder was adamant that if McKinlay had listened to him and sent his camels ahead, they would have found whoever remained of the ill-fated exploring party.[13] This incident made Elder even more determined to source camels of his own, so he and Stuckey took time to rethink their camel strategy.

In 1865, Stuckey returned to India and succeeded in shipping 124 camels and eleven cameleers to Port Augusta, but six weeks after landing, the dreaded scab killed much of the herd. Stuckey shifted the remaining camels to Elder's Beltana Station in the Flinders Ranges and Umberatana, near Lake Hope in the far north of South Australia, where the camels wasted no time in reproducing. Stuckey introduced three different camel strains – the Mekraua strain for speed and the Scind and Kandahar strains for strength.

*

The donkey story also began in central Australia when Elder and Stuckey imported donkeys in 1866. Elder improved the breed with excellent stallions from Spain, and his property, Beltana Station, became similarly famous for its donkey stud. The donkeys multiplied so rapidly that they stocked the stations of the central and western interior for well over half a century.

The donkey cannot claim status as a glamorous animal. Always the butt of jokes and ridicule, it was slow to gain widespread use in Australia. Even at the height of its popularity the donkey was in the beast-of-burden minority and mostly only appreciated in the interior of South Australia and Western Australia. The men who used donkey teams for haulage under the most trying conditions valued the donkey's rugged, hardy, and easy-to-live-with nature. Teamsters working in the rugged north-west of the continent much preferred donkeys to horses and bullocks.

It's easy to think of donkeys as little creatures, and while they can be as small as 61 centimetres at the withers, the largest, the American mammoth, can be over 152 centimetres. The Australian feral donkey is a brawny, well-put-together creature made up of diverse breeds drawn from Asia and Europe, and forms the largest wild donkey population in the world.

*

The introduction of camels and donkeys made the exploration and development of the far regions possible. Camels became the mainstay of explorations and Beltana became the most important breeding station and stepping-off place for exploring parties for camels, donkeys and supplies.

From 1866, camels and donkeys were employed for the transportation of goods to remote sheep and cattle stations and proved of immense value in carrying supplies during severe drought. They established a flourishing transport network between inland stations and mines, railheads and ports, carrying wool, grain, ore, stores, fencing equipment, bore pipes, household furniture and even pianos. Donkeys helped to build the north–south railway to Oodnadatta in 1884, and the railway line to Alice Springs in 1927. Over a hundred camels were engaged in the construction of the Adelaide–Darwin Overland Telegraph in 1872, carrying wire, insulators and supplies. By 1895, South Australia had an estimated 1500 camels and Western Australia had 4000.

Thomas Elder's superior Australian camels found regular employment throughout the arid regions of Queensland, New South Wales, the Northern Territory and Western Australia, where there was strong demand for their services.

Camels are unique among Australia's imported animals in that they brought their own human culture to Australia, one that did not change because of Australian influences. Wherever Sir Thomas's camels went, they were led by the men recruited to work them. These men left their homelands to work the camels in Australia's interior and, though few, they made a significant contribution to the development of the outback.

The cameleers belonged to four distinct cultural and linguistic groupings – Pashtun, Baluchi, Punjabi and Sindhi – none of whom were on the best of terms with meddling Britain or her subjects. They came from Afghanistan and present-day Pakistan but were known in Australia as Afghans or Ghans. They taught the outback camel-sense and made a substantial but unappreciated contribution to the evolving culture of the interior.

The bushies found the Ghans an odd 'breed' and their customs even odder. For a start they didn't drink. It was extremely difficult for anyone in the shimmering mind-numbing interior to ever trust blokes who didn't regularly get blotto. Worse, they got about in turbans and fancy loose clothing and wore jewellery and loved flashing their gold. Like sheilas. Worse still, they even draped their camels in decorations.

The Ghans came to Australia alone, leaving their missuses and their little Ghans behind. They lived in segregated quarters on stations or set themselves up on the fringes of the towns they settled in. Their corrugated-iron enclaves became known as Ghantowns, and each Ghantown had a mosque, which hosted strange turnouts that caused murmurs among townsfolk extremely suspicious of any form of cultural diversity. They could only guess at what kind of shenanigans the Ghans got up to in there!

Yet for all their foreign-ness, the Ghans were straight-dealing, dependable and honest. They earned the confidence and trust of their Anglo-Australian business associates, but only a begrudging, tenuous tolerance from the isolated, distrustful Anglocentric people of the outback.

Indeed, the fact that the Afghans had defeated the might of the British Empire in the first Anglo–Afghan War (1839–1842) wouldn't have earned the Ghans many hearty handshakes and congratulatory backslaps. And when the British had still not learned that it was better to be a live dog than a dead lion and had another crack at the Afghans, their humiliation in the second Anglo–Afghan War (1878–1880) was a complete PR disaster for the Ghans of the outback.

Anti-Ghan and anti-camelism only ever simmered while the people of the outback were dependent on the Ghans and their camels. It was the coming of the motor lorry and a camel-free future of the twentieth century that really cranked up resentment.

# CHAPTER 8

# Motor Vehicles Supersede Camels and Donkeys

In 1891, a member of the New South Wales Legislative Assembly, Mr Nicholas Willis, the member for Bourke, introduced a Bill to prohibit, with certain exceptions, the use or introduction of camels within the boundaries of towns and urban areas. The preamble of the Bill stated that the use of camels on highways or within the boundaries of municipalities was frequently a great inconvenience and source of great annoyance to carriers, drovers and others using the roads. It became law that no person was in any way to use camels upon any highway or elsewhere within the boundaries of any municipality in New South Wales unless it belonged to a travelling menagerie or exhibition.

The new law prescribed a penalty of £20 for every day on which the offence was committed. Mr Willis made no secret of the fact that the Bill was the outcome of recent friction in the west regarding camels as beasts of burden. Granted, camels are grumpy, and at times dangerous creatures, frightening to people and animals unused to them, but so are horses. What the new law really meant was that time was up for the Ghans and their camels in the towns of western New South Wales.

Wild camels were multiplying rapidly in the region west of Bourke and in South Australia. At Dunlop Station in far western New South Wales, camels were damaging the vermin-proof fences and letting in dingoes and rabbits.

A letter from a Bourke resident to *The Bulletin* was a typical example of the rampant anti-camelism of the times and the bigoted belligerence towards the cameleers:

Dear Bulletin. – You seem to think that camels are an absolute necessity in Western N.S.Wales. I'd like you to name one track, from Bourke to any part of N.S.W., which is impassable for horse or bullock teams, even in the driest seasons. Certainly, ere Government tanks and watering places were constructed along the dry roads, the camels would have been a boon. But now their proper place is not N.S. WALES, but the sandy wastes of Queensland, Centralia, and Westralia, where they are almost indispensable.

You off-handedly, suggest that the horse might be abolished in favour of the camel. So it will, when NSW is handed over to the Asiatics, which at the present rate of progress, will be sooner than you expect. You say the fittest is going to survive. Well, the camel is not the fittest now in N.S.W., whatever it might have been 20 years ago. Camels don't take kindly to waggons; they are too slow and stubborn, and their feet were not designed for heavy pulling, and if you advocate the present system of camel loading you advocate barbarous cruelty in many cases – in carrying wool, wire netting, boring pipes, and timber, all of which the poor brutes have to struggle under.

The constant friction causes frightful sores on their backs, which there [sic] and masters, the Afghans, sometimes endeavour to hide from the public gaze by sewing basil or canvass on to the live skin; but as a rule, they don't bother about it at all, as they aren't liable for cruelty to animals, the camel not being an animal 'within the meaning of the Act', according to our local magistrate. For the same reason they have full possession of the Bourke Common free of charge, whereas carriers and others have to pay stiffly for having their horses scattered in all directions.

If, as you seem to wish, the camel gets possession of the roads, half the public watering places will be non-revenue-producing, for the wily Afghans use the camel's great powers of endurance to escape paying water charges. Also, if you were compelled to live on some of the flour that is carried on that smellful animal's back, your enthusiasm would cool considerably.[1]

Anti-Ghanism and anti-camelism was always bubbling beneath the dusty red surface of the outback. It started getting worse when Anglo-Australians realised there were transport alternatives to camels and the writing for the Ghans, and their camels, was on the wall.

The love affair was over because there was no longer any need for them, as this newspaper report, published in the *Wagga Wagga Daily Advertiser* of 19 February 1927 made evident:

It is predicted that the picturesque 'ship of the desert', the odorous camel, will very soon be only a memory in the sandy stretches of Australia. Motor-traction has consigned his slow steps to the limbo of other primitive means of transport, and in a few years the shuffling beast with the hump will probably occupy a place in history alongside Cobb's coach.

Travellers in the far west of New South Wales tell of droves of wild camels that are giving selectors untold trouble and putting them to great expense in repairing broken fences. This, it is said, is the aftermath of the fight that has been waged during the past two years between the ancient and modern means of transport, as represented by camel teams and motor lorries.

The lorries have survived, and the owners of nearly all the camel teams have given up the struggle. As the owners of the teams have gone out of business, the camels, being of practically no value, have been allowed to go bush and in their wild state are breeding rapidly.

The camel drivers did not give up their livelihoods easily. One of the favourite methods of warfare of the camel team drivers was to drag their wagons across the tracks that the lorries ran along in such a manner that the wheels obliterated a length of the ruts. Coming to such a place unexpectedly, the lorries would be thrown right off the track, as the *Daily Advertiser* article also noted:

> The camel teams put up a great fight against the lorries, and made the most of the natural conditions to aid them. Hundreds of miles of the main routes out west are sandy tracks, with hardened wheel ruts. Provided the lorry driver can keep in these ruts he can make a moderately good journey, but once out of them on to the sand, then he must

wait until another vehicle comes along to give him a tow back to the track.

\*

According to official returns, there were 11,728 camels in Australia by 1926, but that did not include the growing number of ferals that were quickly becoming a problem. The feral camel issue came up for discussion in the South Australian House of Assembly in February 1926, when the Commissioner of Crown Lands acknowledged a report to the effect that there were about 2000 camels running at large around Marree in the central east of the state. The government needed only 400 of them to do any work, and then only for about six months of the year. The camels freed to run loose became a nuisance on the big stations so the government proposed a Bill that would give a lessee power, after having given notice, to shoot any camels that were running wild.

Common among stockmen faced with deciding what to do with their superseded beasts of burden was an inability or at least an unwillingness to destroy them. Releasing livestock to fend for themselves, while creating a needless feral problem, is understandable when one considers how attached to their stock these men became. It was no different for the Ghans, who loved their camels, despite nasty claims to the contrary. It was a sad ending for the men and camels who serviced the interior so faithfully for so many years. The cameleers turned their camels loose into a life of unemployed ferality. Thousands of camels were set free by their masters, who had little if any prospects when their trade died and no stomach for destroying their animals. As for the Ghans themselves, they either assimilated or went home when their prospects ended in ungrateful Australia.

Camels are cantankerous, ill-mannered creatures at the best of times, but idle camels are the work of the devil and nothing but trouble looking for a place to happen. A super feral, they are way too big and way too destructive for the bush ... and for infrastructure. Most ferals are destructive, but none are quite as damaging as a big mob of camels faced with a fence. It's little wonder tolerance for them evaporated on the stations where they roamed.

*

Donkeys had cornered a niche in the Kimberley region of far north-west Western Australia. Walkabout disease, which killed horses that ate the rattlepod plant endemic to the region, had no effect on donkeys, who could eat it with impunity. Donkeys held their jobs longer than horses in other parts of the country due to the ruggedness of the regions in which they toiled, in huge teams that pulled inordinately large wagons. Teamsters valued donkeys, unlike camels, into the late 1930s.

Over the heavy sand country, it was not uncommon to see up to ninety donkeys harnessed to a wagon. Occasionally, at bad crossings, more were joined to the harnessed team. A carrier often had a hundred and fifty of the little animals on the road, with a stockman employed to drive the spare ones. Because of the numbers, a donkey team took a considerable time to harness and unharness. But the donkey had a special value in Australia's parched country because it eked out a living like a goat and never wandered far from the night camp.

Stories of the feats of donkey teams are legendary. One concerned a west Queensland carrier who had a donkey team drawing a big load of store goods for a border station and got stuck in a wide patch of loose sand. The top part of the cargo was flour in 50-pound bags, and it was plain that he would have to unload it. But instead of dumping it on the sand, from where he would have had to carry it a considerable distance afterwards to firm ground, he put one bag on the back of each of his donkeys. Then he started the team. The donkeys, with their packs, easily pulled out the lightened wagon.[2]

The donkey's usefulness for carrying supplies in the arid parts of the interior gave a value to even the ferals in their numbers. Feral donkeys introduced to a working team quickly applied themselves to the job and required no extra effort to break them in to the work. Donkeys make good pack and team animals, and in the toughest conditions their hardy constitutions endured when horses and bullocks failed.

\*

The introduction of motor vehicles to supersede the donkeys of the Kimberleys and elsewhere was a stop–start affair. Lorries put the donkey teams out of business, but petrol shortages and wet weather stopped the motorised transport altogether. When the lorries stopped, the donkey teams carried the loads or pulled out bogged vehicles. While they may have been redundant on the transport routes, donkeys were still handy on stations for carting water and other loads, riding fences or mustering sheep. Kangaroo hunters, rabbit trappers, miners and anyone else who didn't have recourse or use for motor vehicles still used donkey-power.

The people who worked with donkeys developed a great attachment to them. A well-known South Australian bushman, Bob Slade, a returned soldier from the First World War, lived and worked out in the Flinders Ranges near Eyre's Depot Springs. Hunting for kangaroo skins and foxes, he said that, except for the war years in France and one trip to the town of Quorn to have a tooth pulled out, he had spent all his life with donkeys.[3] Men like Bob Slade didn't want to know about lorries and never found the need to give up their donkeys. But plenty did and soon the released donkeys of the north-west would become a major feral problem.

By the 1950s, feral donkeys were one of the most serious pests for pastoralists in the Kimberleys. They are great foragers, much hardier than cattle, and not such asses as tradition has labelled them. Their numbers were increasing in both the East and West Kimberleys after the Second World War and they spread to unopened areas of the northwest. The chief vermin control officer for the Kimberley region, Mr AR Tomlinson, noted that shortages and high costs of ammunition during the war years were the main factors handicapping control work.[4]

By 1958, on the Ord River station of three million acres, and running 20,000 head of cattle, there were also 20,000 donkeys. A year earlier, Ord River station had engaged a team of four shooters to combat the donkeys and they accounted for 6000. This number barely represented the yearly natural increase of the hardy animals. They were a damaging burden on the land, and depleted native grasses and fodder.

The civilised donkey looks a harmless little animal that children might climb aboard and take liberties with. But when it goes bush it leaves all its good manners behind. These little beasts charge and fight fiercely with teeth and hoof when molested. When cornered, they can turn on their pursuers and inflict severe damage. Freshly caught, they are savagely resentful of captivity (though they domesticate quickly and become compliant). They are game and nimble and have a testing stubbornness that only eternal patience can conquer. Many stockmen say they would rather deal with wild cattle than angry donkeys.

CHAPTER 9

# Acclimatisation Societies and the Feral Free-for-all

E dward Wilson founded the Acclimatisation Society of Victoria in 1861 with the principle aim of introducing, acclimatising and domesticating all 'innocuous' quadrupeds, birds, fishes, insects and vegetables, whether useful or ornamental from Great Britain and other countries more civilised than Australia (which they believed was every other country).

Many of their planned and actual importations beggar belief, and luckily some of the species slated for acclimatisation could not be obtained in their countries of origin, died in transit or failed to thrive in Australia. But acclimatisation had enough successes to cause Australia more than its inordinate share of unnecessary heartache.

In the early nineteenth century, sporty colonial squires in New South Wales and Van Diemen's Land found the whole place to be inferior to England, and the field sport a bitter disappointment. The native creatures were so substandard as to be appallingly unworthy of a load of shot, and no substitute whatever for English game. No patriotic sportsman could be satisfied with these poor sporting prospects. There was only one thing for it. And that was to import your own.

Dr John Harris imported the first deer into New South Wales in 1802. They were either Ceylonese chital deer – India being a major and close supplier for Sydney – or fallow deer, as records of their behaviour indicate.

Dr Harris owned a property of 34 acres (14ha) near Sydney Cove, which had been granted to him by Governor King in 1803 for his military service and for aiding the governor in curtailing the illegal trading of rum by a corrupt group in the New South Wales Corps, more commonly known as the Rum Corps. In retaliation, the Rum Corps brought court-martial charges against Harris and declared that he had committed an offence 'ultimo' (in the previous month). He had indeed committed the offence, but having done so 'instant' (in the same month), the court martial failed to proceed, and Harris named his property 'Ultimo' after the clerical error, and no doubt as a reminder to his would-be persecutors. Later the Sydney suburb of Ultimo took the name of Dr Harris's property and Harris Street bore his name, as did the Sydney suburb of Harris Park and the Harris Street there.

Dr Harris's deer were not content to remain in Ultimo. They escaped and ran wild in Sydney. He publicly warned anyone from harassing them or setting dogs onto them. It was the earliest attempt to acclimatise a large European game animal. Those deer eventually died out around 1820, probably through formalised hunting on horseback with a pack of foxhounds, predation by poaching, and by dingoes and feral dogs.

Dr Harris's deer might have gone but the acclimatisation bug did not. Twenty years later, on 3 December 1824, the *Hobart Town Gazette and Van Diemen's Land Advertiser* reported that:

A subscription has been entered into by a few respectable
Settlers, and is now in progress, for raising a sum sufficient
to defray the expenses of bringing to and breeding in this
Island, some of the deer, hares, pheasants, and partridges of
the mother country. We publish this intelligence with great
pleasure, for the general information of the community.
The name of those who may be disposed to concur in this
patriotic measure, will be received and registered, at the
Office of this Gazette.

All these ferals made it into Tasmania, though fallow deer and
rabbits are the only imports that survive still in the island state.
Despite attempts to acclimatise pheasants in Tasmania, the
only surviving population is on King Island in Bass Strait,
which is also home to feral peafowl and turkeys. Fallow deer,
which occur naturally in the Mediterranean region and
eastwards to southern Iran, arrived in Tasmania in the 1830s
and a second attempt brought them to mainland Australia later
that century.

*

The 1860s were acclimatisation's great decade, although the
two acclimatisation headliners, rabbits and foxes, gained their
freedom through the actions of individuals in the years either
side. Globally, acclimatisation was most active where the fauna
was different to Britain's, and where acclimatisation societies
were membered by well-meaning, cashed-up enthusiasts.
Australia's fauna was so different to Britain's that it seemed to
goad Australia's acclimatisers into replacing it altogether. But it
wasn't just the fauna of the British Isles that they sourced.

Anything from anywhere was apparently better than what was already here. And none committed greater environmental crime than Edward Wilson, who got acclimatisation organised; Thomas Austin, who was responsible for the release of the rabbit; Professor Frederick McCoy, who was acclimatisation's arch-propagandist and feral bird proponent; and Thomas Chirnside of red fox infamy.

You name it, if it is a long-term non-livestock introduced pest, mammal, bird or fish, it would have sailed into Port Phillip, Victoria, and been liberated in or around Melbourne in the 1860s. There were no laws restricting or prohibiting the importation of foreign animals, or even the export of native fauna. It was open slather for acclimatisation societies and wealthy private individuals.

While Wilson encouraged the formation of acclimatisation societies in New South Wales, Queensland, South Australia and Tasmania, the Victorian Society was by far the best funded, the most half-witted, and the most influential and damaging – determined to change the faunal appearance of Australia.

'No society has ever been started, in the Australian colonies under more favourable circumstances, or with greater prospects of success, than the Acclimatisation Society of Victoria,' gushed the justly proud Victorian newspaper, the *Yeoman and Australian Acclimatiser*:

> And from what we know of the disinterested and patriotic motives of its supporters, we have no hesitation in saying that no society can better deserve the general support and co-operation of the public. We have only to express a hope that branch societies may shortly form throughout the

interior; and to this suggestion we invite the attention of
the patriotic residents in the various districts.[1]

Edward Wilson's acclimatisation motto was, 'if it lives, we
want it', and he had an energetic, evangelistic belief in the
importance of his cause. He owned the *Argus* newspaper in
Melbourne and was a humanitarian, a good man, who used his
newspapers to exert influence on politicians and decision-
makers to improve the lot of Victoria and his fellow man.
Acclimatisation appeared to be his only vice.

It helped that Wilson was extremely well connected and
influential. He had the numbers and financial backing to start
the acclimatisation society, particularly as the Victorian
government chipped in with the handsome amount of £3000
to help kick things off. A year earlier,[1] in 1860, while on a visit
to England to have his cataracts seen to, Wilson wasted no
effort in leaning on his English connections to arrange a
meeting with Henry Pelham Fiennes Pelham-Clinton, the
Fifth Duke of Newcastle.

Newcastle was close to Her Majesty Queen Victoria and,
through the Duke's good offices, the Queen became aware of
Wilson's visit and his quest for animals to supply the Australian
colony named in her honour. Her Majesty was delighted to
assist. She told Newcastle that Wilson 'was welcome to all
Windsor and Balmoral Castles could supply'. That offer
specifically included red deer, which Her Majesty would later
make good on.

Importing Britain's premier sportfish, the Atlantic salmon,
was a vexing problem. The ova would die if not kept at least
moist, and most definitely aerated and cold, and an ocean
voyage of several months to Australia threatened to scupper

Wilson's burning desire to ship salmon ova to Victoria. Anxious to test Her Majesty's commitment to assisting his cause, he straight-out asked the British government, through Newcastle, for the loan of a speedy man-of-war to bring out salmon fry. The Duke of Newcastle gave Wilson and that request short shrift, stating that 'he did not like converting men-of-war into herring-boats!' Oh well, it was worth a try. The salmon and brown trout ova would have to wait four years for a merchant vessel fast enough to get them to Australia alive.

Acclimatisation societies solved importation difficulties by offering to pay ships' captains, sailors and passengers from distant countries to husband exotic importations on their sea voyages to Australia. Dangling the carrot paid off. There was no shortage of arrivals from ships plying from Asia, India and Britain.

\*

The Victorian society held their first annual meeting on 24 November 1862 at the Mechanics' Institute in Melbourne. Sir Henry Barkly, the governor of Victoria, gave the primary address. He was a founder and life member of the Victorian Zoological and Acclimatisation Societies. Barkly had previously been the governor of Guyana and the natural sciences were his passion. He thought Wilson's proposal to release monkeys in the bush was a terrific idea:

> I recollect that we happened to possess at one time a considerable number of monkeys, and that they were exceedingly mischievous, troublesome to look after, and altogether very expensive. The council almost

unanimously came to the conclusion that it would be much better to get rid of the monkeys, but our friend Mr Wilson wrote out to us to the effect that he was a thorough acclimatiser and that he went in for the acclimatisation of monkeys for the amusement of the wayfarer whom their gambols would delight as he lay under some gum-tree in the forest on a sultry day.

And really when I call to mind my South American reminiscences – when I remember the pretty little sakiwinki [squirrel monkey] which used to frolic in the trees near my study window – and when I recollect how my time was beguiled during the boating excursions on the noble rivers of Guiana by the tricks of the large baboons who clambered from tree to tree, and hurled at a stranger whatever they could catch as a punishment for intruding on their solitude – I think Mr Wilson was in that respect right, and I am inclined to concur with him that it is desirable to acclimatise the monkey tribe, if it can be done.[2]

Professor Frederick McCoy added colour to the otherwise tedious proceedings. He would have loved the boa constrictor's carcase, but he would have preferred a whole herd of boa constrictors to release somewhere they could proliferate in peace and feast on the native creatures, taking up all the room in the bush.

The good professor was born in Dublin and studied medicine at Cambridge but switched to natural sciences and palaeontology.

And if he was as proficient at medicine as he was in the natural sciences, then he did humanity a great service by this change of plan. Professor McCoy immigrated to Melbourne where he helped to establish the Acclimatisation Society of Victoria and sought to replace what he perceived as the silence or unpleasant noises of the Australian bush with the sounds of English songbirds. He said that 'English thrushes, blackbirds, larks, starlings, and canaries when liberated would enliven the savage silence, or worse with their varied, touching, joyous, strains of heaven-taught melody.' In 1862, he celebrated the successful introduction of the European rabbit, 'so thoroughly acclimatized that it swarms in hundreds in some localities and can at any time be extended to others', and agitated for, and stoutly defended the release of the thrush, blackbird, starling and the sparrow.

Professor McCoy was just the fellow for a crackpot theory, including the preposterous hypothesis that dogs and cats were both derived from the marsupial lion. He was a robust supporter of creationism and an implacable enemy of the theory of evolution.

At the first annual general meeting of the Acclimatisation Society of Victoria, Professor McCoy took the lectern to inform the members present of the status of the society's acquisitions and its bright prospects for obtaining more, including:

Three Ceylon elks (sambar deer). Three Indian spotted deer (chital deer). Two Indian hog deer and nineteen fallow deer. Thirty-seven crossbred llama alpacas. Three pure alpaca bucks. Eight angora goats. Three Abyssinian sheep. One Bengal sheep. Sixteen Chinese sheep. One cape sheep. Ten monkeys. One jackal. Three mongooses. One wild boar. And one screwtail.

Whatever that is!

Out of all the species Professor McCoy rattled off, only the fallow deer brought from Tasmania, and the sambar, hog and chital deer, all imported from Asia, became ferals. It could have been worse. Over the years Australian acclimatisation societies introduced eighteen deer species. Luckily, twelve species – the bawean, Chinese water, Eld's, mule, muntjac, musk, reindeer, roe, sika, swamp, wapiti and white-tailed deer – failed to strike roots.

Sambar deer are native to South-east Asia, and the ones in the society's collection came from Ceylon (now Sri Lanka). The deer were kept for a time at the society's zoo at Melbourne's Royal Park. The zoo had two purposes, the primary one being public exhibition, but it also served to house the society's imported animals prior to their release into the wild.

Eventually the sambar deer were released into Victoria's east Gippsland, after which they established themselves along the Great Dividing Range and tablelands northwards. In 1867, a man named James Kelly from Sale in Gippsland forwarded a £10 cheque to the society and requested some sambar deer.[3] Tracing the sambar's liberation is just a matter of joining some dots.

Sambar often make nuisances of themselves when they come in contact with human habitation. Feral sambar are big animals and damage forestry plantations, crops, infrastructure and the environment through over-grazing and killing trees as they rub their antlers and creating boggy wallows. They are also a major motorway hazard due to their size and semi-nocturnal behaviour.

Chital or axis deer are gregarious and can form groups of more than a hundred individuals. Feral chital deer were imported and distributed by the Acclimatisation Society of

Victoria, and after being held as exhibits were sent northwards and now occur in areas throughout north Queensland, pockets of New South Wales, and the south-east of South Australia. Chital deer are diurnal, and feed and get about during the day, unlike all the other deer species in Australia.

The little hog deer are another Indian subcontinental species brought to Australia by the Victorian society for hunting in Gippsland. They are commonly found in coastal tea-tree swamp areas. They are usually solitary animals but may congregate in feeding areas. Where they are regularly disturbed, they may become nocturnal. Hog deer reproduce irregularly, however calves are most frequently seen between August and October. Male antlers may be cast around this same time. Hog deer get their name from their habit of running through the forest with their heads low and ducking obstacles rather than jumping, much like a wild hog in the northern hemisphere.

Feral hog deer are a growing pest problem. They cause browsing damage to coastal vegetation and other sensitive areas. The can damage plantations and ornamental gardens. They can spread both native and exotic plant seeds. Feral hog deer can carry and spread livestock diseases, which reduce farm productivity and increase management costs.[4]

Red deer were introduced into Australia between 1860 and 1874 by European acclimatisation societies. The Queensland population derived from gifts from Queen Victoria, as promised to Edward Wilson, the father of acclimatisation in Australia. In Queensland they are chiefly found in the Brisbane Valley. They like mixed grassland with the nearby security of woodland. They may be seen in the open but usually only when nearby to thick timbered vegetation. Red deer occur in New South Wales, Queensland and South Australia and are becoming more widespread and bigger pests than they once were. They might be a majestic creature but like all deer in Australia they carry disease, compete with livestock and fauna for feed, and spread parasites and disease.[5]

Deer are graceful creatures, and are a gentle-looking novelty for people who don't usually encounter them. They certainly have a more appealing image than any of our other feral pests.

\*

The acclimatisation societies had high hopes for exotic birds, but none of the gamebirds they released ever managed to form viable populations. Professor McCoy rattled off the following species held and ready for release:

> One marabou crane. One Indian pelican. Three Indian peafowl. Twelve golden pheasants. Twenty-one English pheasants. Seventeen silver pheasants. Eight white swans. Six Canadian geese. Twenty Muscovy ducks. Two white-throated geese. Two Egyptian geese. One New Zealand duck. Seventeen Chinese geese. Sixteen English wild ducks [possibly the mallard duck]. Five shell ducks. Four Carolina ducks. Ten call ducks. Three Indian partridges. Two English partridges. Eight Californian quail. Two Fiji doves. Two Ceylon doves. Two Manilla doves. Twenty-one turtle doves. Eleven curassows. Twenty thrushes. Twelve blackbirds. Eight linnets. Ten goldfinches. Five Java sparrows. Twelve canaries. One skylark. Eight ortolans [European bunting]. Thirteen Indian finches.

And a partridge in a pear tree.

Of that lot, only the thrushes, blackbirds, sparrows, goldfinches and skylarks would succeed in acclimatising to Australia. Canaries are hard enough to keep alive in a cage, let alone in the open. The good professor nonetheless confirmed that the thrush, skylark, blackbird and starling 'could now be considered permanently established amongst us, the three former being heard in all directions'. Soon they'd range throughout the bigger towns in Victoria and further afield, causing problems for gardeners, and in vineyards and orchards wherever they went. These pointless bird pests would cause plenty of trouble and damage but the worst of the lot, the Indian or common myna, was yet to arrive.

Great care ensured the English songbirds not only survived but increased, with the other object of their release being the destruction of garden pests such as caterpillars. Snails were not on the list of pests they were to destroy at the time of their introduction, for one good reason: at the time, Australians had no garden snail problem; the nice little native snail wasn't interested in disturbed environments such as gardens.

The common garden snail hitched a ride to Melbourne with the imported thrushes and blackbirds. Quantities of live snails provided food for the birds on the voyage out, especially for the thrushes. To make selected gardens in Toorak, Melbourne, even more English-like and to provide food for the thrushes, the snails went free with them. The two have thrived together ever since, but the spread of the colonising snails was extremely slow.

Caterpillars on the other hand, continued to decimate market-garden crops until pesticides did a more efficient job than sparrows, starlings and mynas. The feral birds that disdained the caterpillar prospered and are now the most disliked, drab and annoying birds in Australia.

When orchardists complained about the dramatic increase and widespread destruction of fruit by sparrows, Professor McCoy told them to harden up and put 'inexpensive' netting over their orchards. Problem solved! Yet the problems became so severe across south-eastern Australia that a Sparrow Pest Association of New South Wales – nothing less than a We Hate Sparrows Club – operated until 1904, and Professor McCoy's name became mud.

It's impossible to pinpoint when the feral pigeon arrived in Australia, but the acclimatisers had something to do with it. There are brief mentions in the contemporary press, usually in shipping intelligence columns that captain so and so of a certain ship had brought pigeons in. The feral pigeon is the descendant of the rock dove and has a renowned homing ability, but it was clearly asking too much of it to find its way back to England when released here in the mid-nineteenth century.

It is a familiar sight in Australian cities, where it desecrates the statues of our past heroes of empire with droppings, and its nest sites spread lice and other nasties. As there is no such thing as a 'native' inner-city-dwelling bird species, it is hard to suggest any native bird that city-based feral pigeons may have displaced. They are preyed upon by peregrine falcons, which hunt them in and high above the CBDs of Australia's biggest cities, and by foxes and feral cats. Feral pigeons inhabit silos and grain-handling facilities, making nuisances of themselves in the bush as well.

Various gun clubs found their own uses for sparrows, starlings and pigeons. In the first decade of the twentieth century, the Melbourne Gun Club staged live shooting every

Saturday. Birds flew from cages called traps and were shot on the wing by armed participants.[5] The Benalla Gun Club, at the turn of the century, ran a popular £10 handicap aimed at starlings, and a Mr Hyland made himself a little pocket money by supplying the birds.[6] Live shooting remained a common activity until public outcry forced gun clubs into adopting the more humane clay pigeon, a small round hard clay frisbee that shattered into a thousand biodegradable pieces when shot and never needed neck-wringing.

The feathered ferals are a fact of Australian urban life. We're all familiar with them and aware of their impact on our gardens and parklands and what natural environmental remnants remain around our cities and towns. Everyone whinges about them, and every so often councils encourage ratepayers to trap and destroy Indian mynas, but it's all piecemeal and hasn't made one scrap of difference. We're stuck with the birds it appears, and poorer for it.

*

Once Professor McCoy had finished discussing the merits of birds at the first annual meeting of the Acclimatisation Society of Victoria, he moved on to fish. He stated that the Society had released 'a quantity of carp, dace, roach, goldfish, and tench' into Victoria, and had generously shared them with acclimatising colleagues in the newly renamed Tasmania. Anyone a fan of tench, roach or dace? Thought not. Few people are, other than dedicated coarse anglers in Victoria. Not even admired in Britain, these highly undesirable and – frankly – ugly, pointless fish were an uninspiring lot scraped from the bottom of English municipal ponds.

It wouldn't be long before the society would import and release redfin or English perch into the cooler reaches of the Murray Darling system. How anyone could think redfin a superior fish in any way to any of Australia's beautiful native perch is anyone's guess. Redfin are a medium-sized freshwater fish native to northern Europe, first introduced to Victoria through the 'energetic kindness of Mr Morton Allport' as a gift to the Acclimatisation Society of Victoria.

Thanks to those singular gentlemen, redfin infest the cooler waterways of all southern Australia. Although redfin are a passable sport fish and alright eating, they are voracious predators of other fish and invertebrates, and can destroy recreational fisheries in enclosed waters by building up to plague numbers and eliminating other species. There are few people in mainland Australia still thanking Mr Allport for his energetic kindness.

*

The Acclimatisation Society of New South Wales was the Victorian society's impoverished relation. Victoria's Acclimatisation Society thrived on the generosity of the colonial government and its wealthy members. The New South Wales society's members were big on talking but small on donating, and the first colony's government was even tighter fisted than the society's stingy members – and that's saying something. We should always be grateful they could not raise the capital to fund their more stupid ideas, yet they did damage enough on a shoestring. There is no telling what they could have inflicted upon the colony if parsimony hadn't been their chief objective.

The New South Wales society held its second annual meeting at Mort's Wool Stores, Circular Quay, in September 1862, where a Mr EL Layard, the curator of the museum at Cape Town, addressed the members. He urged them to import from southern Africa numerous gamebirds, 'well able to cope with vermin, such as snakes' and that ate vegetables, bulbs and the like. In addition, the Cape pheasant principally favoured low scrubby bushland, and the members believed New South Wales had more than enough of that lying around doing absolutely nothing.

Mr Layard then recommended the society purchase various antelope and goats, including the bontebok, ibex, rhee bock, bush bock and klipspringer, 'whose skin makes the best saddle cloth', and the hyrax, a little vocal rodent, 'the flesh of which was much esteemed among the Dutch settlers at the Cape'. The South African visitor said he could supply them all from Cape Town, but that the principal expense would be to provide a depot there, to keep them in until shipping.[7] The mere notion of that mounting expense would have been sufficient to ensure that not one of the species Mr Layard was trying to flog the society ever made it to Australia.

As Mr Layard sat down, up jumped Mr C Moore, pleased to tell the meeting that he'd heard from Mr Phillips, the director of the Botanic Gardens in Calcutta, who was willing to send birds and animals from India if he first received kangaroos and emus from the New South Wales society. Ignoring Mr Phillips's terms, the chair directed that they write to the director and ask him to first send his best black partridge and jungle fowl, and if he did, the society would send kangaroos and emus.[8] That lopsided swap never occurred, the director wisely insisted on taking his kangaroos and emus up-front.

The society spent the rest of the meeting discussing and debating the fascinating merits of their silkworms and yam seeds, which, other than releasing rusa deer in the Royal National Park in the early twentieth century, was about as interesting as things ever got with them.

# CHAPTER 10

# Thomas Austin and the Rabbits of Barwon Park

Three years before the acclimatisation societies would set their various scourges on Australia, another budding 'entrepreneur' set his own sights on importing a bit of Mother England to Australia's shores. On Christmas night of 1859, the ship *Lightning* berthed off Point Gellibrand in Port Phillip. Amongst its cargo from Liverpool, England, were sixty-eight partridges, four hares and twenty-four wild rabbits in the care of a man surnamed Mack. They were bound for Mr Mack's uncle Thomas Austin, in Barwon Park – his little piece of England down under – and arrived at their new and very temporary home on Boxing Day. Mr Austin's rabbits would prove to be the Christmas present Australia should never have received, and we can't blame Santa for this one.

Mr Austin was a prominent and successful grazier and, in his exclusive social circle, much loved. He was born at Baltonsborough, England in 1816. At fifteen years of age, he immigrated to Tasmania to join his brothers, who were stockbrokers. Early in 1837, Thomas moved to the District of Port Phillip and occupied land near Winchelsea, on the banks of the upper reaches of the Barwon River, just west of Geelong. With financial backing from his money-merchant elder brothers, Thomas developed Barwon Park into a productive estate of 29,000 acres (11,736ha). He got rich off the fat of the land and had money to spend.

Victoria, young and rolling in the wealth of the pastoral and gold-mining booms, was keen to show the world, and New South Wales in particular, just how well it was doing. Some of that new money built grandiose manors that were little more than monuments to self-congratulation, and vain replications of the estates of the English upper class that once had no room for them.

The importation and release of English game upon these new estates was the final addition, and in the late 1850s there was no finer example of the faux English estate than Thomas Austin's Barwon Park. In starchy old Victorian-era Victoria, the fowling-piece-happy sporting fancies, who craved the opportunity to blast English game, were excited about the possibilities acclimatisation offered. And the men who made it happen, jolly good fellows like Thomas Austin, were the heroes of the day.

Along with the rabbit, Austin also bought bird stock including blackbirds from upper society's favourite importer, Mr H Brown. Mr J Rennie, in an article in the *South Australian Weekly Chronicle* of 24 February 1859, wrote that he feared for Mr Austin's blackbirds:

> In the notice of Mr Austin's importations, I see blackbirds
> are enumerated; but I fear we shall not easily succeed in
> naturalizing them here. If let loose in the open woodless
> country of the Barrobool Hills, along with partridges, etc,
> they could not thrive for want of food, though it is
> possible, if they were to make their way to the banks of

the Barwon, about Fyan's Ford, or to the wooded shores of Lake Connewarre, they might find some sort of congenial food.

It strikes me as rather singular that the taste of importers should run upon blackbirds, whose notes, though sweet and plaintive, are unvaried and somewhat monotonous, while their time of singing is as brief as that of the nightingale – seldom longer than four or five weeks, and not even so long unless their nests have been robbed; for if I mistake not, they only breed once a year, and only sing when breeding, and not from mere gaiety, like the redbreast in winter.

No person who has not tried, as I did, for years, can have any idea of the incessant care and trouble in feeding and managing blackbirds, nightingales, and other soft-billed birds; and hence we rarely see them thrive in confinement, and if not thriving, how could they be expected to breed?

Mr Rennie need not have worried. The blackbirds did almost as splendidly as Mr Austin's rabbits.

Mr Brown had arrived in Melbourne in early 1857, where he wasted no time in setting up shops in Melbourne and Sydney, running this ad through January in the *Argus* and *Sydney Morning Herald*:

NOTICE to Bird fanciers – The undersigned begs to inform the bird fanciers of this city, that he has just arrived again in the clipper ship *Bielefeld*, from Hamburgh, with the following extensive assortment of European singing birds: 70 genuine German Canaries, raised at the Hartz Mountains by amateurs, and taught to sing the nightingale and lark notes, the waterbubble, flute, trill, and bell notes, to the greatest perfection; 100 pure Belgian Long Breed Canaries, of the finest stock of Brussels and Antwerp. Also, a great number of Thrushes, Blackbirds, Larks. Robin Redbreasts, Nightingales, Black caps, etc, all in full song and perfect health. Every bird warranted. Also, a small number of fancy Pigeons, best Canary and German summer Rapeseed, and a great assortment of wooden and metallic cages. For SALE at reasonable prices, at H BROWN'S, No 98 Bourke Street, opposite Theatre Royal.[1]

You name it, Brown had it. And he didn't have to look far for a sale. The acclimatisation societies and Thomas Austin wasted no time in snapping up his stock, and everyone who bought birds bred them up and released them. They may as well have just paid the money and opened the cage doors.

Thomas Austin was the acclimatisation megastar of his day, and Barwon Park was his stage. Edward Wilson's Melbourne newspaper, *Argus*, was ever ready to keep the public up to date with his successes:

It may no doubt be satisfactory to those who take an interest in the introduction of English game into this colony to know that, through the exertions of Mr Thomas Austin, of Barwon Park, great things have been accomplished towards the end in view ...

The rabbits introduced by Mr Austin have proved themselves to be as prolific, if not more so, than in the old country, and may be said now to number in thousands, and, unfortunately, prove highly destructive to the young trees planted in the various plantations intended for the pheasants and partridges. ...

In the meantime we wish success to Mr Austin in his endeavours to benefit the public by introducing the game. We cannot too highly compliment the keeper, Mr Myles, in charge of the birds and animals, for the exertion made by him in the cause, and for his kindness and urbanity to visitors in affording every information desired.[2]

What Edward Wilson failed to note was that Austin's rabbits had long been at large. Within a year or so of releasing the rabbits on Barwon Park, the top popped off the bottle and the cotton-tailed genie was happily hopping out over the boundaries. Austin wouldn't have been happy about that. He was too much of a snob to want to share them with the common yeomanry and the landless multitudes who found the newly arrived rabbits a pleasant sporting novelty. It was at this point that Austin could have cleaned up the mess he made. He did nothing. And his rabbits were now unstoppable because no one lifted a finger.

Interestingly, though Austin was feted by Wilson and the Acclimatisation Society of Victoria for his successes, he was not a member for several years. Why? No one knows. It was a decision that would absolve the society of the sin of original release of the rabbit, which, as we shall see, is but a minor technicality.

Austin eventually bought himself life membership of the society in April 1864 for a sum of ten guineas. Now that Barwon Park had had such astounding acclimatisation success, he modestly added in his membership application that he 'had done perhaps a little towards introducing game and birds'. He proudly stated that he had thousands of wild rabbits on Barwon Park.[3] As did everyone within twenty miles of the place. By June 1864, at the Acclimatisation Society of Victoria's second meeting of the year, Thomas Austin was the evening's honoured member, acclimatisation's role model and greatest benefactor.

Melbourne newspaper *The Yeoman and Australian Acclimatiser*, the Edward Wilson-owned PR arm of the society, beamed that the whole evening was successful. It was not only a fitting tribute to the cause of acclimatisation, but it was also a 'complete triumph of gastronomy'. And the gastronomic marvels were a bizarre and stomach-churning array of mostly Australian native creatures.

The entrees contained wombat, bandicoot and lorikeet, but everyone agreed that the *vol-au-vent* of frogs was the best dish of the evening. Yum. There were also dishes of Australian bustard, kangaroo, brolga, mallee fowl, black swan and wallaby, Murray cod and Murray crayfish, trumpeter from Hobart Town, eels caught at Yan Yean (north of Melbourne), and perch (Australian bass) from Gippsland.

After polishing all that off, the interminable round of toasts commenced. Mr WC Haines prepared to toast the society on behalf of the Victoria Legislative Assembly. 'In aiding the work of acclimatisation,' he slurred, 'the Legislature is conferring a substantial benefit upon the country. The history of successful colonisation in Australia is the history of acclimatisation.'[4] And that was true enough in its way.

The society then found Mr Austin rightly celebrated as the man who had done more than anyone in Victoria to not only draw gentlemen around him, but to show them great sport. The young men of Victoria 'who took to shooting, fishing, and hunting as naturally as ducks took to water' ought to be grateful to Mr Austin, they said, he who had been so successful in introducing game into the colony and so developing its resources.

'Hear! hear!' cried the members.

Glasses were charged, and a toast was drunk to Mr Austin's continued good health. Mr Austin responded, intimating that in his efforts at acclimatisation he had met with both success and failure. Last year, he confessed, he'd lost 200 gamebirds from various causes; but this year he had reared about 100 pheasants, and, amongst other acclimatisation triumphs, he had been successful in breeding blackbirds, thrushes and hares. Lucky members of the Acclimatisation Society had had the pleasure of shooting at the birds he'd so lovingly reared; and if any of the members wanted to promote those field sports, which were so popular in the old country, he would be happy to give them a pair of birds for breeding purposes, if they would take the same care in the feeding and management of them as he had done.[5]

Mr Austin was also happy to hand around the rabbits. He could afford to. By mid-1865 he and his fellows had shot around 20,000 rabbits on his estate and reckoned on there being at least 10,000 there still. He would happily give a pair to anyone who would release them on their properties for future sport. In that he was as good as his word. He donated rabbits to the Acclimatisation Society for further dispersal, as well as rabbit coursing clubs, which held field meetings where wild rabbits were released to be hunted down by dogs and killed. Members placed bets on which dogs would win.

# CHAPTER 11

# Royal Rabbit Routs and the Stately Shooter Shot

T he purpose of stocking Barwon Park with exotic game like rabbits was to provide gun sports for Thomas Austin and his rich mates. Austin's game keeper, Myles, went to pains to remove every predator that as much as looked sideways at his game preserve. In 1866, shooting on Barwon Park netted 14,253 rabbits and the 'vermin' destroyed included 448 hawks, 23 wedge-tailed eagles, 622 quolls and 32 domestic (probably feral) cats. Barwon Park was nothing more than a grotesque killing field, but it was one that was irresistible to the wealthy sporting ghouls of the day.

*The Yeoman and Australian Acclimatiser* published a full description of a typical Barwon Park shoot-meet in June 1865. The seven guests arrived at nine o'clock and enjoyed a hearty breakfast. They, and the station hands who were to function as beaters, numbered around twenty-five. Myles the gamekeeper and his assistants would have been up since midnight, blocking all the entrances to the warrens to keep the rabbits aboveground during the day.

Shotguns and ammunition were handed out to the guests at Myles's lodge. Next, they were shown around to the huge wire-netting-enclosed pheasant aviaries and the hare enclosure, which proved to be interesting exhibits. The pheasants, blackbirds and thrushes, which had recently arrived aboard the *Yorkshire*, were still acclimatising and could not in good conscience face the shotguns until they had properly adjusted – ethical sportsmanship being bywords for shooting on Barwon Park.

The scythed grass on the shooting grounds gave the sportsmen the best opportunity, and instructions were given to only shoot cock pheasants. The beaters had to yell 'Ware hen, ware hen!' if a hen pheasant rose, thus warning the shooters not to shoot the hen, and hopefully not them either. The beaters armed themselves with sticks and, beating the ground and grass, drove the rabbits towards the waiting line of guns.

The party retired to the Barwon Park mansion for luncheon, the shooters dining inside, and the exhausted beaters, like faithful dogs tired from a morning's work, were fed on the lawn. After lunch, the party shot rabbits along the bank of the Barwon River. The tally for the day was 173 rabbits and five cock pheasants.[1] Small change in Barwon Park's scheme of things.

The most prominent sporting ghoul to shoot up Barwon Park's obscene number of rabbits was Prince Alfred, the Duke of Edinburgh, second son of Queen Victoria. In 1867, he became the first British royal to visit Australia. The Acclimatisation Society, loyal patriotic brown-nosers to a man, were all over him like silver gulls on a chip:

To His Royal Highness Prince Alfred Ernest Albert, Duke
of Edinburgh, Knight of the Most Noble Order of the
Garter [Etc, Etc, Etc.]

May it Please Your Royal Highness,

We, the Members of the Acclimatisation Society of
Victoria, do ourselves the distinguished honour of

approaching your Royal Highness with sentiments of loyalty and attachment to Her Majesty's throne and person, and we humbly offer our most sincere congratulations on your safe arrival in this distant part of Her Majesty's Empire.

We presume it is unnecessary to remind your Royal Highness of the deep interest your late illustrious and ever-to-be-lamented father, the Prince Consort, took in the cause of Acclimatisation, and also His Royal Highness the Prince of Wales, as evidenced by His Royal Highness' acceptance of the presidency of a kindred institution in Great Britain.

We further do ourselves the honour of presenting to your Royal Highness the published reports of our Society, and we do so with the hope that you will find that our past labours have not been in vain.

We have the honour to be, with the most profound respect,

Your Royal Highness' most obedient servants,
Signed on behalf of the Society,
Thomas Black.[2]

His Royal Highness was enormously popular and his tour was a great success. So impressed and pleased was he with the sycophants of the Acclimatisation Society of Victoria and their published reports, which would have made fascinating bedtime reading, that as soon as he found a little spare time, he headed straight for acclimatisation's showpiece, Barwon Park.

In December 1867, after attending a range of civil functions in Geelong, His Royal Highness and his entourage attended the property of Thomas Austin. After luncheon, the Duke and his party went out shooting, and enjoyed magnificent sport, killing almost 1000 rabbits in three and a half hours, HRH bagging 416.

The Duke left the following afternoon for William Robertson's property, Glen Alvie, near Colac, where he stayed the night. William Robertson senior had a bit in common with Thomas Austin. They were both successful pastoralists, they were both members of the Acclimatisation Society of Victoria, both were rabbit and small-game enthusiasts, and they were both high in royal favour. And it just so happened that William Robertson was having self-inflicted rabbit issues of his own. It is probable that, HRH, being such a mad-keen rabbit shooter, may well have helped Robertson thin out a few of his rabbits while he was there.

The Duke of Edinburgh's second visit to Barwon Park was a real hoot. The day's death toll began when the Duke's train, approaching Geelong, ran over and killed four sheep, but the carriage ride out to Barwon Park from Geelong was uneventfully bloodless. There were seven guns participating: HRH, Austin, and five hangers-on, all of whom covered themselves in 'haloes of sporting glory'.

Everyone, with the probable exception of the rabbits, had the best time. *The Mercury* of Hobart, reporting on the festivities, even suggested the rabbit was morally obliged to get itself shot: 'after all, the end and aim of a bunny's existence is that he should be shot for somebody's amusement, and so how, when, or where he does get shot cannot much matter.'[3] Which is more than any rabbit could reasonably hope for.

Over two sessions on consecutive days, the party shot more than 1500 rabbits, of which the Duke accounted for over 600.

In a live pigeon shooting match in Melbourne, the *Horsham Times* reported, HRH was the best shot on the ground.[4] Of course he was. And luckily for HRH, he was a better shot than Henry James O'Farrell.

O'Farrell wasn't a Fenian; he was just another disaffected Irishman, one of millions who would have happily shot the entire British royal family, but you have to start somewhere. At a public picnic function at Clontarf, Sydney, on 12 March 1868, O'Farrell shot the Duke in the back, but he was such a remarkably bad shot that from just five or six feet away he only mildly wounded the Duke, who nevertheless fell to the ground crying, 'My God! My back is broken!' The bullet missed his spine and all his vital organs, followed the course of a rib and lodged beneath the flesh on the right side of his chest. HRH was extremely lucky. The New South Wales government tried its best to uncover a Fenian conspiracy and failed, but O'Farrell did not get a taste of the Duke's good luck.

This was Australia and you don't walk about Sydney taking pot-shots at His Royal Highnesses like you're His Royal Highness walking about Barwon Park taking pot-shots at rabbits, no matter how angry you are that the Brits allowed your entire family to starve to death in the potato famine.

O'Farrell was duly hanged on 21 April and the Duke, who had recovered completely by 26 March, and who, to be fair, requested clemency for O'Farrell (but not all that stridently), left for England on 26 June 1868. He wouldn't be gone for too long. Not while his big mate Thomas Austin was breeding up all those rabbits for him.

In October 1870, the Duke was back in Australia on an unofficial visit and wasted no time in making off for Barwon

Park and Mr Austin's legendary hospitality. In the Duke's absence Thomas Austin had procured a beagle pack and these worked alongside the beaters to drive the rabbits towards the waiting muzzles of the Duke's side-by-side shotguns. The dogs were probably fed on the lawn along with the beaters.

The Duke shot with three breech-loading shotguns and kept two men loading for him as quickly as they could, the barrels getting so hot the loaders could only grasp the guns by the forearm woodwork. The slaughter (it wasn't hunting) lasted for three and a quarter hours. The Duke shot 333 rabbits out of about 500 dispatched. That's about one rabbit every 35 seconds. His aide, Lieutenant Haig, shot about half that, and wisely so because everyone's happy when a Royal Highness is the best at everything. During the progress of the shooting the occasional pheasant rose from cover, but HRH let it be, intending to deal with them the following day. However, it poured rain all the next day until three o'clock in the afternoon forcing the Duke to bid Mr Austin adieu and reluctantly return to Melbourne.[5]

His Royal Highness would not visit Australia again. He succeeded to the Duchy of Saxe-Coburg and Gotha in 1893 and thereafter lived in Germany until his death in 1900.

*

Obviously, Thomas Austin is not solely responsible for the release and distribution of the rabbit in Australia. Lots of people got in on the act. But it is indisputable that the real rabbit trouble started with him. Thomas Austin was a ubiquitous promoter of acclimatisation, and an energetic supporter of releasing rabbits. And he encouraged, aided and abetted anyone of his social standing to do the same. Even when rabbits were causing huge problems in the late 1860s, Austin was still insensitively holding obscene shoots on Barwon Park, slaughtering thousands, catering for the rich, famous and powerful, still trying to play the English lord.

Austin died suddenly in December 1871, aged just 56. It was long before the rabbit plague went coast-to-coast, but they were a plague in central and western Victoria sure enough. Not that Austin ever acknowledged his part in it. His obituary and the article recalling his life and achievements were so thoroughly rabbit-sanitised you could eat your dinner off them.

His rabbit-less obituary in the *Argus* was glowing in its praise for his energy, community spirit and kindness for all men. He 'loved a joke', and was 'possessed of a considerable amount of shrewdness, detested all kinds of snobs and humbug, and had a kind and cheery word for every man – rich and poor ... During the past twelve years he twice paid a visit to England, and we all know of his importation into this colony of pheasants, partridges, hares, and other game.'[6]

An article commemorating his life also masterfully omitted any reference to the rabbit, besting even the *Argus*'s euphemistic 'other game': 'he became possessed of that beautiful estate called Barwon Park, which in after years became famous as the home of the pheasant, the partridge, and the hare.'[7]

Both articles appeared in newspapers that were at one time owned by, or associated with, Edward Wilson, who much admired Thomas Austin. It is understandable that those loyal to him chose to ignore the big, grey, buck-toothed, long-eared, cotton-tailed elephant in the room, but that his entry in the usually reliable *Australian Dictionary of Biography* is so neglectful surprises this writer at least.[8]

By the time Thomas Austin had been gone for a decade his rabbits had beset three colonies. The fight against them and the losses to agriculture cost millions of pounds a year. Some legacy, but great good did come out of Barwon Park.

During that decade, Thomas Austin's widow, Elizabeth, lived in quiet obscurity in her lonely mansion. But in 1880, Mrs Austin became involved in philanthropy. Her interest in helping those struck down by incurable disease began when her cook, Louisa, an English immigrant, contracted tuberculosis. Louisa told Elizabeth that she would have to cease work and seek admission to the prison hospital, which was poorly equipped but the only hospital for immigrants with incurable illnesses.

Elizabeth's concern for Louisa and other immigrants was the impetus for her donating £6000 to assist in the building of a hospital for incurables in Melbourne. Her example prompted others to donate to the cause and the Austin Hospital for Incurables opened in 1882 on her birthday. She made further donations, and in 1898 she paid for the establishment of a children's ward.

Elizabeth Austin was also the benefactor of the Austin Homes for Women at South Geelong. She supported many other benevolent societies and local charities. Hers was a household name throughout the colony of Victoria in the 1890s. She died on 2 September 1910 at Winchelsea. Elizabeth Austin was the preeminent woman philanthropist of her generation, and a pioneer of female benefaction in Victoria.[9] Her family remained involved in the hospital for many years – three of Elizabeth's granddaughters served on the hospital committee until the 1960s.

Melbourne's Austin Hospital, along with the other facilities under the Austin Health umbrella, is renowned for its specialist work in cancer, infectious diseases, obesity, sleep medicine, intensive-care medicine, neurology, endocrinology, mental health and rehabilitation. Austin Health is an internationally recognised centre of excellence in hospital-based research, and is the largest Victorian provider of training for specialist physicians and surgeons.[10]

Out of everything bad comes something good. The fruits of Elizabeth Austin's philanthropy have certainly counterbalanced the destruction wrought by her late husband's rabbits, which in 1880 numbered in their millions and had crossed the mighty Murray north into New South Wales.

# CHAPTER 12

# Barwon Park's Rabbits Conquer Victoria

Wild rabbits might look Easter-bunny cute, but they are a surprisingly tough creature that, in numbers, can withstand the harshest environmental conditions and predation, and still proliferate. To do so they need to be aggressive enough to out-muscle native Australian fauna, and it didn't take a lot for the pushy rabbits with the weight of numbers on their side to do just that. They immediately took advantage of native-animal burrows and have clearly contributed to the decline or loss of southern and northern hairy-nosed wombats and the greater bilby, and displaced and out-competed the yellow-footed rock wallaby, the mallee fowl, the Australian bustard, several species of quail, and the plains-wanderer.

In the complicated social structure of rabbits, large dominant males defend territories savagely and gain mating rights to the best females by beating up the opposition. And dominant senior females claim and defend nesting sites in warrens. Fights between rabbits of the same sex are vicious affairs. In densely populated areas, different social groups can share common warren or feeding areas amiably enough. Their territories range up to around two hectares depending on the population, provided there is enough food to support the population.

Rabbits have a small mouth and rodent-like teeth for close grazing. They are selective feeders — searching out tiny seedlings of the most palatable species and removing them before they can grow and reproduce. Rabbits don't fell giant ancient trees; rather, they seek out and eat the seedlings of their preferred species; so, once mature trees die, there are no younger plants to replace them. The immediate impact of rabbits may go unnoticed, but the lack of plant recruitment can change the whole structure of vegetation communities, with flow-on effects for the native birds, reptiles, invertebrates and other animals that live within.

Rabbits prefer deep, well-drained, light sandy loams, with warrens typically larger on deeper soils and smaller on sandy soils. Rabbits are quite easy to please and can occur anywhere in temperate regions except in dense forests, on heavy, black soil plains or in alpine regions above 1500 metres. Warrens are the key to the rabbit's survival. They provide protection from predators and the extremes of the weather. Without protection from the elements, rabbits are not able to breed successfully, because newborns are susceptible to temperature extremes and predation. Living aboveground doesn't bother them if there's enough cover, and the hollow trunks and branches of Australia's fallen eucalyptus trees have made excellent homes for bush bunnies. On the whole, though, successful breeding usually requires them to be underground.

Rabbits become sexually mature at three to four months. They require fresh protein-rich growth to stimulate breeding, which starts in autumn and continues until vegetation dries off in early summer. Breeding stops and rabbit mortality is particularly high during summer months due to diseases, lack of food and water, and extreme temperatures.[1]

The rabbit is all about quick reproduction. The doe's gestation period is around thirty days and they have litters of four to six kittens, which are born blind, deaf and almost hairless. The doe bears her kittens in short nesting burrows or aboveground nests. Mating can take place again immediately after giving birth. Because of this, rabbits are highly prolific, and a single pair can increase to nearly 200 individuals within eighteen months of first breeding. A doe can have five-week-old kittens playing outside the warren nest at a dead-end, have the same number in a fur-lined chamber, and still be carrying five in the womb. The wild rabbit needs to reproduce quickly because it doesn't live much longer than two years. More than eighty per cent die before reaching three months of age.

Young bucks and does of no social standing move off in search of new digs as testosterone-charged battles commence at the beginning of the breeding season. Most dispersal is never any further than it needs to be. Those on the move always try neighbouring warrens as their first choice. The quicker they find safety, the longer they'll live because being homeless increases a young rabbit's vulnerability.

Rabbits are neither migratory, nomadic nor given to venturing far from home. They feed in areas of short vegetation within about three hundred metres of the warren but will travel further when food or water is scarce.

Dispersed youngsters will usually only venture a matter of metres further, and in the mid- to late-nineteenth century, the colonisation of Australia was a simple matter of moving on a little and digging a new burrow, then further burrows, which became a new warren. Why rabbits picked one spot in a paddock for a warren no one could tell. It was just the rabbit's choice.

\*

Hares by contrast, are wild animals that do not respond well to attempts at domestication. They are always nervous and unhappy in captivity and often fret themselves to death. Hares do not burrow like rabbits. The doe, when ready to deliver young, digs a crude scrape and gives birth to three to five fully formed young called leverets, which can mostly fend for themselves soon after birth − a naturally developed compensation for the young not being sheltered in the safety of a warren.

Tasmania received Australia's first introduced European hares in the late 1830s but that initial attempt to establish wild populations failed. The first successful colony of hares to get a foothold in Australia was by William Lyall, who imported them in 1856.[2] Austin also raised hares at Barwon Park.

The hares released in and around Melbourne by William Lyall and the Victorian Acclimatisation Society became a widespread and nomadic species throughout Victoria by 1870, and a sporadic agricultural problem in northern and western Victoria through their habit of stripping plants of their bark. Hares have been big trouble locally at times, but away from orchards and young plantations, they did little real damage.

Spreading at an approximate rate of 60 kilometres per year, hares crossed the Murray River in 1875, where they made their way along the western slopes and southern tablelands of New South Wales. Many found themselves caught up in the rabbit wars, the poor old hare was an innocuous fellow and caused comparatively little damage, but it was a bad time to have long ears and buck teeth. Generally considered to be one of the least troublesome ferals released in Australia, the hare still overran the southern half of the continent. That's a plague by any other name.

*

It was in late 1867 that the first reports of the budding rabbit environmental disaster emerged from the western district of Victoria at Warrion Hills, north of Colac. The epicentre was William Robertson's property, Glen Alvie. William Robertson and Thomas Austin were both members of the Acclimatisation Society of Victoria and there is no question Robertson sourced his rabbits from Barwon Park. Now they had come home to roost.

In 1859, police charged a man and fined him £10 for shooting a rabbit 'the property of one William Robertson' on Glen Alvie. A couple of years later, Robertson's son John spent £5000 in a year in rabbit control.[3] That was small beer.

Rabbits so trashed Victoria's western district that property prices dropped by half. *The Times* of London even reported on the rabbit invasion, stating that rabbits were 'starving the sheep out of their runs' and referred to William Robertson's property and the costs of the rabbit war. The western district was in crisis, and the rabbits – Thomas Austin's handiwork – had become an unstoppable alien force.

In 1867, Austin's rabbits were at Barwon Heads, sixty kilometres away from Barwon Park, and twenty kilometres north and west of Winchelsea, and they were spreading west rapidly. The rabbits infuriated local farmers. The farmers blamed the Acclimatisation Society of Victoria, which stoutly denied any involvement, although by this time, Austin was a society member.

We know Thomas Austin wasn't the only rabbit liberator, but he seems to have been the supplier for the others in Victoria, New South Wales and South Australia. In the early days, only the landed gentry had the money to mess around with expensive hobbies like rabbits. And Austin was in the habit of gifting pairs of rabbits to his wealthy sporting friends and acquaintances, which they dutifully bred up and liberated all over the country.[4] This explains the almost simultaneous population explosions in Victoria, southern New South Wales and South Australia.

In 1867, two graziers named Mills and Mogg, who farmed in the Mallee country of western Victoria, got hold of four pairs of wild rabbits directly from Austin or indirectly via Colac or South Australia. They released the rabbits on their property, Morton Plains, just north of Donald. In New South Wales, Thomas Holt, a New South Wales parliamentarian and acclimatiser of Marrickville in Sydney, bred and released rabbits during the 1860s. Nothing is certain but the timing works perfectly with Austin's. The South Australia rabbit outbreak occurred at Kapunda to the north of Adelaide between 1865 and 1867. No one knows who released the Kapunda rabbits, but they would have fitted the standard profile of the sporty, wealthy, well-connected grazier. The South Australian rabbits proliferated, as all the wild liberations did. All outbreaks would eventually join forces and move north and west into the interior.

By this time, William Robertson was up to his eyeballs in rabbits. In 1869 he spent £9500 trying to clear Glen Alvie of over two million rabbits. Glen Alvie's hired trappers were killing 4500 rabbits per week. A hundred men were employed filling wombat holes and shooting and dogging. A neighbour estimated that he had hundreds of thousands of rabbits on his own land. The rabbits had got started by occupying wombat burrows, and there was no shortage of these.

Joseph Connor, a member of Victoria's Legislative Assembly, told the Assembly that 'the rabbit nuisance in this colony promised to be as great as that of the locusts in the land of Egypt'. He was wrong about that. The locust plague of Egypt came and went. The rabbit plague of Australia was the worst bio-invasion the world had ever seen, and still is. Mr Connor tried to introduce rabbit control measures into the Local Government Bill. It went nowhere, unlike Thomas Austin's rabbits, which went everywhere.

*

Australians might have had some chance of halting the rabbit's advance had it always progressed by just feet and yards, which is how the creature naturally advances when seeking new territory. Each of the colonies flung up a multitude of barrier fences to halt the invader's advance, and these should have stemmed the tide or at least bought time had they not been built too late. And even if those fences were completed before the rabbits arrived they were never deep enough, high enough, and crucially, wide enough, to stop the broad advance. And they were certainly no barrier to human mischief. The bush was thick with credible rumours of professional rabbiters seeding new areas with rabbits to ensure their livelihoods for years to come.

The people who didn't have rabbits eating them out of house and home loved them. Bunnies were once solely the preserve of the posh. Now they were as thick as flies, and compared to the native animals, they were great sport. Little environment wreckers they may have been, but there was money in them too. A lucrative industry sprang up in the turbulent, acrimonious wake of the rabbit's advance; a genuine get-rich-quick industry that exploited the graziers' get-poor-quick predicament. Men hunted the destructive creatures with muzzle-loading shotguns and gundogs, and boys chased them with all sorts of dogs, fast and slow, and some boys even had ferrets that they put down warrens after them.

Australians found rabbits to be good eating. And that was useful because they'd be eating millions of them before long. Rabbiting was a flourishing, unregulated industry, foisted on landholders as a legislative requirement and a desperate practical response. It created a compromised workforce dependent on the flourishing of the bio-invader, even though their work's ostensible purpose was the rabbit's extermination.

What the rabbits didn't need was a hand to proliferate. Yet rebel foot soldiers of that compromised industry collaborated with the enemy and facilitated their advance, carrying them, in the end, hundreds of kilometres, and releasing them in virgin country. If that virgin country was the other side of a barrier fence, or a river, or even in another colony, then so be it.

Though most rabbiters were decent folk doing the best they could for themselves, the devastating actions of the few caused an air of suspicion and distrust to hover over the industry. Graziers were the meat in the lamb-and-rabbit sandwich with no greens, and the only ones out of pocket and staring at a loss of livelihood. Some graziers received threats from people threatening to release rabbits on their land if the grazier ignored their extortionate demands.[5] Ugly times in merino land.

Fittingly, the rabbit industry started in Victoria near the massive outbreak on Glen Alvie and other stations in the region. A rabbit-preserving factory at Colac commenced processing rabbits in 1871 and canned over six and a half million rabbits in fifteen years. The company opened a branch factory in Camperdown in 1881, and there treated up to one million rabbits from April to October each year. Up to ninety men and boys worked in the factory and hundreds of trappers supplied it. At least someone was making a buck, but it wasn't the graziers, and as the rabbit commerce took place on their land and at their expense, it must have rankled.[6]

Rabbits sold in markets in Sydney, Melbourne and Adelaide. To get an idea of the size of the local market for rabbit, consider that in 1875, trappers from Colac were sending 8000 rabbits a week to markets in Melbourne, Geelong and Ballarat in the winter months alone. Between 1872 and 1874, 150,000 rabbits were dispatched from trappers at Bacchus Marsh to the Melbourne Fish Market. Butcheries everywhere stocked fresh wild rabbit.

The Melbourne trade grew rapidly from the early 1870s. In 1884, a Melbourne syndicate formed the Stonyford Pastoral and Preserving Company. Their rabbit-processing works and cannery at Stonyford in Victoria's rabbit epicentre commenced operations in 1885. It was soon processing 600,000 rabbits annually and proved to be serious competition to the Colac works.

South Australia got its own rabbit works in 1877 when the Northern Rabbit Meat Preserving Company commenced canning that colony's over-abundance of our hopping friend. It churned through 45,000 rabbits a month, a mere drop in the endless rabbit ocean, before ceasing production a short two years later.

Australian rabbits fed more than just local markets. Rabbirs were shipped of to England as tinned meat.

In November 1878, syndicated newspapers around Australia ran the story of the ship the *Aconcagua*. While on her homeward trip to London with a large shipment of 20,000 tinned South Australian rabbits, as she steamed up the Red Sea towards the Suez Canal one balmy evening, a resounding explosion from deep within the ship's bowels shook the ship, swiftly followed by an odour of unimaginable offensiveness.

Gagging passengers ran about in vain trying to escape the grotesque smell. The dreadful stench of putrescent processed rabbit lingered for days. The ship's doctor had disinfecting fluid sprinkled liberally about, so that between the two overpowering odours the passengers had an exceedingly unpleasant trip. Most on board believed the heat of the Red Sea had caused the tinned rabbit, all 2000 cans, to explode. There was conjecture that the bursting of the tins occurred because of neglect, by allowing them to get too hot. Yet tins of preserved meat exposed to the heat of an African sun for years on end were found on another occasion to be quite palatable when discovered and opened.[7]

Perhaps the closure of the Northern Rabbit Meat Preserving Company in 1879 was related to the *Aconcagua* public relations disaster.

It was the newish refrigerated rail wagons that allowed rabbiters in the New South Wales interior to supply the city markets. Frozen lamb dispatched in a refrigerated rail car at Narrandera in the Riverina district of New South Wales in 1890 had arrived in Sydney 30-hours later in 'excellent condition'. The successful frozen lamb experiment showed rabbit carcases could be transported the same way, and insulated rail opened the rabbit-infested rail-serviced country to the hungry Sydney market. By 1895, Sydneysiders were eating 20,000 rabbits a week, and by the turn of the century that number had grown to 30,000.[8]

Refrigeration was a major threat to the rabbit canning industry. In the late 1890s, when the growing export trade in frozen rabbits caused a major downturn in demand for export canned rabbit, and a reluctance for rabbiters to supply the canning works. The frozen-rabbit exporters were paying double the money for rabbit carcases.

Following the 1870s, not only was everyone eating rabbit, they were wearing it. Rabbit skins for felt and fur was in high demand. Private enterprise sent over 3 million skins to auction in London in 1878, and close to 6 million skins in 1879, and that only ramped up. Around four billion rabbit skins were exported between 1904 and 1947. In 1905 just over 67 per cent of rabbit skins went to America, with Britain taking the other 33 per cent.[9]

Local manufacturers, including the Akubra hat company, processed around 20 to 25 per cent of all skins annually. The Australian Army slouch hat was made of rabbit fur felt, as were hats for general use, while cashed-up Aussies paid through the nose for rabbit skin faked to look like a finer fur imported back from America.

Rabbits became the great levellers of Australia's colonial classist society. While wool remained the nation's major export earner, the profits from wool ended up in few hands, while the rabbit industry provided cash daily to thousands of trappers and workers. Even youngsters were getting into the act and cashing in on rabbit skins and carcases. The profits from the rabbit industry stayed in the local economy, and unlike other rural industries, the rabbit industry prospered during war, depression and drought.

# CHAPTER 13

# Victoria's Rabbits Breach Colony Lines

In the early 1870s, rabbits proliferated in and advanced across southern Australia. In Victoria they were established from Geelong in the east to Colac and Donald in the Mallee, down to Cape Otway in the south. In South Australia they ranged from Kapunda to Adelaide on the coast. And in New South Wales, they appeared around Balranald and Wentworth, where humans deliberately seeded rabbits just north of the Victorian border. There were without doubt plenty of other areas where this environmental vandalism occurred.

In South Australia, liberated rabbits on Anlaby Station had eaten out the grasses there and on surrounding sheep runs by 1872. Farmers in the Kapunda and Julia Creek region were bracing for the onslaught as the rabbits headed towards the crops north of the Mount Lofty ranges, where they made nocturnal attacks on the summer crops and retreated to the safety of their warrens by daylight when their enemies sought them.

In Victoria's Mallee district, the rabbits that Mills and Mogg released were making headway in all directions. They'd learned to extract water from the mallee roots, and the sandy, well-drained soils of the sand hills were just what they loved for their warrens. Rabbits in Australia were learning to adapt. It was bad news for the Mallee country.

Mills and Moggs's neighbouring property, Curyo South Station, carried 15,000 sheep when their four pairs of rabbits were liberated to Morton Plains in 1874. Four years later, Curyo South was unstocked and barren. You wouldn't imagine Mills and Mogg were all that popular with their neighbours.[1]

Twenty-two rabbiting gangs employed by the South Australian government were working throughout the colony. Each party had a foreman and six men (although where practical two boys substituted for two men and reduced costs). Different extermination methods including carbon disulphide fumigating, shooting, dogging, netting, trapping and donging them on the scone with a waddy all proved to be ineffective. The cost was about £10,000 per year.[2] It didn't make any difference to the rabbits, but it kept a few men and lads in work. And it all made zero difference to the commercial value of the rabbit. Private enterprise sent over 3 million skins to auction in London in 1878, and close to 6 million skins in 1879.

South Australia was drowning in rabbits and the profits from them went nowhere near meeting the damage bill. In April 1877, *The Advertiser* recognised the elimination of native predators for the environmental disaster it was:

> Owing to the dingo and the native cat, the rodents
> [rabbits] made no headway for a very long time, but as
> strychnine did its work, and the dogs and cats disappeared,
> the rabbits increased enormously, and then it was seen what
> an evil had been imported and established in our vast
> territory ... We have destroyed the balance of nature in
> two ways simultaneously, by destroying the carnivore and
> introducing a new herbivorous animal of immense
> reproductive powers.[3]

The rabbit had been on the loose in Victoria for twenty years and in South Australia for around fifteen. In the early 1880s, the two populations merged and began to move northwards in a broad front that stretched from around Adelaide across the whole of the Murray River to the Great Dividing Range. Rabbits got so bad in the Victorian Mallee country that people were walking off their properties, eaten out and defeated.[4] The rabbit's conquest of the grazing lands of Victoria was complete, the colony defeated from within. New South Wales was next.

Western New South Wales now looks nothing like it did before the coming of stock and the rabbits. It is hard to believe, but pioneers of that region described the west as once being a something of a dry wonderland. It was the damage caused by overstocking that weakened the west, making it harder to recover from the consequences of droughts. And it was the livestock mixed with the rabbits that virtually killed it, ably assisted by the foxes, cats, brumbies, pigs and goats that came after. The feral horror story doesn't get any scarier than western New South Wales, and in the 1880s the destruction was building momentum. It was the one place that could ill-afford the rabbit.

The rabbits found the going easy by following rivers and spreading out either side as they moved northwards. Their advance along the Darling and Lachlan rivers was assisted by people travelling in the paddle-wheelers that plied the rivers, delivering supplies to and taking wool bales from Hay, Wilcannia, Bourke and Brewarrina. This seeding established rabbit colonies well in front of the main body of the advance. Eventually all the populations would join.

To begin with the rabbit initially spread slowly in south-western New South Wales. By September 1880, rabbits had reached Hillston on the Lachlan River, over 300 kilometres north of the border. But their numbers hadn't increased to a level that would prompt graziers to spring from their cane-bottomed chairs and exterminate them while they had the opportunity. Even in 1881, with rabbits increasing over new territory, the annual report for the Chief Stock Inspector recorded that New South Wales graziers had destroyed 2250 dingoes, 581,753 kangaroos, 43,724 wallabies, and just 3999 rabbits. Two years later, parliament admitted that rabbits occupied 60,000 square miles (15 million ha) of New South Wales. Some graziers kept their rabbit problems on the quiet, put their places on the market and got out before the rabbits ate them out. That may not have been honest, but it would have been prudent. The western division of the colony was heading for a fall.[5]

It seems there is always a Thomas involved in Australia's feral woes. By 1883, Thomas Holt's rabbits, once confined to a fenced warren in Marrickville, Sydney, had spread west to the Cowpastures of Camden and south to Bulli. Mr Holt, a New South Wales parliamentarian, wasn't backwards in describing his rabbits at liberty as a 'perfect nuisance'. Eventually this population would blend with the northward moving horde from eastern Victoria.

It is probable that Holt's rabbits were partly domestic stock, though if they carried Austin blood no one would be surprised. For a time, the story went that Thomas Holt sourced his rabbits from Tasmania and New Zealand, but there does not appear to be much genetic difference between the Sydney rabbits and those of Barwon Park origin. A study into the matter concluded 'it is unlikely that any ecologically significant, genetically-based, differences would be found between the rabbits in Sydney and those elsewhere in Australia'.[6]

Out west, regional New South Wales towns formed

graziers' groups to try to plan how to best protect themselves from the coming invasion and lobby the government for assistance. At Cobar in June 1883, a meeting of the squatters considered a proposal for erecting a rabbit-proof fence on the southern extent of the district. Although the rabbits were still a long way off, the group members all correctly concluded that exclusion was their only hope. They thought it 'wise to take time by the forelock' and try to keep the dreaded pest out of Cobar. The proposal was to erect a rabbit-proof fence extending east to west from the Macquarie River to the Darling River. A couple of their more prominent and influential members signed a memorandum to the government asking for subsidies to assist in building the proposed fence.[7] Macquarie Street ignored their plea for help. Like the rest of the unprotected colony, Cobar had to fend for itself.

In 1884, with no barrier fence built, the first reports came of rabbits near Cobar, across to the west on the Darling River, and to the south-east at Mudgee. It was a moving front half the width of the state. Though a drought that year slowed them, by 1885, the rabbits were on the hop again and had reached Bourke on the Darling. They made Dubbo on the Macquarie in the central west of New South Wales in the same year. Someone actually shot a pair at Angledool (almost on the Queensland border) in 1885, but these must have been deliberate seedings as they were over 240 kilometres ahead of the advancing front.[8] In their desperation, those faced with the rabbit inundation thought that releasing predators would fix the problem – that thousands, even tens of thousands, of small predators would eliminate millions upon millions of rabbits. Just like the writer in the *Advertiser*, farmers in New South Wales were waking up to what the elimination of the small native quolls, dingoes and wedge-tailed eagles meant. But you don't know what you've got until you've exterminated it.

The *Goulburn Evening Penny Post*, of Thursday 16 April 1885, ran a small advertisement on page three, right above the Important Notice for Ferguson's Renowned Cholera Mixture:

### Live Native Cats for Rabbit Nuisance

Wanted, sound and in good condition, young or old. State price; delivered on spot, or at Goulburn, Yass, or Bungendore Railway station.

F. Campbell

Yarralumla, Queanbeyan

The quoll entrepreneur who set the ad was none other than Frederick Campbell, a grazier whose sheep station at Yarralumla became the location of the future governor-general's residence in what would become Canberra.

Meanwhile in Wagga Wagga, attendees at a pastoral meeting debated what to do about the rabbit problem and decided to introduce improbable numbers of rabbit predators, starting with 100,000 cats, 100,000 quolls and 200,000 goannas. Where they were going to find that many quolls and goannas was anyone's guess. Certainly not in sheep country, that's for sure. Campbell's quoll trade never amounted to anything, and neither did the campaign of the wool-growers of Wagga Wagga. Graziers like them had been flat-stick killing off the predators with strychnine for decades. Now they thought they'd just say abracadabra and pull a rabbit predator out of the hat.

Mongooses were another suggestion for rabbit-hunting predators. Kilfera Station near Ivanhoe in western New South Wales first received and released mongooses to prey on their rabbits in August 1883. Mr Richardson, the local rabbit inspector, visited Kilfera to report on the mongoose activity and while he made no mention of problems with the mongoose around Kilfera's fowl yards, he did mention its excellent predation on the Kilfera bunnies.

To his delight he found a vast improvement. In the three kilometres around mongoose central he counted seven burrows at work, compared to over ninety burrows before release. In other portions where the mongoose was not employed, the rabbits had increased. Richardson believed the mongoose would be a success.[9]

Mr Crystal of Torrumbarry Station in the Echuca district of Victoria was importing mongooses from India and turning them loose on the parts of his run most affected by rabbits. They had been most effectual in destroying the rabbits, he wrote, and he intended to try the experiment of withdrawing the trappers and using the mongoose exclusively for rabbit destruction.[10]

Out Hillston way, just a little east of Kilfera, where mongooses were doing their bit to slow down the rabbits, the editor of the *Hillston News* referred his readers to *Chambers Journal*. While impressed by the mongoose's ability as a vermin killer, the journal was concerned about what all the mongooses would be doing with themselves when they'd polished off the last of the billions of rabbits. The mootest of moot points. Still, there could be no question that the idle mongoose would be Trouble with a capital T. And as eggs and poultry are mongoose family favourites, and as mongooses are fierce gluttons, and 'fearless as a rat' when at bay or pressed by hunger, they would not hesitate to attack fowls and even sheep when rendered desperate by famine. The good people of Hillston received fair warning.[11]

Word was getting about that mongooses were getting on with the job. During late 1883 and early 1884 mail steamers were bringing large consignments of mongooses out from Ceylon. They had found steady employment in south-western New South Wales and were doing their bit to destroy the rabbits, but the jury was still out as to their total effectiveness.

The added benefit of mongooses was their decided partiality for snakes which, in a snake-infested country like Australia, added to their appeal. Australian snakes may have also ensured the mongooses would never become a feral problem[12] Mongooses readily attack, kill and eat cobras on the Indian subcontinent. They often allow cobras to bite them as they have a resistance to the venom. Perhaps they took a liking to the Australian venomous snakes that also preyed on rabbits and were known to loiter around their warrens. And perhaps the mongoose had no resistance to Australian snake venom.

Luckily for Australia, the mongoose failed to thrive and eventually disappeared, but not before instituting a wholesale poultry massacre and making a nuisance of themselves in Perth, of all places. Someone had introduced them there as pets and, as usual, they had escaped captivity and bred prolifically, playing old Harry among poultry farmers' chickens. They didn't last long. All Australia's mongooses were destroyed early in the twentieth century; whether that was by the venom of Australian snakes we can only speculate, but we do know there was a mass destruction of mongooses by rabbiters looking to protect their patches.[13] Our starchy old friends in the acclimatisation societies would have been very upset about that.

\*

On 1 October 1885, at the direction of the New South Wales Minister for Mines, delegates from all the district sheep boards of the New South Wales colony met in Sydney for a rabbit gabfest. Its purpose was to provide suggestions to the government as to the best mean of dealing with the rabbit pest. They needn't have bothered.

There were notable attendees including John King from Wagga Wagga and Mark Tully from Bourke, men deeply involved with the development of the kelpie in the Riverina during the 1870s, and great stockmen both. Also present and representing Walgett was Frederick Wolseley, the inventor of the powered hand shears that revolutionised the Australian wool industry. Many of the other delegates were prominent graziers of the day.

The first day's discussion centred on netting fencing and the conference heard from speakers who testified to its effectiveness elsewhere in Australia and Britain. The meeting supported a suggestion that a proposal should go to government to construct a fence between the infested west – say, for example, Cobar – and the supposedly uninfested east of the colony.[14]

Day two was a livelier affair. The chair told the meeting that the minister for mines had received thirty-one letters regarding rabbit solutions. Only eight were worthy of consideration. Three were 'particularly absurd'. One correspondent proposed catching rabbits with hooks, another suggested using baited canvas traps into which the rabbits would fall, while a third genius advocated 'catching all the rabbits and putting them in wire cages'. Why didn't someone think of that before?

Several other submissions suggested using the rabbit's 'natural enemies' such as the Indian grey fox, the ferret and the domestic cat. Chief among them was a professionally printed pamphlet titled *The Rabbit Plague in Australia, and a Scheme for its Suppression* by RJ Murchison,[15] who proposed releasing thousands of ferrets from specialised breeding stations all around Australia.

Countering Mr Murchison and other enthusiastic ferretists, Dugald McLellan, a Scottish gamekeeper, related his experience with ferrets on Green Hills Station in Kaikoura, New Zealand, and told of the greater environmental disaster of using them as rabbit killers. Playing on a familiar tune, another bright spark put forward a motion that the release of large numbers of iguanas (goannas), domestic cats and native cats (quolls) would reduce the numbers of rabbits. The unnamed fellow then proposed that residents of Sydney and other large towns could breed up moggies and deliver them to government agents, who would ship them to regional rabbit infested areas for release.

From there the pro-cat plan descended into farce, as supporters compared the economics of a human rabbit catcher with the cat. Their argument was that, rather than hiring 10,000 men at eight hours a day and £100 per annum to eliminate the rabbits, it would make economic sense to have a million cats on the job working 24/7. The downside would be a bit of predation on native birds ('no biggie,' they said) and 'a little excessive poultry predation', but avoiding that problem was easy if one just built 'cat-proof fowl houses and trained one's fowls to use it.'[16]

As stupid as the cat idea sounds today, someone in the New South Wales government took it seriously, and contrived to herd together 400 cats and had them railed to Bourke for transport to Tongo Station on the Paroo River, 200 kilometres south-west of Bourke. Feral cats were everywhere British Australians had settled, but now that population would receive a boost with Sydney's feline dregs. Nice.

It was typical of the biological ignorance and desperate actions of the times. Desperation forced graziers into the questionable embrace of the cats. Thousands of cats trapped in cities and towns ended up on trains all over Australia, to be dumped in the bush near rabbit warrens in the vain hope that, left to their own devices, they'd eliminate the rabbits. Cats killed rabbits, especially young rabbit kittens, no question, but they never had a hope of seriously reducing the population. They failed to slow the rabbits – as everything failed to slow the rabbits – preferring to prey on native animals and killing thousands by the day every day. The cats themselves eventually multiplied to unsustainable numbers.

\*

The smartest bloke in the New South Wales Rabbit Conference room was Dr Creed of Woollahra, Sydney. He suggested that all the colonies should combine to establish and fund a panel of bio-specialists to investigate inoculating rabbits with infectious diseases. If the colonies could get their act together, he suggested, they could get French germologist Louis Pasteur to visit Australia and set them on the right path. Creed's suggestion sparked great interest from delegates, and time would prove him right. But it would be a slow and tortuous journey.

Debate about fencing dominated day three. Attendees supported a motion that recommended that rabbit-proof fencing should isolate all railway lines. It was a good idea, but a little late. Rabbits followed the construction of railways as they spread web-like across and throughout rural Australia. They dug warrens under the tracks, which made beautifully drained (if noisy) homes for millions of them.[17]

After two further days defining rabbits and making recommendations as to the offence of seeding rabbits beyond rabbit-proof fences, the conference concluded with the delegates taking a tour of Lysaght's wire-netting works on the Parramatta River.[18]

Lysaght Bros Ltd (previously John Lysaght Ltd) knew a rabbit-inspired market opportunity when they saw one. It had established a manufacturing plant in Sydney in 1884 in response to the prospect of rapid growth of demand for galvanised wire netting because of the rabbit plague. Working in the company's favour was a process for mechanical wire weaving developed by John Lysaght himself, which compensated for higher labour costs in Australia. The new mechanised process left the competition behind for fourteen years. Between 1885 and 1890 demand in Australia grew from 1600 to 10,000 kilometres of standard gauge netting a year.

Defects in the galvanising and transportation of imported products helped. Lysaght's netting from the mid-1890s was high-quality German netting wire, which was specially prepared and sorted to accept a smooth zinc coating – the key to the manufacture of long-lasting netting. To facilitate handling and minimise freight costs, imported netting also needed tight rolling. However, this tended to crack the galvanising, which led to rapid rusting during the sea voyage. Fencing contractors and DIYers found tight-rolled netting extremely difficult to manage because of its propensity to roll back up again unless forcibly kept unrolled. That recoiling made straining more difficult and time-consuming. Most men in the bush hated the imported wire. Lysaght's loose-rolled local netting was cheaper to erect.[19]

The delegates met again the following year in June and got straight down to the business of a barrier fence to separate the east and west of the colony and keep all the rabbits to the western half. They agreed that the fence would begin on the Queensland border and run south to Bourke, then parallel with the railway and road south-east straight down to Nyngan, where it would turn due south down to Condobolin. From Condobolin it would run south-east to Cootamundra, where it would follow the railway line south-west through Junee, Wagga Wagga, Henty, Culcairn and on southward to Albury. There it would terminate at the Murray River and Victoria border.[20]

By December of that year, 1886, the barrier fence's first section from Bourke south to Byrock had been completed.[21] The entire fence took around seven years to complete and was of course a pointless expense. Rabbits had already made themselves at home on both sides of it.

Some items on the second conference's agenda that second day reprised topics from conference one; on the efficacy of 'iguanas' (goannas) as merciless rabbit destroyers. Mr Wreford, a big fan of the goanna's work, thought they were the answer to the rabbit plague. He produced evidence that proved beyond any reasonable doubt that goannas were so effective in destroying the rabbit horde that professional rabbiters, fearful for their prospects, had been going out of their way to destroy them. One impossibly pessimistic and sceptical curmudgeon demanded that Mr Wreford explain how so many rabbits had managed to invade New South Wales if goannas were so good on the job.

Mr Wreford had come prepared. He calmly swatted that prickly query aside by explaining that the rabbits swam across the Murray into New South Wales in winter 'when the iguanas were all slumbering in their nests, and consequently got a couple of month's start'.[22]

So stout was Mr Wreford's support for the goanna, despite the fact it bundled off for its winter hibernation, that the delegates supported Mr Wreford's proposal to add the virtuous reptile to the official list of useful natural enemies of the rabbit – a great victory not only for Mr Wreford but iguanaphiles Australia-wide. It's a pity that, at the same time, iguanaphobes Australia-wide were poisoning them off in their thousands.

The Rabbit Conference closed by signing off on Frederick Wolseley's recommendation that landholders not pulling their weight in rabbit destruction should receive a summons to the Court of Petty Sessions, where the police magistrate could take such necessary steps as to ensure the owners paid for the destruction work. He recommended that in no case should that expense exceed two shillings per rabbit. Fred Wolseley's genius lay in developing powered shearing apparatuses, but not fair or workable legislation.

Wolseley's recommendation somehow became enshrined in law and caused a whole mess of problems in its interpretation and execution. Fines were issued to some farmers as their numbers grew, while not to others. In one noteworthy example of the dangerous zeal of minor officialdom, one farmer in New South Wales had applied for professional rabbiters to attend his property and clean out the rabbits. He had also ordered enough rabbit traps, two hundred native cats (this must be a misprint – they would have been domestic cats, not quolls), and sixty mongooses. He ordered disulphide of carbon as a poison fumigant, and a ton of carrots for poison baits. While all this was in transit to his property, a rabbit inspector inspected his property, found he had rabbits – such a revelation – and summonsed him to court. The court fined the farmer £2 and imposed £4 court costs.[23] It was all quite arbitrary and useless in the war against the rabbits. But there's your state legislature for you.

By 1878 Victoria, the colony that had started it all, had its own faulty rabbit legislation. Although graziers and Victoria parliamentarians were pushing for rabbit laws that would require their compulsory destruction, no one seemed too determined to do anything about them. It was a dilemma for the law makers. On one hand, rabbits were destroying the place, and powerful pastoral lobbies were piling the pressure on to do something about the plague. On the other hand, there was no business like the rabbit business, which was employing and feeding the colony.

Queensland adopted and passed something equally as toothless and unjust as New South Wales had, just months later. Rabbit legislation came and went, replaced by new rabbit legislation even more exasperating and impotent. Laws were tedious and complex, and none worked, because laws that threatened people were never going to defeat the rabbit.

Most people ignored the laws – the rabbits certainly did, and kept on multiplying and forging further ahead in their quest for new country. Rabbits proliferated because they were united in their biological drive to survive and multiply, and people weren't united in the effort to stop them.

# CHAPTER 14

# Thomas Chirnside and the Foxes of Werribee Park

I n the early 1800s, England had a vibrant and thriving class
system that was much appreciated, unsurprisingly, by its
rich people. The class system preserved their rights and
privileges, affording the sporting squire all manner of country
pleasures, such as shooting and angling, and the great rural
social pursuit, foxhunting. Few contented and entrenched
members of England's sporting rural upper class were ever in a
hurry to leave. The men who left England and made good in
Australia were only ever those who would never have been
able to achieve or enjoy their 'great man' status had they
remained in their homeland.

It was these colonial great men with their self-indulgent
class elitism and desperate need to play the English lord down
under that was behind all the foreign animals released for
recreational hunting in colonial Australia. And aside from the
rabbit none has caused as much damage, heartache and expense
as the European red fox.

During the mid- to late-nineteenth century there was
strong demand in the Australian colonies for wild-caught red
foxes to satisfy those who pined for the society, excitement,
and mindless cruelty that is English fox hunting. Before foxes

became available, hunts released kangaroos, wallabies and dingoes for their foxhound packs to chase, kill and devour.

The first recorded instance of a fox running free in Australia was an exhibit from Sydney's Zoological Garden at the Domain in 1835. The fox escaped from its enclosure and two young fellows riding in the park saw it running at large. They gave chase for an hour during which time the fox made repeated but ineffectual attempts to get over the boundary wall. It eventually evaded capture, but the next morning 'presented himself at the entrance gateway of its old quarters, and quietly surrendered himself a prisoner'.[1]

The earliest mention of a fox used in fox hunting in colonial Australia is from Sydney in 1836, and its tone suggests this foxhunt may not have been the first:

> After drawing the back of the training stables in the
> direction of the Waterloo Mills, a fox was found at the
> furthest extremity of the Steeple Chase ground and broke
> away in the direction of Point Piper ... after a beautiful
> run through the enclosures of Shepherd's Garden. Here he
> was compelled to yield to his pursuers, after the most
> brilliant run ever witnessed in the country.[2]

In September 1860, the ship *Heather Bell* brought three foxes from England to Hobart. One fox died on the passage out.[3] The other two foxes met their ends before packs of foxhounds. It was an ugly dispatching for any animal, but Tasmania has never regretted those losses and, until recently, has miraculously remained fox free. Imported foxes probably went to many destinations in Australia. We just haven't heard about them. It is certain that these early importations were for the purpose of 'sport' and viable wild populations never took root.

On 30 April 1863 in Rockhampton, Queensland, the police court heard the matter of *Paton v Murphy*, regarding the theft of of all things, a fox. The facts of the case presented to the court were as follows. Mr Paton imported two foxes. They escaped his property and were running at large in the local area. Mr Murphy captured one of them on his own property. Paton, upon hearing that Murphy had one of his foxes, demanded its immediate delivery, but Murphy said he would not give it up without a reward. Paton, obviously ungrateful for his fox's redemption, refused to reward Murphy, and complained to the wallopers, who had a search warrant issued and executed. Paton regained possession of his fox, had Murphy clapped in irons, shuffled off into custody, charged with theft and bailed to appear at court.

The court dismissed the charge, but the local press said that the charges brought by Paton cast a slur upon Murphy's reputation. Naturally, Murphy, vindicated after his ordeal, felt a little miffed. Paton was apparently miffed, too, and felt slighted that the outraged public thought his actions against Murphy to be a little on the draconian side of ridiculously severe.

A journalist from the *Rockhampton Northern Argus* also had the temerity to report the matter, which further incensed Paton. Too furious to heed the adage that it's better to keep your mouth shut and let people think you're a bigoted snob than to write a bombastic letter to an editor and confirm it, he sharpened his quill and dashed off a diatribe to the *Northern Bulletin*.[4]

The *Northern Bulletin's* large stablemate Brisbane's *Courier* smelled blood and got in on the act, outing Paton by suggesting he was culpable of 'allowing destructive animals to roam at large to the terror of poultry-rearing housewives', not to mention their fowls. It was in the public interest, the *Courier* suggested, that Paton's actions of importing and releasing foxes should be a matter for the authorities to determine.

Paton and his captive foxes went to ground and obscurity, but his free-ranging fox didn't. It continued its unwelcome depredations until it too, disappeared.[5]

\*

Australia dominated the world wool trade in the 1870s. It was the decade that saw the widespread introduction of wire fencing, the great game changer, and it heralded the development two of wool's most potent innovations: Wolseley's powered hand shears and the kelpie. The national sheep population jumped to seventy-five million. The ride on the sheep's back had never been more comfortable, and it seemed like the good times would last forever.

The truth is the wool industry developed a misplaced confidence in the future because no one appears to have appreciated the dogged persistence of drought, how much environmental damage sheep were doing, and the eventual scale of the rabbit disaster. But in central Victoria, the developing rabbit plague was cementing a rival industry and providing opportunity for the townsfolk who did not get to share in wool's runaway success.

The origins of the longstanding rivalry between New South Wales and Victoria is rooted in the resentment of Victoria's rabbit and fox plagues. New South Wales did the unpleasant heavy lifting during the convict transportation era.

Victorians were the new wool- and gold-rich kids on the block, who loved to show New South Wales and South Australia just how good their good times were. But pride goeth before destruction, particularly after rubbing one's older sibling-colonies' noses in it.

Victoria's failure to eradicate their pests when they had the chance riled their neighbours, whose farmers faced great hardship, went broke, or worse, because of Victoria's feral fetishes. Of course, Victorian farmers suffered just as badly, but the greatest of ironies was that it was all the work of successful Victorian graziers.

Graziers had purged the detested dingo from the prime sheep lands, and for a time it was a smart move. Then, right on cue, with central Victoria's environment reeling from years of rabbit pain and that pain increasing, the second feral genie escaped from the bottle.

*

Thomas Chirnside was born in Berwickshire, Scotland, in 1839. He sailed from Liverpool on the *Bardaster* and from Sydney he overlanded cattle to Adelaide, before joining in business with his younger brother Andrew, with whom he remained partnered for life. He was a successful pastoralist, who settled much of what would become Werribee west of Melbourne.

In April 1842, the brothers established a station in the Grampians, and that same year Thomas acquired a station on the Wannon River, where he was one of the first to employ Aboriginal stockmen.

The elder Chirnside settled in Werribee just before the gold rushes, eventually buying 80,000 acres (32,000ha) of land and building a grandiose bluestone mansion on the now heritage-listed Werribee Park Estate. He loved horse racing and won the Melbourne Cup in 1874 with Haricot.[6]

Thomas Chirnside was an independent acclimatiser who acclimatised for his own sport. No records of the Acclimatisation Society of Victoria show him to have ever been a member or supporter. He imported fallow and red deer and released gamebirds on his properties. He also imported quality horses and was mad keen on traditional fox hunting, hosting the Geelong and Corio hound packs. He also imported and released foxes on his property around 1871.

Chirnside's foxes were never going to stay put on his land. They kept on running beyond his boundaries, seeking a better life than having to run for their lives from packs of foxhounds and mounted red-swathed ghouls.

Foxes would have been fairly tripping over rabbits in the region where they first found freedom and the absence of dingoes greatly enhanced their chances of establishing themselves. Exposed native animals with no skills at avoiding foxes were also easy meat. Released into acclimatisation's epicentre, there was nothing to prevent the fox doing as it pleased. It would expand its range on a path smoothed for it by pastoralism and Thomas Austin's rabbits.

Foxes had the frightening ability to cover quite long distances when looking to establish new territories. And once they settled in they weren't going anywhere. Depending on the type of country and the amount of available prey and other food, a fox with an established territory can range up to 500 hectares. Foxes are defensive of their territory and like dingoes and dogs mark it with urine, faeces and anal scent. Territorial squabbles are common.

While foxes are usually solitary creatures, they pair up at mating time in winter and both parents contribute to the raising of litters. Foxes are independent by six months, when they leave the family group to find new territories.[7]

Foxes are hunters and scavengers. Almost omnivorous, they'll eat fruit if they're hungry enough and they don't mind chowing down on insects such as grasshoppers, locusts and beetles. But like all the canids, foxes will always take the better offer, and that regularly brings them into conflict with humans because human activities make for an easier living.

In the early days, all the fox outrage was about fowl and lamb killing. But mostly unseen and irrelevant to agriculture and the householder was the fox's toll on native animals. Foxes kill and eat more rabbits than any other prey – when they're readily available. But foxes have never put so much as a dent in the rabbit population. When rabbits or domestic animals are not available, or are hard to get, foxes go for the next best thing: ground dwelling creatures – mammals and birds preferred. You name it, foxes kill it.

By 1882, foxes were doing it easy in the rabbit's slipstream. Dead lambs of a morning, attributed to the dreaded wedge-tailed eagles, were fox victims. Just like when the rabbit began its spread, some people at first considered foxes something of a novelty, until caught in flagrante. In a carbon copy of the rabbit, the fox spread through a merging and northwards advance of the Victorian and South Australian releases.

*

Dr JE Taylor was the editor of *Science Gossip*. In 1885 he wrote an article for *The Argus* in which he made relevant observations about the fox's dingo-like tendencies:

> The fox has changed both his ideas and his tastes. He now prefers young lambs to poultry and allows the rabbit to go scot-free. The latter is too much trouble to catch and is not worth going after. Consequently, the English fox is assuming the propensities of the dingo.[8]

Dr Taylor was right. There isn't a fox born that prefers rabbit to lamb. But the graziers gleefully eliminated the dingoes, and their tracks hadn't even gone cold before foxes took their place. Graziers found it a lot harder to get rid of the foxes. They were too small and mobile, at times not strictly tied to defined territories, solitary rather than social pack animals, and they bred faster.

It was obvious that after the catastrophic release of the rabbit, just 80 kilometres away, that the release of the fox was another developing environmental disaster. The *Weekly Times* published a lengthy but strong condemnation of Thomas Chirnside and his foxes and demanded the government act while it had the chance, unlike its inaction in eliminating the rabbit while it had that chance. The article concluded:

> Foxes … are a most unmitigated evil. They have not a single redeeming point in their favour; and, as we have shown, wherever the slightest cover is to be found, there they congregate in numbers, to the annoyance and suffering of the surrounding districts.

The fox can only be of value for sport; the rabbit is an article of food. The rabbit has cost the country tens of thousands of pounds; the fox is likely to become an even more expensive pest. It would be well if the nuisance were taken in hand before it assumes greater dimensions. Mr Tucker has informed the [Legislative] Assembly that the foxes are to be treated the same as other vermin, and that licensees of crown lands are to be compelled to kill them as they kill rabbits and wild dogs; but this is an inadequate measure.

There was a time when rabbits could have been killed off, but the opportunity for doing it was neglected, and the rabbits have since entailed enormous loss on individuals and the State. Today foxes may be destroyed. All that is wanted is a stringent destruction law. If the vermin can run wild, increase, and multiply for another six months, thousands of pounds will have to be spent to exterminate them. If the Government delay the matter longer, they will afford an admirable exemplification of the penny wise and pound-foolish idea.[9]

Two days after the *Weekly Times* article, the Legislative Assembly of Victoria, stung into action, declared foxes as vermin under the *Mallee Pastoral Leases Act 1883*. In practical terms it meant nothing to the graziers who were up to their necks in rabbits. No law was going to stop foxes killing lambs over winter in the mallee. In summer when the lambs were too big and the rabbits thinned out, they kept themselves busy digging up mallee-fowl mounds and raiding clutches of eggs and in autumn picking off chicks. The native fauna in Victoria, like everywhere else the fox invaded, paid an awful, unseen price. Killing native quail and bilbies and kangaroo rats were the least of the grazier's problems with foxes.

Foxes are nocturnal hunters and do their killing under the cover of darkness. Stockmen killed three foxes in August 1886 near Mount Elephant and believed if they had spread that far into the interior there was no doubt they would overrun the colony unless vigorous steps ensured their destruction.[10]

Further north at Wagga Wagga in the New South Wales Riverina district, in October 1889, a stockman shot a fox. It caused something of a stir and raised suspicions that someone may have seeded them in the region for either rabbit control or sporting purposes.[11] That was all they needed.

On 13 June 1889, during debate in the Legislative Assembly of Victoria, a Mr Highett asked the premier if he would take steps, as a matter of urgency, to have a short Bill introduced giving local councils the power to pay bonuses on fox scalps. Mr Woods jumped in before the premier had a chance to answer and replied that he thought it an unusual thing to ask for public funds to pay for private issues, because it was well known the Chirnside brothers had introduced the foxes and they certainly had the wherewithal to eradicate them themselves. The onus, he stated, lay on the Chirnsides, not the state to exterminate the foxes.

The premier, Duncan Gillies, stood and said that the government would not entertain paying for fox bonuses, but that members could discuss the possibility of councils doing that and passing the cost on to the ratepayers, when they debated the Local Government Bill a little later.[12] The buck, not the proposed Bill, was effectively passed, and nothing was done.

The Victorian government sat on its hands, but the South Australian parliament acted. In the south-east of the colony foxes had become almost as big a nuisance as dingoes, it was told, and 'there were districts in the south-east ... that were infested'. The South Australian Legislative Assembly passed the *Wild Dog and Fox Destruction Act 1889*, and paid scalp money for dogs and foxes killed outside council areas, the bounty being fixed annually by the Commissioner of Crown Lands. Claimants had to produce scalps as evidence for payment.[13]

By 1890, foxes were at large throughout Victoria, making enemies no matter where they went. The lamb slaughter went on unabated, but the tell-tale sign of foxes colonising a new area was a nocturnal raid on the fowl houses. Quolls had always been terrible fowl-killers, but when the dingo war eliminated the quolls, the fowl houses once again became targets, this time for foxes. In time there'd be more foxes than there ever were quolls.

Wherever dingoes had been extirpated, foxes assumed the role as wool's great persecutor. Still, the sheep population was growing exponentially. And so were the foxes. The Victorian shires of Euroa, Benalla, and Shepparton placed bounties on their heads. But paying bounties has never solved regional feral animal plagues. It just pays people for killing the creature in question and does nothing to reduce the populations.

The wool industry, now at its height, waged a constant battle against the land itself, the weather, and the social and economic disadvantages of isolation. The early 1890s should have been prime seasons. But sheep had weakened the land, and rabbits were wool's death by a billion cuts. The fox plague merely rubbed salt into the wounds.

The year 1894 held odd weather for eastern Australia. Western New South Wales and Victoria, and south-western Queensland enjoyed heavy rainfall, but the area to the east, particularly between Melbourne and Sydney, remained dry. It was the beginning of a long period of drought for the eastern half of the continent. Hot, dry summers decimated the rabbit population, but that was bad news for the native fauna. Foxes and cats turned their attention to the birds and ground-dwelling fauna instead.

In June 1904, farmers around Ganmain in south-western New South Wales's Riverina district complained of the havoc wrought by foxes. Some wool growers were losing up to twenty-five per cent of their lambs to foxes. Lamb killing became a matter of surplus killing – killing for 'sport', not food.[14]

By 1911, foxes had conquered New South Wales and were well and truly on the loose in southern Queensland. Not everyone thought foxes were entirely a problem. Affected graziers thought the fox needed extermination. Others – the Western Land Board Commissioners among them – saw the fox as an enemy of the rabbit, and deserving of credit for the mitigation of the rabbit pest. With the country's rabbit population then approaching ten billion and climbing, nothing and no one was doing any mitigating. Especially not foxes during lambing. Still, in their wisdom, the Western Land Board Commissioners recommended against war against the fox, no doubt leaving their constituent landholders staring at dead lambs of a morning wondering whose side their commissioners were on.[15]

If that wasn't enough, the same board of commissioners reported that the rabbit population had not increased in 1914. They must have gone out and counted them. They were convinced that the decrease in the rabbit was due almost entirely to the increase of that jolly good fellow, the fox.[16]

\*

Foxes were heading west, and the West Australian government came up with the idea of dingo- and fox-proofing the rabbit-proof fence on their border. Sheep men wanted to know how the government proposed to pull that one off. They knew that no fence could be dingo- or fox-proof. One wrote in 1914 that his parent's property in South Australia had almost six-foot-high netting fences and dingoes regularly scaled them to kill sheep. It made absolutely no difference to foxes at all either. He had seen a fox climb a nine-foot fowl-yard fence with a chook in its mouth.[17]

In May 1917, Mr CP Murray of Windimurra Pastoral Lease, Mount Magnet, 580 kilometres north-east of Perth, caught a fox in a dingo trap, well on the east of the rabbit-proof fence. He sent the skin to the Chief Inspector of Rabbits as proof of their existence in the region. He had seen fox tracks about often, and the same day he caught that fox, he had seen another to the west side of the fence.[18] Foxes were in Western Australia to stay.

By 1920, foxes had reached Longreach in north-western Queensland, not far short of their northernmost limit on the eastern half of the mainland. The Great Dividing Range in New South Wales appears to have slowed the dispersal of foxes into coastal districts, sometimes by as much as six to ten years, but elsewhere foxes spread throughout Australia at an estimated seventy-three kilometres a year. By 1934, they had invaded the south-west and the north-west as far as Derby. In 1943, they were shooting foxes in the Kimberley, their northernmost limit in the west.[19]

A small fur industry grew around the fox – nothing compared to the rabbit skin trade, but enough for townsfolk to make a spare pound or two from dragging a dead animal as a scent bait, then trapping foxes along the trail in the manner used to trap dingoes before they got wise. Later, strychnine and then cyanide became popular fox baits. Spotlighting foxes and dispatching them with .22 calibre rifles was also a popular method of thinning-out numbers. The fox skin trade in Australia was a winter pursuit, until clamour from green groups opposed to the fur trade finished the fox season.

Foxes achieved complete colonisation of the continent in around seventy years. They spread out faster than rabbits, but their path to continental ubiquity was rabbit assisted. If you take a look at the mainland distribution maps for the rabbit and the fox, they are nearly identical. The rabbit, as we have seen, only moves short distances to start new warrens, but the fox is a highly mobile creature and needs to get on the track and move a fair way from home to find new territory, sometimes up to hundreds of kilometres.

CHAPTER 15

# Alpacas, Buffalo, Banteng and Ostriches

The first alpacas to arrive in Australia were imported not for their guardian capabilities, but for their wool. In 1852, Charles Ledger, a British farmer, adventurer and entrepreneur, visited Sydney and returned to his estates in Peru convinced that the colonies were ideally suited to alpacas. He must have convinced the New South Wales graziers of that as well, for he made a deal with them to import alpacas to their shores.

Ledger had been an agent for the wool trade in Peru for fifteen years, collecting alpaca wool from indigenous alpaca farmers and exporting it to Britain.[1]

Unfortunately for Ledger, the Peruvian government had prohibited the export of living alpacas, so Ledger assembled a flock of hundreds of alpacas and llamas at his estate near Peru's southern border and smuggled them across the Andes Mountains into the Argentine Confederation (now Argentina) to ship them to Australia.

It was no mean feat. Ledger endured incredible hardship and adversity in fulfilling his part of the bargain. South American countries had no love for Britain or its dominions, and made life difficult for anyone trying to export alpacas. Two hundred of Ledger's flock supposedly perished from drinking leech-infested water. Disaster struck twice more when he found himself caught in an Andean snowstorm and lost half of his remaining animals, and a 'negligent Indian' caused the loss of two hundred more of his alpacas. As well as enduring the privations of the high sierra, the Peruvian and Bolivian authorities arrested him twice and threatened to destroy the remainder of his flock.

With the courage and guile typical of the plucky Victorian-era adventurer, Ledger eventually managed to outwit his captors. He embarked 322 alpacas and llamas on the *Salvadora* for the trip to Australia in July 1858, of which 256 survived the four-month voyage to Sydney.

It took Ledger six years to fulfil his agreement with interested New South Wales farmers, and by the time he landed his stock in Sydney, they declined to buy them at auction. Admittedly, Ledger had kept them waiting, but the farmers' reluctance to fulfil their part of the bargain was poor form. The colonial government stepped in and purchased the animals, arranging pasture for them at properties in the southern highlands and paying Ledger an annual salary of £300 to look after them.

Ledger nonetheless persisted with the experiment and set to work interbreeding his animals, hybridising the alpacas and llamas, hoping to eventually cross back to the alpaca for superior wool. Just over 400 alpacas in July 1862 would be about as good as it would get for Ledger in New South Wales. Alpacas were expensively hard work in Australia, where the cheap, hardy, bomb-proof merinos already ruled. They sounded a good idea at the time and given what we know now about their guardian capabilities, might not have been a bad idea, but their time had passed. A severe drought in 1862 to

1863 killed a lot of Ledger's flock, while an outbreak of sheep scab broke the alpaca's back.

Eventually, the New South Wales government sacked Ledger and tried to auction off his flock without success. The Acclimatisation Society of Victoria bought some eventually, and the rest found buyers here and there.

Ledger, meanwhile, returned to Peru bankrupt and embittered, finding himself 'at 48 years of age without one shilling of my own, having lost all I had in the realisation of an enterprise that I fondly hoped would have conferred great benefits on a thriving colony of my own country, and a just recompense for my capital and labour.'[2]

\*

Alongside the alpaca, the water buffalo is perhaps the most exotic of Australia's feral livestock. The New South Wales colonial administration established an outpost at Port Essington on the Coburg Peninsula in the Top End of the Northern Territory in 1827. About eighty buffalo made the boat ride to Melville Island and the Cobourg Peninsula from Java for meat, along with around twenty banteng cattle brought from Bali. Banteng are attractive cattle, smaller than western beef cattle, and have distinct white patches on their rump and lower legs.

When the British abandoned these settlements in 1843, they turned the buffalo and banteng loose. The buffalo soon colonised the permanent and semi-permanent swamps and freshwater springs of the Top End. Meanwhile, the banteng survived as a feral population, unknown to anyone other than the locals, until rediscovered in that isolated area in 1948. Banteng are critically endangered in South-east Asia, and the

Australian feral population is free of domestic cattle blood. This poses quite a dilemma for environmental managers in Coburg national parks, as the Australian bantengs are vital to the species' survival, although they are quite damaging to the lands in which they now reside.

\*

Some feral problems have been created by the well-meaning ethicists who sought to protect a species. It was like that with ostriches, which first arrived in Australia in 1868, imported by our friends at the Acclimatisation Society of Victoria.

Ladies' hats decorated with ostentatious feather displays were all the rage in the late nineteenth and early twentieth centuries, a period notorious for its barbarous exploitation of wildlife around the world. So, rather than releasing the ostriches into the wild, the society intended that a farming industry should develop to serve the great demand for plumage. It was one of their better schemes. However, it was a dodgy time to be a bird furnished with large attractive plumage in Australia and many native waterbirds were caught up in the feather-hunting frenzy.

A 'Save the Birds' campaign launched in Europe raised awareness among consumers, who stopped buying plumage-decorated hats after seeing graphic evidence of the distasteful business. The plumage trade died in 1914 and native waterbirds got their reprieve, though it caused the ostrich-farming industry in Australia to go belly-up. Ostriches from New South Wales and Victorian farms went to zoos and other wildlife parks as exhibits. Many ostrich farmers in South Australia released their birds to fend for themselves.

Thankfully, feral ostriches never became much of a problem. The odd remnant is still out there roaming around, survivors from the brief resurgence in ostrich farming in the 1970s. They've wandered as far north as the Birdsville track, and can turn up anywhere in the interior, but ostriches have always had difficulty reproducing in Australia and it won't be long before they eventually die out.

# PART THREE

# The Federation Plagues

The twentieth century should have been a new dawn for Australia, and politically it was. The Australian colonies, other than Western Australia, had by 1899 twice voted in favour of federation. The west followed suit a year later. Federation was to unite the colonies as a nation on New Year's Day 1901. But wool's ugly fall, the rabbit's devastation and the fox's wanton reign tempered the joy of the forthcoming birth of nationhood. Drought wracked the eastern interior with the barren consequences of three decades of environmental torture.

During the first three decades of the new century, all the major feral species consolidated their grip on Australia. Rabbits had been wrecking the joint for sixty years, foxes fifty, cats possibly longer, and all thrived in the purged absence of the dingo and other native carnivores. The feral livestock species –

goats, pigs, camels, donkeys and horses – all expanded their ranges, and the national sheep flock was recovering. Foreign animals, feral and domestic, became just a part of bush life.

During the early-century periods of economic depression, drought and war, rabbits were a free and accessible food source for many Australian families. Impoverished rural people relied on rabbits to survive. During the 1930s and 1940s, young boys and girls often provided the family's daily meat needs by trapping or shooting rabbits. The Australian bush culture of the time wasn't about kangaroos and emus, it was about the merino and the rabbit. If you lived in the bush and were not engaged in some sector of wool growing, you were usually dependent on the rabbit in one way or another.

In the cities and towns, while rats and rabbits ran riot underfoot, starlings, sparrows, feral pigeons, imported doves, and Indian mynas flew around like they owned the place, because they did. Anyone who didn't know better would assume they were native to Australia because there was not a capital city or major town without them. Even the wheat belts suffered starling, rat and mouse infestations and remarkably, remote grain silos, usually the domain of the endemic galah, had a resident flocks of feral pigeons. How that came to be is anyone's guess.

The picture of the trashing of rural Australia in the late-nineteenth and early-twentieth centuries is not complete without colouring in the background with the bland green of the prickly pear. First grown at Sydney and Parramatta in the early to mid-1800s in a failed effort to start a cochineal industry, prickly pear became Australia's vegetal rabbit. Its infestations covered 10 million acres (4 million ha) by 1900 and 58 million acres (24 million ha) by 1920. Australia was fighting desperate environmental wars on different fronts. Despite every control effort, the plant's rate of advance was 2.4 million acres (1 million ha) per year.[1] The country was a complete mess.

Invasive-species control was high on the new national agenda and, fortuitously for Australia, the twentieth century heralded the dawn of biological control mechanisms. It doesn't matter how smart the scientists are when the people with the right of veto aren't. Australia stupidly missed the opportunity to destroy the rabbit early in the new century but somehow the country landed on its feet and stunned the world with the incredible insect bio-controller that flattened the prickly pear. The difference being that the rabbit had friends in business and the prickly pear had none. Buoyed by that success it was decided the Queensland sugar-cane beetle problem would be best dealt with by toads − a strategy we still struggle with today. By mid-century, everyone was so rabbit-worn that a deadly virus finally loosened the rabbit's stranglehold on Australia. Two out of three ain't bad.

# CHAPTER 16

# The Destruction of Western New South Wales

Prior to European invasion, Australia's eastern interior had evolved over millions of years to carry only a sparse population of specialised, soft-footed creatures on spongy moisture-retaining drought-resistant country that required but a minimum of rain to survive El Niño's regular dry cycles.

James Cotton, the stock inspector for the Cobar sheep district, giving evidence to the 1901 Royal Commission on the Western Lands of New South Wales, declared that in the years 1880 and 1881, before the district was stocked, the country was covered with a heavy growth of natural grasses – 'kangaroo grass, star grass, blue grass, mulga, and other grasses. The western half of the district abounded with salt bush and cotton bush, together with the grasses mentioned. The ground was soft, spongy and very absorbent. One inch of rain then, in spring or autumn, produced a luxurious growth of fresh green grass.'[1]

As pastoralism spread into the newfound grazing lands of the interior, graziers saw the west's wide-open spaces, which encouraged gross mismanagement from the start by overclearing and overstocking. A horde of destructive wool-clad bio-invaders tens of millions strong overran the region, stomping across a rugged-looking, but surprisingly delicate, ecosystem and obliterating the grasses, compacting the subsoil and trampling the fine layer of topsoil to fine powder.

Then came the rabbits – millions and millions and millions of them. What remained of the west, the rabbits stripped bare, sending the region into irreversible decline. Dry spells that the native ecosystem once took in its stride became pastoralism's devastating droughts. And the droughts' scorching winds blew the powdered topsoil away in ferocious dust storms, leaving the landscape scalded and barren.

There has been appalling environmental destruction everywhere sheep and rabbits reigned, but nowhere copped it worse than the western division of New South Wales. The federation of Australia coincided with the Federation Drought – a dry spell that withered eastern Australia from 1896 to 1902 and resulted in the destruction and death of the semi-arid sheep lands that had briefly supported tens of millions of merinos.

Leaseholders went to the wall and the newly proclaimed state's sheep population reduced by two-thirds. According to official returns, the number of sheep in the western division in 1891 was 15,406,000. In 1900, the number had fallen to 5,704,000, all due to the exhaustion of feed and water. Things were so dire that the state government established a royal commission on 11 August 1900 to investigate the causes of the devastation, the state of the landholding leases, and how the merino could regain its feet before being steadied and pushed off again on its tottering way.

The evidence provided only a year later by the men at the sharp end makes compelling reading. It is apparent that they understood the causes of the crisis and the horrific extent of the damage to the environment quite well. Even the wholesale killing of trees and fauna rated a mention as a contributing factor. Mr E Quin of Tarella Station summed up the problem with this vast land clearing when he gave evidence to the royal commission that the removal of the bush had exposed the topsoil. The plant roots held the earth together, he wrote. Once the plants were removed, the wind blew the soil away.

Nonetheless, other than reducing the size of holdings which did reduce the damage, no plan emerged to recover the environment and protect the fauna. The emphasis was on regenerating the western district as a wool-producing money spinner.

The commission's findings summarised the causes of the 'present depression and the general unprofitableness of the pastoral industry in the western division as the result of a combination of low rainfall, the rabbit, overstocking, sandstorms, and the profusion of non-edible woody vegetation.' The 'gloomy state of affairs in the west' was due to the pastoralists' failure to recognise that what they called drought was the just the meteorological norm for the west, and not intermittent obstacles. The meteorological history of the region proved it to be a country of constant low rainfall and recurring dry spells. These periods of low rainfall only became an issue in western New South Wales when millions of hungry and thirsty ungulates needed to be kept alive. In other words, the western division was only suitable for the native creatures that the graziers were doing their best to eliminate.

The wool industry was sent enough warnings but couldn't hear them for the deafening ka-ching of cash registers echoing out of the canyons of the wool-bale mountains. The effects of overstocking had been obvious and newsworthy since the

1870s, when drought years exacerbated its effects. A conference of the Chief Inspectors of Stock in Sydney in November 1874 reported to the New South Wales Minister for Lands, as part of their report on pleuro-pneumonia and its treatment:

> The Conference desires to point out that the system of overstocking, so generally carried out over the whole of the colonies, has had a most injurious effect on the pastures and stock; that it has reduced the size and injured the constitution, and is a great source of disease in stock generally.[2]

Warnings or no, graziers were hell bent on growing wool while the sun shone. And they got more than their share of sunshine in the 1870s. Even the graziers' newspaper, *The Sydney Mail and New South Wales Advertiser,* tried to get through to them:

> As to the droughts, it is only to be expected that their effect should be severe where overstocking has been the rule instead of dam-making, well-sinking, and improvement generally. In the Albury district it is said that fully one-half the damage done by late droughts is attributable to overstocking; and if this be true, it is to be hoped the lesson will not be entirely thrown away. The pastoral interest would be in a sound position for learning, even by sharp experience, the necessity for caution, foresight, and care, and the dangers of that kind of speculation which arises from the over-eager desire to become rich speedily, and the concurrence of circumstances which seem to promise its fulfilment.[3]

The commonly expressed view was that overstocking was the main cause of the trouble in the west, and when the rabbits invaded, graziers wasted huge sums of money trying to stop their advance. However, for the thirteen rabbit-entrenched years from 1885 to 1897, the average number of sheep in the region went up forty-two per cent, even while competing with the rabbits.[4]

With the grasses gone, the enterprising rabbits ringbarked trees and ate the roots of any edible plant. It was the final nail in the west's coffin. Before the rabbit there was always hope of recovering from drought in the unlikely event the cocky didn't overstock. The rabbits completely nullified the effects of most rains, nipping off the grass as soon as it stuck its head above the ground, and digging up and consuming the living seed and roots of everything that tried to grow.

Although sixty centimetres of rain fell over the district in 1891, no grass was able to grow. Whenever new grass shoots or edible shrubs appeared, the rabbits ate them, and the sheep starved. Cobar's stock inspector James Cotton was emphatic in his evidence to the commission, stating that a gradual deterioration of the country was caused by stock, which had transformed the land from its original soft, spongy, absorbent nature to a hard, claylike, smooth surface that, 'instead of absorbing the rain, runs it off in a sheet as fast as it falls, carrying with it ... the seeds of all kinds of plants, sheep manure, sand &c., to enrich the lower-lying country, and plant it with pine, box, and other noxious scrubs.'

It wasn't just rabbits removing the tree cover. Many graziers thought their paddocks had too much natural shade. Axe-wielding men ringbarked eucalypt and acacia trees in their millions. And it wasn't as if most graziers had a malicious set on the native fauna and flora, even if it appeared personal. Ten thousand outback acres was supposed to function like a hundred stonewalled acres of lush English competition-free fertility. Graziers just eliminated anything that got in the way of their sheep – animate or inanimate, native or not.

\*

Wire netting on sheep and cattle fences, dug into the ground, are a common feature in rural Australia. In the nineteenth century, it was the only hope of keeping rabbits off one's property. Rabbits learned to scramble over them. The dingo fence between Queensland and New South Wales started its life in 1884 as a rabbit-proof fence that wasn't rabbit proof. Fencing a property, a region or a state might provide exclusive protection but it does nothing to address the bigger issues.

The royal commission noted that such fencing was only ever as good as its construction.

Mr LA Chambers, inspector of Pastoral Properties for the Agency Land and Finance Company, submitted to the commission that in sandy country – and in country prone to floods – rabbit netting was useless. That was eminently true. Netting fences were about the only decent rabbit preventative, but their very nature meant they caught all kinds of debris and were particularly damaged during floods.

The prevailing westerly winds blowing over the trampled, denuded land produced sandstorms of such enormity that they could only be described as calamitous. The wire-netting fences collected the wind-blown debris, which then banked wind-blown sand, rendering the fences, in many places, useless.

Submissions to the commission spoke of instances where sand and debris completely buried rabbit-proof wire-netting fences. Bourke's stock inspector, Mr DWF Hatten, confirmed that there were places in the west where you could drive over the fences, so buried in sand were they.

Mr N Sadleir, Manager of Albermarle and Victoria Lake Station in the Menindee district, wrote that his experiences with wire netting fences had been 'a total failure'. Workers built 180 kilometres of fencing, but he eventually had it demolished because of the shifting sand. Three fences erected one on top of the other could not keep the sheep in, let alone the rabbits out.

With the ground compacted and the topsoil trampled to dust and blown away, the vacant sub-standard earth found itself invaded by small trees and woody shrubs – natives, but weeds nonetheless. Those woody weeds still dominate the red country of the western lands, and not just in New South Wales. What was once lightly timbered, open-grassed red country is now barren forests dominated by mulga and woody weeds like budda and hop bush.

The royal commission also acknowledged that the woody weed infestation that replaced the depleted grasses and filled the empty niche was due in part to the cessation of bush fires (possibly due to Indigenous people no longer carrying out traditional burning), which destroyed weeds and promoted the growth of grasses and other edible herbage. But with flammable pastoral infrastructure and equally flammable stock in place, fires were the last thing any grazier wanted to see sweeping across his already devastated country.

In other locations also, bush fires that previously swept through the land every year and kept down the scrub and undergrowth, stopped, and the scrub grew to an enormous extent, becoming a harbour for feral goats, pigs and horses.

No living Australian has ever seen the western division in its pristine state. The poor old west has limped along in its altered state for well over a century.

Even now, the papers of the royal commission make for depressing reading. The commissioners trotted the dingo out for dishonourable mentions, and the fox for just one. Curiously, the feral horses, goats and pigs, which were certainly creating havoc back then, didn't rate a mention.

From the furthest north-west corner of the state, Mr R Dawes of Yandama Station wrote that the bad seasons had driven the dingoes in from the 'back country', and no less than 750 had been destroyed on Yandama in one year. In that same year, 2500 sheep had been destroyed by dingoes.

There were other political, practical and administrative causes for dissatisfaction among the lessees of western lands. The Royal Commission addressed these in the report, but the real focus was solely on getting wool back on its feet. No one mentioned the fate or future of the native fauna that had been displaced or eliminated by sheep and rabbits. No one cared. This wasn't about them.

Men went broke and wool took its dive, fewer producers wrung smaller fortunes out of the emaciated west, but the environment and biodiversity were the biggest losers. The exact toll in native animal lives and natural vegetation is impossible to calculate. And fittingly, the runners-up in the contest for biggest loser were the graziers. All their wounds were self-inflicted. Their short-sighted management of the western division helped to propel New South Wales towards prosperity and federal unification, no question; but, axe in one hand, strychnine in the other, they paved the way for their sheep to flog their properties to death.

To be fair, environmental considerations rated lowly on about everyone's priority list in those days, not just the graziers'. But effective conservation is simply a matter of common sense, moderation and a little empathy for the country. They couldn't muster up any of that.

The rabbits and sheep died in their millions as they joined forces to bring about their own destruction. Yet the rabbit also created a startling social and economic transformation in the bush. The increased demand for rabbits and their by-products offset the sharp downturn in wool production. The rabbit usurped wool as the economic mainstay of many bush communities. While the grazier watched his topsoil blow away, praying for rain and hoping for better times, his one-time seasonal labourers turned to rabbit-trapping and emerged from the environmental, social and economic disaster as the real winners.

# CHAPTER 17

# The Rat, Mouse and Cat Plagues

T he fledgling Australian colonies had their animal problems, but none had been more persistent or damaging than rats. The black rat, which had colonised the British Isles was as comfortable in a barn as it was in a city tenement as it was in a ship. It was an enthusiastic seafarer and an uninvited guest on every ship, merchant or naval, where it raided bread rooms and food stores.

There would have been thousands of rats in the eleven ships of the First Fleet, and they came ashore in quick time, the proverbial rat on a mooring rope. The conditions were quite to their liking and they soon bred to plague proportions. Initially, the imported rats and the local native rats may have joined the quest for a free feed. The native bush rat looks strikingly like the black and brown rat. Anything edible, or anything that looked like it was edible, was liable to attack.

Captain John Hunter, the captain of the flagship HMS *Sirius* and Governor Phillip's second in command, wrote that attempts had been made by several men to establish little farms, but no sooner had the corn formed into ear than the imported rats and native herbivores destroyed the entire crop in a night.[1]

The rat attacks were just the beginning of a constant war with that enterprising rodent and the local native fauna. It would also place a serious drain on the colony's limited provisions. On 15 February 1788, Governor Phillip directed Lieutenant Philip Gidley King, seven soldiers and fifteen convicts to settle Norfolk Island, which lies 1412 kilometres east of Evans Head on the New South Wales north coast.

James Cook had observed Norfolk Island on 10 October 1774, on his second voyage to the South Pacific on HMS *Resolution*. The British administration considered the island to be of the highest strategic importance to the New South Wales colony on account of the tall pines and the flax that grew there. A great danger for ships supporting an outpost so far away from Europe was to its timbers, masts, spars and sails. Britain was dependent on Russia for flax for its ships' sails, and for its masts and spars, which came from Baltic pine forests. Russia had been getting ever more difficult to deal with. As such, annexing Norfolk Island was considered imperative for the success of the Sydney colony.

Norfolk Island appeared to be a godsend. Unfortunately the pines proved to be useless for ships' timbers and the flax substandard. It was good luck for Norfolk Island, however. Based on their attitude to resources in New South Wales the British would have stripped the place bare of pines and flax in truly short order, as they did the providence petrel, the mutton bird that roosted there in their millions, and most of the native forest.

Nonetheless, King landed on 3 March and brought his small party and their stores safely ashore. The rats came with them. King had the party build a secure storehouse for the island's provisions. The flour was safe from the rats, but the newly sprouted grain crops didn't fare so well. Rats destroyed the germinating corn, which was three inches high and had been growing strongly, and worse, they completely dug up the freshly sown wheat two days later, and consumed every grain. King wrote in his journal, 'As I had no cats, and only one dog these vermin were likely to prove a serious nuisance; however, in order to rid ourselves of them as much as possible, I caused all the empty casks to be converted into traps.'[2]

King reported that the casks worked. For a while. Initially they caught thirty or forty rats each night over several nights. 'These were killed, and scattered about the garden, to deter the rest from coming to the place; but they soon grew too cunning to be caught in the traps, and too bold to be intimidated by their dead companions.' In desperation the colonists smashed bottles and finely ground the glass mixing it with oatmeal, which they spread about the gardens and 'killed vast numbers of them'. Not nice, but such were the times. After that, the rat population on Norfolk Island abated to something less than plague status and agriculture was able to succeed despite some rat raids.

Back in Sydney, the pillaging and despoiling of stores of flour by rats was a serious issue. The colony was running short on rations and had resorted to hunting kangaroos and emus to supplement their food. On 2 October 1788, Governor Phillip dispatched the *Sirius* under the command of Captain Hunter to the Cape of Good Hope to collect more stores for the colony.

While the colony impatiently waited for the *Sirius* to return, David Collins, the colony's judge advocate, wrote that in March 1789 'the gardens and houses of individuals, and the provision store, were overrun with rats. The safety of the provisions was an object of general consequence, and the commissary was for some time employed in examining into the state of the store.'[3] It would be just one of several full-scale assaults the rats would make on the flour stores.

The *Sirius* returned to Port Jackson on 6 May 1789 and brought with her 6450 tonnes of flour for the settlement. It was well-received but calculated at full rations to only last around four months. Unfortunately, 6450 tonnes of flour also looked appealing to the burgeoning rat population, as David Collins ruefully recorded:

> Our enemies the rats, who worked unseen, and attacked us where we were most vulnerable, being again observed in numbers about the provision store, the commissary caused the provisions to be moved out of one store into another; for, alas! at this period they could be all contained in one. These pernicious vermin were found to be very numerous, and the damage they had done much greater than the state of our stores would admit. Eight casks of flour were at one time found wholly destroyed. From the store, such as escaped the hunger of the different dogs that were turned loose upon them flew to the gardens of individuals, where they rioted upon the Indian corn which was growing and did considerable mischief.[4]

Rats rioting upon the corn reduced the daily ration to two-thirds per man – women and children exempted. The flour and other stores had severely diminished, and Collins noted that there was a 'great uncertainty as to the time when a supply might arrive from England, and from the losses which had been and still were occasioned by rats in the provision store.'[5]

Australia, like the rest of the world, was bedevilled by the two most common species of rat: the black rat (or ship rat), which originates in India and South-east Asia and which is brown; and the brown rat, also known as the Norway, sewer or wharf rat, which is not Norwegian at all, but is believed to have originated in China and is also brown. It was the black rat that beset Sydney – the same rat that carried the nasty flea *Xenopsylla cheopis*, which brought the bubonic plague from Asia to Europe, where it killed tens of millions of people.

By 1795, the colony had built secure storerooms with tile roofs. Rats had previously gained access through thatched roofs, but even when built with solid tiles, the rats (being rats) dug their way in.

The administration might have hoped their cats would eliminate the growing rat plague, but there weren't enough cats to put a dent in the ravenous horde, if they were even all that interested. Sydney's penal colony cats had a far more diverse selection of helpless victims than the rats. The Reverend Johnson's cats (which arrived with the First Fleet) were presumably too overburdened with their rat-catching responsibilities at home – or too pre-occupied killing blue-tongue lizards and superb blue wrens while avoiding the local dogs – to lend a hand in protecting the government stores from rats.

Little terriers are much better and more dedicated rodent killers and were frequently used by Sydney's marines for pest control. The dog's propensity for surplus killing has much to do with this. But the sheer numbers of rats meant that the dogs did a fat lot of good.

Finally the colonists resorted to poisoning the rats with

arsenic. It may have helped. The rats seem to have reduced in number, though they never disappeared entirely.

Somehow, despite the rat deluge, the Black Death spared both Sydney and Norfolk Island during the early days of the colonies. But the threat never totally went away. While there were rats and poor hygiene there was always the risk bubonic plague could appear as it regularly did elsewhere in the world. It would take it over a hundred years, but eventually the disease did appear.

By the late 1800s, the plague was sweeping through south-east Asia. In 1899, Australia-bound ships made port to take on supplies in plague-infected Chinese cities and took on infected black rats. And so the Black Death came to Sydney.

Early in 1900, dead black rats began to appear around the wharf areas of the harbour foreshore and the plague started killing people. In 1900 alone, there were 303 human cases of plague. One hundred and three people died. Sydney's chief medical officer, Ashburton Thompson, showed considerable foresight in establishing a campaign to rid Sydney of rats to prevent the spread of the disease. Within ten months of the first human case of plague appearing in Sydney, workers killed 108,308 rats, and poison and fumigation killed a large but unknown number. A general rat persecution continued for years because of the bubonic plague epidemic.

Thousands of rats died during the black rat pogrom, but it wasn't just the black rat that suffered. The black rat had long competed with the native bush rat around Sydney Harbour. Bush rats ordinarily lived in forests, woodlands and heath, sheltering in short burrows under logs or rocks and lining their nests with grass. They, like so many others, found city life an easier way than bush life. Bush rats and black rats are extremely difficult to tell apart, and poison and fumigation is an undistinguishing method of control. The bush rat numbers never recovered from the Black Death pogrom, and black rats moved into the vacant territories.

*

Alongside the black rats, the First Fleet would also have carried a number of non-native mice as stowaways. Mice are associated with human activity all over the world, especially in agricultural and urban areas. Normally population levels are low; however, when conditions are favourable, mouse numbers can increase exponentially to plague proportions and they become a serious pest.

The earliest reported mouse plague in Australia was in 1917 on the Darling Downs in Queensland, and they have been occurring, with increasing frequency, ever since. In 1993, Australia's worst ever mouse plague caused an estimated ninety-six million dollars' worth of damage. The mice destroyed thousands of hectares of crops and, when they left the grain fields barren, they moved off and attacked livestock in piggeries and poultry farms. They chewed through rubber and electrical insulation, damaged farm vehicles, and ruined cars and buildings. Another plague in the summer of 2010/2011 was as bad, affecting three million hectares of crops in the New South Wales central west and the Riverina, as well as parts of Victoria and South Australia. Mouse plagues now erupt in the grain growing regions of Australia on average every three years, causing massive disruption to communities and losses to farmers. The mouse plague of 2021 in New South Wales (following drought, bush fires and pandemic) has affected more than twenty per cent of the state and caused untold damage to crops, infrastructure and the psychology of rural residents. Videos of plague mice are easy to find online and vision of the creepy little things swarming over everything in their path at night is just ghastly.

Mouse numbers have multiplied in the grain belts through the improved food supply caused by the planting of summer and winter crops. Mouse populations now don't suffer the annual setback of deep tilling. Reduced or no-tillage practices these days don't destroy underground nests and their occupants as they used to. And that means more mice.

Plagues begin when grain growing seasons are long and bounteous in spring and continue, with increasing numbers, through summer and autumn and end in the cold of July when food is scarce and weakened mice in their millions die from disease and starvation. Plague populations crash so suddenly that the crisis can end within just two weeks.[6]

Mice can squeeze through the tiniest gap and like most creatures are wholly appreciative of the comforts of someone else's home. Pantries are raided, food containers – opened and unopened – are breached and the contents consumed, droppings are deposited without any thought for their flabbergasted hosts, and mice seek out and occupy every warm or cool niche inside the house depending on the season. They like dark places, nest in shoes and clothing, and are not in the least repelled by snoring or sleep-talking. Being sociable by nature, they don't mind cosying up to a human in repose and regularly cause children, and some less staunch adults to wake shrieking and leg-slapping from their slumber when awakened by questing mice invading their bedclothes and venturing up a pyjama pant leg.

There are some upsides to mouse plagues. In true Australian famine-feast fashion, anything that preys on small critters takes advantage and does very well on the swiftly moving here-today-gone-next-month feast. Reptiles, birds, native mammals, foxes, and feral cats, dogs and pigs hoover them up one after the other and even large native fish like Murray cod have been seen taking mice (and birds and reptiles) that find their way into waterways through misadventure.

Naturally, there are more downsides to the mouse plague than up. And while all predators large and small feast on the little suckers, that can be fraught with danger, particularly around human habitation. True, your field mouse doesn't have a terribly long life expectancy but they live long enough to make a few mortal enemies, and when they turn their hands to home-invasion, they can set off a whole chain of unhappy events. Predators wild or domestic naturally prefer to prey on the slow or weak, and the slow or weak mouse loose about the house is more dangerous that it seems.

There is a troubling amount of collateral damage caused by mouse plagues, and wild animals and pets die through secondary poisoning every time. In a futile attempt to stem the mousy flow, poison – the go-to agricultural response to any biological threat – gets thrown about with little thought about the consequences. The mouse takes the poison bait, it is weakened and becomes attractive to whatever eats mice, or it kicks its tiny little bucket and the carcase is subsequently consumed, resulting in the predator (quite often inquisitive puppies) being poisoned.

Mouse plagues are an inadvertent but unwelcome by-product of broadacre farming. Plagues can't be prevented but there is much sufferers can do to lessen the mouse's effect around the home. Judicious poisoning, trapping, clearing or removing cover and harbourage, mowing and keeping grass short, and eliminating food supplies can all help to convince the furry little piranhas to move on.

\*

The First Fleet's animal manifest is a little abstract in regard of cat passengers. It listed only 'kittens and the Reverend Johnson's cats'. We do not know if the kittens were of an independent age, if they constituted one or more litters, how many there were, or if their mother accompanied them. Other than the ones owned by the Reverend Richard Johnson we don't know if anyone else brought cats to New South Wales. You'd think there would have been plenty unaccounted for on the eleven ships of the First Fleet.

Cats have certainly been in Australia since British settlement, but it is possible they arrived earlier. For an animal that hates water, cats are accomplished sailors. They are common on ships and other vessels for their on-board rodent control.

There are theories that cats could have made their way to Australia through any number of planned and unplanned visits spanning several thousand years. First there were the travelling colonising Lapita people who passed by the tropical north, and latterly the Macassans, who for centuries came to Arnhem Land in the Northern Territory annually to fish for the sea cucumber. The Dutch plying to and from the East Indies made intermittent visits, and shipwrecks of various nations litter Australia's west coast. Cats may certainly have come ashore because of any of these events, but it is highly doubtful they would have lasted, for the same reason there is nothing heard about the cats that arrived in early colonial New South Wales: canine predation.

Dogs chase cats because they prey on them, not because they hate them, and back then the Reverend Johnson's cats and the other kittens that came ashore would have needed more than nine lives to survive Sydney's dogs and dingoes.

On the other hand, small birds such as willie wagtails and wrens, small marsupials such as antechinus and bandicoots, little skinks ... you name it, the cats that arrived with the First Fleet would have been killing all of them. Although the cats would not become a real nuisance until Sydney's feral dog and dingo problem ended.

The native fauna was naïve to the wicked wiles of the moggie and the slaughter went mostly unnoticed. Cat predation most often happens at night and their prey is usually devoured by dawn. A sad scattering of feathers or fur in the morning is the only sign of nocturnal depredation. None of the early colonists would have been concerned if they saw a cat playing with a small grey creature. They'd just think it was a mouse or a rat.

Today feral cats constitute one of Australia's greatest feral disasters and perhaps the one feral species that the average Australian has most contributed to, due to their popularity as pets and an ill-placed faith in them as vermin controllers that would do their duty and nothing else.

The cat's dispersal throughout the continent matches the colonisation settlement of modern Australia. Their full range had been achieved by 1890 and covered an area of 760 million hectares in only seventy years. Letting cats roam uncontrolled, dumping the unloved and unwanted, and the deliberate release of cats as prospective bio-controllers have all provided thousands of willing recruits to the feral horde.[7]

The Australian feral cat is an impressive beast. Usually grey or ginger, they occupy every habitable part of the mainland, Tasmania, and 4856 of Australia's 5448 off-shore islands. They are the perfect predator and are murder on native creatures. They are known to have preyed on over 400 vertebrate native creatures, which translates to 272 million birds, 470 million reptiles and 815 million mammals each year. There are no figures for invertebrates and amphibians but the true extent, while unknown, would be horrific. This is an appalling toll on our fauna and is in addition to the cats' steady but ineffectual toll on ferals such as rabbits, hares, rats, mice and imported birds.

No one knows for sure how many feral cats plague Australia. Terrain, resources, and seasonal and weather conditions all affect feral cat populations, which vary markedly from region to region. The feral cat population probably fluctuates from around two to five million, though wild estimates have at times ranged as high as eighteen million. At any rate, even just one is too many for Australia.

Australia's unique environments were never cut out for feral invasions. All the ferals are death to native creatures, directly or indirectly, and the predatory skill set of the feral cat is appallingly diverse. Nothing is safe from a feral cat. They can climb trees and raid the nests of birds and arboreal mammals. They have been blamed for over forty extinctions of native birds, mammals and reptiles. Unsurprisingly, it is the little native mice, rats, bandicoots, bettongs and the like, and birds such as the plains wanderer and quail that mostly fall victim to cats, but nowhere are cats more destructive than on small islands with captive populations of ground-dwelling or ground-nesting fauna. These occur all around the continent and Tasmania, as well as far-flung sub-Antarctic outposts like Macquarie Island.

The full extent of the cat problem is being revealed as the effects of feline predation on native fauna become better known. Research is ongoing as to the best approach to tackle this massive issue. Only cutting-edge science will have any hope of reducing feral cat numbers to somewhat sustainable levels, but as uncontrolled domestic cats do very much the same sort of damage to native fauna, we should expect considerable pushback from cat lovers and animal rights groups to any biological controller being developed and released. Which raises another question: What has priority? An uncontrolled domestic cat or the hundreds of native creatures it will kill in its lifetime?

# CHAPTER 18

# The Prickly Pear's Green Hell

Australia's feral rogue's gallery is not solely the domain of mammals, birds, fish and amphibians. The weeds are legitimate invaders that have done their bit to degrade their adopted homeland.

*Weeds Australia* profiles 398 weeds of national significance. Gorse, lantana, pampas grass, bitou bush, privet, camphor laurel, blackberry, Bathurst and Noogoora burr are some of the worst that pastoralism and civil authorities have had to deal with. All of them are trouble, and all have had local nibbles at Australia – a bite here and there – but none can compare with the aggressive advance and environmental devastation of the prickly pear's mind-boggling spread in the late-nineteenth and early-twentieth centuries. It was in every sense a feral that ate Australia – and not just any feral, but one of the worst that we've ever had to deal with.

The Australian prickly pear story – or myth – began innocuously enough, with the First Fleet. The wind-dependent nine-month journey of the Fleet from England to New South Wales comprised just three stops: the Canary Islands off the north-west coast of Africa; Rio de Janeiro in Brazil, south-west right across the Atlantic Ocean; then the Cape of Good Hope, south-east back across the southern Atlantic.

Phillips's first two ports of call were particularly significant in relation to the challenges in keeping his Royal Marines looking ship-shape on the far side of the world. Marines were deployed in Royal Navy ships to help preserve order and to assist in fighting and, at times, handling and maintaining the ship, particularly in emergencies. Once they arrived in New South Wales the marines would be required to act as prison guards while maintaining the spit-and-polish military standards of dress.

The red dye needed for maintaining the bright scarlet of the marines' coats was derived from the carminic acid produced by the female cochineal insect, which lived only on certain cacti. Phillip planned to start cochineal production at Botany Bay (where he thought he would be establishing his penal colony), and his plan was to collect his cochineal cactus, the cochineal insects, and presumably a how-to-guide from the Canary Islands, which at the time had a thriving cochineal industry. But once there, he was advised to collect his cochineals and cactus from Rio instead, to minimise the time the insects and their hosts were to spend at sea. Phillips's journal confirms he took that advice, and also took onboard indigo seeds or plants to produce the dye from which the navy blue of Royal Navy officers' uniform coats were produced and maintained: 'Provisions were here [Rio] so cheap, that … such seeds and plants procured as were thought likely to flourish on the coast of New South Wales, particularly coffee, indigo, cotton, and the cochineal fig.'[1]

The cochineal fig (*Opuntia cochenillifera* or *Nopalea cochenillifera*) is native to Mexico, but has been taken to many warmer parts of the world for cochineal production. *Opuntia cochenillifera* is thornless and safe to work around and was obviously selectively developed for cochineal production. The 'fig' referred to in Phillips's journal is the red fruit produced by the opuntia family.

Several prominent works on Australia's prickly pear problem claim that Phillip collected the variety *Opuntia monacantha* from Rio and refer to it as the smooth tree pear.[2] Smooth? It is anything but – more like a vegetal echidna, furnished with an armoury of nasty single and double thorns three to four centimetres long. It is hardly the *Opuntia* variety favoured for cochineal production, where the larvae need to be collected by hand. *Opuntia monacantha* certainly made it to Australia, and it did make something of a localised pest of itself, but it is highly unlikely to have made the trip with the First Fleet.

Despite the beat-up that fingers Arthur Phillip for the introduction of the cactus that devastated eastern Australia, his prickly pears seem to have been relatively harmless, and faded into obscurity. No one knows what happened to them, but they were certainly not the common pest pear, *Opuntia stricta*, which was responsible for the bulk of the devastation. When it and the several other *Opuntia* varieties now found in Australia arrived no one knows, nor do we know who imported them, but arrive they did, and they constituted the greatest botanical bio-invasion ever known.

The first record of this common pest pear in Australia appears to be the anecdotal account of a prickly pear brought from Sydney to Scone, in the Hunter Valley of New South Wales, in about 1839. 'Sydney' might have in fact referred to Parramatta in Sydney's west, where the variety is believed to have been growing for some time. The Hunter Valley infestation can be attributed to the Scone planting of cuttings for hedges at a time when stock fencing was crude zig-zag brush and logs, or horribly expensive and ridiculously labour-intensive post-and-rail fencing. The prickly pear was similarly first introduced into Queensland at Yandilla, in the Warwick district of the southern Darling Downs, about 1843 for fencing or hedges, and most likely sourced from the Hunter Valley or Parramatta.

Between 1840 and 1850, landowners throughout what would become the affected regions obtained cuttings from either the Scone or Parramatta source, and grew them as hedges around their homesteads. Not being a plant given to staying put, these hedges became burgeoning problems. When they were hacked back into line, the discarded cuttings were just 'tossed across the flat', where they started new colonies that radiated unopposed because, like most weed infestations, no one could be bothered doing anything about them until livings were threatened. Once prickly pear appeared anywhere, new colonies were quickly established, aided by humans, the elements, native animals and livestock.

The segments or pads of the prickly pear can be detached from the parent plant by animals, wind and flood waters. They are able to withstand considerable exposure and immersion without drying up or rotting, and every broken off portion is liable to take root. But at the time, most reproduction was by seed. The prickly pear fruits are palatable to humans and animals, and during the regular drought years they provided much sought-after feed. The fruit seeds, viable for at least 15 years, passed undamaged through the consumer, who then deposited it in its own fertiliser-rich germination medium. It was not uncommon to find dozens of pear seedlings springing from one such source, and such was the problem of prickly pear spread by birds that Queensland introduced a bounty in 1924 on currawongs, magpies, crows and emus. The bird slaughter as a means of slowing the spread was nothing new. It had been going on for years and bounties were paid by landholders.

In *The Birds of Australia* Volume 1, Gregory M Mathews, a member of the Australian and British Ornithological Unions, wrote that emus in particular were much attracted to the prickly pear fruit. He quotes a correspondent, James Scrymgeour of Callandoon Station, south of Emerald, Queensland, who wrote:

Emus were plentiful when Messrs Ross and Scrymgeour took possession of 'Callandoon'. The contractors were paid 6d per egg and 1s 6d per head for the birds, and during three months destroyed sixteen hundred eggs and nine hundred birds. I have seen three hundred and sixty-seven pear-seeds taken from inside of a single bird, and most of the digested food was coloured red with the pear-juice. They prefer this food, when they can get it, to any other.

By 1863, the common pest pear was established in the Darling Downs, Queensland, and further west at Goondiwindi, and at Scone and around the Gwydir River region of northern New South Wales. About 1870, a prickly pear hedge was planted at Blackall, Queensland, which started the rot there as did the one planted near Rockhampton about 1870.

Alarm bells were ringing by the 1880s. The *Brisbane Courier* in August 1884 wrote that the prickly pear was spreading so rapidly that it was causing serious apprehension. By the early 1890s, many thousands of pounds had already been spent in vain on pear eradication and it was finally declared a noxious weed in Queensland.

In 1900, an area of 4 million hectares was affected – not just by the common pest pear but also by several other varieties that, on a much smaller scale, contributed to the destruction. That would have been devastation enough, but the spread of the prickly pear was greatly facilitated by the federation drought. Being a succulent plant low in nutrition but high in water content, the spiky pear pads were not deterrent enough for thirsty livestock, and the tasty fruits provided some nutritional value. The science of the day concluded that, despite the enormous quantity of fruit produced during the height of the infestation, only a very small percentage of seeds succeeded in forming viable plants.[3] And the prickly pear was surprisingly vulnerable as an infant and needed sheltered conditions to thrive. Among light eucalypt, acacia and casuarina forests, and those dominated by box, brigalow and belah trees, there was no stopping it, but it had real trouble propagating in open, exposed areas such as grasslands.

However, as a mature plant, it seemed virtually indestructible. Conventional weed-control measures were useless against the apparently invincible pear. Infestations became impassable flesh-tearing barriers up to six metres high. And since the prickly pear is mostly comprised of water, it becomes incredibly heavy. As a comparison, a hectare of green wheat 90 centimetres high and heavy with grain and leaf weighs around 33.6 tonnes. A prickly-pear-infested hectare with growth of 90 to 200 centimetres weighs between 1120 to 1800 tonnes.[4] Manual removal was dangerous, back-breaking work.

At the height of its dominance in 1925, the pear commanded 24 million hectares of good grazing country in Queensland and

New South Wales, extending from around Mackay, Queensland, to Newcastle, New South Wales – as great an area as the entire United Kingdom. Scattered plants and patches occurred from Townsville in far north Queensland to the south coast of New South Wales. The western limit of the pear belt was usually around 320 kilometres from the coast in central Queensland, and 650 kilometres inland from the coast at the Queensland–New South Wales border.

The return on unimproved farming land at that time was between £1–3 a hectare, but the same land infested with prickly pear could not be manually cleaned up for less than £25 a hectare. Farmers were engaged in an endless battle against the rapidly advancing scourge, digging it up and burning it, crushing it, or using horses and bullocks to drag it out by the roots. Many settlers found it cheaper and less painful to walk away from their green hell, leaving their family homes to the tender mercies of the remorseless invader.

Something had to be done, and in 1912 the Queensland government established an experimental station at Dulacca, about 400 kilometres west of the Sunshine Coast. The scientists there concluded that arsenic pentoxide was the best available poison for controlling the prickly pear. Under experimental conditions it probably was. But arsenic pentoxide came too late and was too expensive and difficult to apply to a triffid-like invasion that was too big and too quick to recover from the ineffectual setbacks applied by mere men with poison sprayers.

However, just like every monster in every horror story, the prickly pear had a mortal enemy – one that could end its reign of terror. It lay ready to strike, wanting for nothing but discovery. In 1912, the Queensland and New South Wales governments, realising manual methods of control were never going to work, concluded that a biological response was the only way to tackle the prickly pear. The Prickly Pear Travelling Commission was established, comprised of a group of eminent scientists charged with finding the plant's nemesis.

The travelling commissioners certainly travelled. They went to the home of the *Opuntias* – North, Central, and South America – and to India and South Africa, countries with their own prickly pear problems. The commissioners' research recommended several promising insects, including the Argentinian moth called *Cactoblastis cactorum*, but Australian research work on the moth, like all the struggles against Australia's ferals, took a back seat to the Great War in 1914.

Despite being on a war footing, the prickly pear clean-up still happened on the local level and, surprisingly, it seems the green hell even found favour with some farmers, who used it for stock feed despite the inevitable environmental consequences.

In 1915, the Glengallan Shire Council in the southern Darling Downs of Queensland sent out a notice to a farmer in the Emu Vale district requiring him to destroy the prickly pear on his property within a month. The enraged prickly-pear-dependent farmer wrote an impassioned response to his local newspaper, the *Warwick Argus*:

> I am not going to destroy one pear at present. I have a man
> doing nothing else but roasting pear for my cattle and
> cutting it for my pigs. After losing all my labour and wages
> and expenses last year without getting one shilling's worth
> of crop in return, I am not going to destroy the only plant
> I can grow, and let my cattle and pigs die, if I have a
> chance to save them.[5]

It was reported by the *Argus* that the council took no action against the farmer, but the days of using the prickly pear for anything were numbered. After the Great War, a strategic alliance between the Queensland, New South Wales and Commonwealth governments formed the Commonwealth Prickly Pear Board, which formally convened in April 1920. A biological response was firmly on the agenda and a laboratory, breeding station and quarantine station was established at Sherwood in Brisbane.

Several species of various pear-eating insects were imported from the Americas in 1921. They were eventually released and had variable success, chiefly due to their reliance on specific pear varieties. But the research team, among whom was Reginald Mungomery, an up-and-coming entomologist whom we shall meet later, were on the verge of making a remarkable discovery and advance in sustainable biological control.

In 1924, Mungomery and the Sherwood scientists decided to re-investigate the promising *Cactoblastis cactorum* moth that their predecessors had unsuccessfully tried to breed back in 1914. They requested more insects from Argentina and the consignment reached Sherwood in May 1925 in tip-top condition ten weeks after its dispatch from Buenos Aires. The half-grown larvae were removed to cages in the quarantine insectaries and were supplied with plenty of prickly pear to feed on. The *Cactoblastis* proved to be good doers and prospered during the winter, pupating in late winter and early spring. The adult moths emerged in September and October numbering over a thousand, representing an emergence of ninety-four per cent. The moth was off and flying.

The *Cactoblastis* proved to be the most helpful of insects. It was a breeze to reproduce and it very considerately laid its eggs in convenient, easy-to-handle strings. These eggstrings were rolled cigarette-like into paper quills and packed in boxes each containing 100,000 quilled eggstrings, complete with printed how-to instructions for pinning them to the cactus. Why pins were needed to secure paper quills to a cactus covered in spines is anyone's guess, but the system was a spectacular success.

The researchers found the *Cactoblastis* a voracious destroyer of most types of prickly pear but completely harmless to any other form of vegetation – and the scientists tried just about everything. The larvae bored into other fruit but soon died. So in 1926, confident that the *Cactoblastis* was totally *Opuntia*-specific, they deployed 10 million eggstrings in around sixty locations throughout the affected areas. The results were immediate and devastating for the prickly pear, which collapsed under the *Cactoblastis* larval onslaught.

One hundred blokes working shifts in seven trucks carted the packed eggstrings to all the affected areas. Local entrepreneurs began collecting eggstrings in the field and were marketing them to farmers desperate to get rid of the green hell. On the outskirts of one Queensland town, a couple of boys wagging school set up shop in an old hut and in chalk above the door announced themselves as 'Cactus Blastis Agints'!

By 1931, an astonishing 2.2 billion eggs had been deployed and by 1936 the prickly pear invasion was just an awful memory – for the most part. After the initial collapse of the pest, the *Cactoblastis* died off too, there being nothing other than pear remnants left for it to live on. But prickly pears being what they are, the remnants tried to stage a comeback. It was doomed to failure, as the *Cactoblastis* naturally bred up again and finished the job soon after.

The *Cactoblastis* was Australia's first successful attempt at bio-control of an environmental pest. While spectacularly successful, environmentally safe and easy to produce and deploy, it may have created an ill-placed confidence in the efficacy of bio-controllers in some of the Queensland entomological community. Because, as we all now know, there are bio-controllers and there are *bio-controllers*, and the next bio-controller to be set loose by Queensland entomologists would produce an entirely different outcome to that that of Australia's busy little insect mate *Cactoblastis cactorum*.

CHAPTER 19

# The Great Cane Toad Con Job

It is hard to accept, given the circumstances leading to the cane toad's liberation in Australia, that their release was an act of good faith. It was an act so lacking in scientific foundation and process, so reckless, so arrogant and so aggressively dismissive of rightful criticism, that it defies belief that it was a project of Australia's scientific community.

That it happened at a time when the country was still struggling with the rabbit plague and recovering from the prickly-pear mass infestation just demonstrates how disastrously wrong and compromised industry plus science can get. The Queensland state and federal governments could have easily avoided its greatest officially sanctioned feral disaster by impartially dealing with bio-controller importations, and properly investigating what the watchdog was barking at. And then, behaving like a parent ignoring the tantrum, saying no and meaning no.[1]

All the toad trouble began because the larval grubs of eighteen endemic and one introduced species of beetle developed a taste for the roots of sugar cane. The most infamous are the larvae of the Australian greyback cane beetle and his little mate French's cane beetle. The grubs live underground and feed on the sugarcane's roots, which eventually distresses and kills the plant.

The next step on the road to trouble was the fourth Congress of the International Society for Sugar Cane Technologists convened in Puerto Rico in 1932. The attendees heard a paper read by scientist Raquel Dexter on the use of *Bufo marinus*, the American giant toad, as a biological controller for cane beetle infestations of sugar crops. The paper referred to the toad's introduction to Puerto Rico in 1920 and 1923 to control a white grub plague which was devastating sugar cane there. The white grubs dramatically declined in the years after the toad established itself in Puerto Rico.[2] Dexter's glowing paper lauded the cane toad as the saviour of the local sugarcane industry. But out in the cane fields, all was not as reported – because Dexter's paper was based on nothing more than guesswork and supposition.

The success of the toad population in Puerto Rico coincided with its highest ever recorded rainfall. It is now apparent that the big rains severely limited and reduced the reproduction of the white grubs. The cane toad received completely unwarranted credit for the white grub's demise and was proclaimed the best thing to happen to the sugar industry since the sugar cube. But unlike the sugar cube, there was nothing sweet about this warty, poisonous amphibian.

The cane toad's Puerto Rican fraud even sucked in the esteemed British scientific journal *Nature*, which published an article that proclaimed, 'TOADS SAVE SUGAR CROP'.[3] Suddenly, no sugar producer in the Pacific region, Australia included, could live without the heroic toad. Even highly respected Hawai'i-based entomologist Cyril Pemberton and his boss, John Waldron, got themselves well and truly sucked in by the toad PR job. Their unscientific gullibility would have massive repercussions for Australia.

At one stage during discussion on Dexter's paper at the conference, entomologist Harold Box from Antigua, where the toads had had plenty of time to show their true colours, countered that in fact the toads ignored cane grubs but ate the local bees. Pemberton side-stepped that correct observation and replied that, 'there were still in the Hawai'ian cane fields a few insects not yet under complete control ... and the introduction of toads offered possibilities for improving this state of affairs'.[4]

Impressed by Dexter's paper and ignoring Box's warnings, John Waldron pressured Pemberton to ship toads to Hawai'i. It appears Pemberton needed only a little convincing. After debating the pros and cons and somehow satisfying himself that more good than harm would come to Hawai'i from the toads, Pemberton carted thirty-six of the ugly suckers home with him in modified suitcases and had another ninety-six sent over later. That was more than enough to eventually swamp all the main islands of Hawai'i.

Cane toads eat anything. They eat pupa and grubs that live in the soil, although they are incapable of digging them out. And they certainly eat cane beetles that live on the tall sugar cane, but are likewise incapable of climbing sugar cane or jumping high enough to catch any beetles except those on or very near the ground. The best opportunity for a meal of cane beetles is when the grubs emerge from the soil as mature beetles, but these opportunities don't happen with enough regularity or volume to keep the toads on the job. And in any case, even if they were great grub and beetle destroyers, it was asking too much to expect they'd clean up such large infestations as the Hawai'ian cane fields hosted. So, in Hawai'i the toads did what they did in Puerto Rico: they hung out into cane fields for as long as they could make a living there then moved to town or out to the broader environment.

Not that the toad's propensity for deserting its post and environmental pillage was enough to deter people who should have known better. Because looking on the Hawai'i toad experience with interest and apparent envy was the Queensland government's Bureau of Sugar Experiment Stations (BSES), which was losing an ongoing battle with the beetles and grubs decimating Queensland's sugar crop.

The fellow in charge of plant pathology and entomology at the BSES was Arthur Bell. He had attended the 1932 Puerto Rico conference on behalf of the bureau. The following year, cane farmers in Queensland's north, who were copping it from the grubs, heard all about the toad's 'success' in Puerto Rico and Hawai'i and wanted a slice of the action. The harried BSES management were happy for them to have it. It was the job of this bureau to do something about the beetle and grub problem and Bell thought he had the answer.

After digesting the proceedings of the Puerto Rico conference and a report from Hawai'i on the toads there, Arthur Bell asked his staff for their opinion on using the toad in Queensland. BSES assistant entomologist Reginald Mungomery, who had been instrumental in combating the prickly-pear problem, responded by doubting the toad would work. 'The habits of cane beetles are such,' he wrote, 'that this insect is not likely to be controlled by a predator on the adult stage, for the reason that adult females are in evidence for only ½–¾ hour on the night of their emergence, hence a predator would have to be particularly active and be present in very large numbers to effect any appreciable control.'[5]

But that was not all Mungomery had to say. He noted that the common green frog was already known to eat beetles, with little overall impact on populations, and before any attempt were to be made to introduce the toad, the BSES should investigate the habits of the native green frog.

However, with cane growers breathing down his neck, Arthur Bell was in no mood to listen. He spoke with the BSES director and filled him in on the Hawai'ian toad experience, suggesting they send Mungomery over there so that he might better learn to understand and appreciate the ecological virtues of the toad ... and also bring some toads home. In two years, Brisbane would be hosting the fifth annual sugar conference and he figured it behove Queensland to flash the latest tech advances to the visiting sugar movers and shakers of the world. The latest technology sweeping the sugar cane world at that time was the toads, and so the BSES duly dispatched Mungomery to Honolulu.

Talented and likeable, Mungomery was your man for cane grubs. He had grown up in Childers in Queensland surrounded by sugar cane. And he knew a thing or two about sugar-cane pests and feral pest bio-controllers, having worked, as we recall, in the 1920s with the Commonwealth Prickly Pear Board at Rockhampton on their successful search for the *Cactoblastis cactorum*.

There was the slight hurdle of importation prohibitions which required circumvention before Mungomery's Hawai'ian trip could be rubber stamped. As we will soon see, Australian scientists trying to import myxoma virus into Australia in the hope it would help in the desperate fight against the rabbit faced unsympathetic opposition from the Director-General of Health, Dr John Cumpston. His concern was that myxoma virus might actually kill the rabbit pest and the industry that went with it. Working on that premise, the Director-General of Health should not have bent the rules and allowed the importation of the toad. But he did.

Mungomery was excited by the prospects of his voyage across the Pacific and it appears that as every nautical mile slipped away in his ship's wake so too did his apprehensions about the toad and his support for the native green frog. It was a new, pro-toad Reg Mungomery who arrived in Hawai'i. Reg had his work cut out for him soon after he arrived. One of his tasks was to write to Bell about down-playing the tragic news that a small girl in Hawai'i had died from ingesting toad poison in a case of mistaken amphibian identity. He couldn't let that story cause bad toad publicity back home.[6]

Then, after recovering from a bout of appendicitis that saw him spend over a week in hospital, Mungomery, in company with entomologists Cyril Pemberton and Harry Denison from the Hawaiian Sugar Planters' Experiment Station, set out to collect cane toads for Australia.

On that night of 1 June 1935, did Mungomery's hosts lead him on a torch-lit safari into the steamy undergrowth of the darkened cane fields to snatch toads from their conscientious nocturnal cane grub destruction? No, dear reader, they did not. Pemberton and Dennison took Mungomery toad collecting where the toads were thickest: on the front lawns of homes in suburban Honolulu. Alarm bells, anyone?

The Hawai'ian cane toads hadn't fixed the cane grub problem and they never would, because nature drives every creature to make the easiest living it can. The toads went where life was cushiest, which was anywhere but a cane field. The premise that cane toads released into cane fields would diligently remain there exterminating cane beetles and grubs was just fanciful and undeserving of conventional science.

The implications of cane toads hopping about in the Honolulu 'burbs certainly didn't ring any alarm bells for Mungomery. Because this was how the Queensland BSES intended to shut the cane growers up: by setting in place an indiscriminate and broad-scale amphibian bio-invasion of eastern Queensland. Honolulu's cane toads should have clearly demonstrated to Mungomery their great attraction to the easier living provided by human habitation. It should have been obvious to him and all his scientific colleagues that the cane fields would end up being but a fraction of the eventual range of this amphibian monster in Australia. Still, mission completed, Reg Mungomery sailed for home two days later aboard the *Mariposa*, armed with just over a hundred cane toads, fifty-one of either sex packed in ventilated suitcases on moist wood shavings.

And Australia had no idea what was coming.

# CHAPTER 20

# Walter Froggatt
# Tackles the Toad

On their arrival in Sydney on 17 June 1935, the toads were skinny and dehydrated and unfortunately alive except for one male who'd had the decency to croak on the voyage. When Mungomery and his toads reached the BSES research station at Meringa, they went straight to the pool room (a toad gazebo that they'd had purpose-built while Mungomery was away). It was an octagonal wire-netted affair complete with rockery, fountain and water-hyacinth-fringed pool (for charm). The toads found their first tiny patch of northern Australia much to their liking. They piled the condition back on and, demonstrating the cane toad's notorious fecundity, laid fertilised eggs in the pool just a week after taking up residence.

Australia's first toadpoles – the first of billions – hatched three days later. The country's second biggest but ugliest bio-invasion was ready to launch. The only thing these seeds of environmental catastrophe needed was someone reckless enough to propagate them.

Monday 19 August 1935 will forever live in Australian bio-invasion infamy. That day, when thousands of Australians were struggling to survive under the weight of the rabbit plague, Mungomery, aided by his underling James Buzacott, released

2400 toadlets at sites around Little Mulgrave in the vicinity of the Mulgrave River south-west of Gordonvale, Queensland. Just like that. No quarantine. No studies and research. No supporting scientific evidence. No formal approval or bureaucratic hoop-jumping. Nothing.

A little over a week later, the Fifth Congress of the International Society for Sugar Cane Technologists came to Brisbane. Sugar daddies from all around the world arrived and, though the worldwide depression limited the number of delegates, Hawai'ian entomologist Cyril Pemberton was able to attend. His colleague and friend Reg Mungomery, excited by his speedy toad reproductions, wrote a late submission paper, 'A short note on the breeding of *Bufo Marinus* in captivity'. Mungomery was proud of his breeding success, which was the first time cane toads had bred in captivity, and he believed a breeding program would hasten the distribution of toadlets to other regions for release. But he demonstrated his ignorance of toad biology when he recommended breeding the toads behind the protection of small wire netting and in a managed pond so as to protect the toadpoles and toadlets from 'predatory water beetles and larvae of different kinds, snakes, birds, which are sure to prey on either the eggs, tadpoles, or the toads themselves'.[1] He needn't have put such protections in place. Cane toads are poisonous at all stages of life.

After the conference, the organisers herded the delegates onto a chartered train for a tour of the north Queensland sugar industry and the cane fields. They visited the Meringa research station at Gordonvale, where they got to see the stars of the show in their pool room. Their support act was FW Bulcock, the Queensland Minister for Agriculture and Stock, who officially opened the Meringa research station later that afternoon. The BSES fellows basked in the attention while along the nearby Mulgrave River, Mungomery's sown seeds of bio-invasion were swiftly nearing the time when they would do a little sowing of their own.

After the chartered Sugar Daddy Express returned to its terminus in Brisbane, Cyril Pemberton took another train to Sydney. While waiting to embark his ship back to Hawai'i, he met with an old friend and colleague, Walter Froggatt, an eminent Australian entomologist. That appropriately named gentleman knew an impending environmental disaster when he saw one. He was the former New South Wales Department of Agriculture's chief entomologist and founder, president and member of a list of prominent wildlife and zoological societies as long as your arm. When Froggatt heard about the goings on at Meringa he was astonished and utterly appalled. Pemberton, a card carrying pro-toader since Puerto Rico, could not understand Froggatt's anti-toad attitude. It was the beginning of the end of a long friendship.

Pemberton's ship wouldn't have made it past Sydney Heads before Froggatt began firing off letters to newspaper editors to warn Australia about the impending cane-toad disaster. Those letters eventually found their way to Canberra. Froggatt also enlisted the help of his influential contacts in the New South Wales government. Such was Froggatt's reputation and standing that the already suspicious federal Director-General of Health, John Cumpston, when given a full account of the actual consequences of the release of the toad, at once banned further releases. Cumpston's ban was effective as of 9 November 1935 and it went down like a lead balloon in Queensland.

The unfortunate truth is that the toads had been on the loose for a couple of months already. They had gained the foothold they would never relinquish, no matter what Canberra said or did. Still, if the authorities had it in them to stare down the BSES and the cane growers there was a chance they could have reversed the limited damage done with prompt action. But no one other than Froggatt had the stomach for that.[2]

BSES's director, Bill Kerr, went whingeing to the Queensland Under Secretary for Agriculture and Stock and his boss, the Minister for Agriculture, assuring them that 'in Puerto Rico and Hawai'i where these toads have been bred as extensively as is possible, nothing but good has resulted'.[3] The 'nothing but good' was based on Kerr's spin and nothing else.

Kerr then pooh-poohed Froggatt's dire but precise predictions. 'Mr Froggatt predicts the extermination of ground nesting birds, many lizards, certain frogs which supply water for famished blacks in the interior, some of the rare and peculiar insect life of Australia, etc. etc. He anticipates a tremendous epidemic of toads, which will greatly alter the fauna complex over much of tropical and semi-tropical Australia.' Total over-reaction according to Kerr.[4]

After the disasters of the rabbit, fox and introduced birds you'd have thought the scientific community would have at least done their due diligence. But the BSES had desperate cane growers breathing down its neck and Kerr was building support wherever he could find it. Even the CSIR (the early version of the CSIRO) supported the importation of the toad.

As we all know, Professor Froggatt was in the right of it, but the ban was to be short-lived. The Queensland Agriculture Minister was a veterinary surgeon who should have known better. But promptly submitting to Big Sugar's pressure, the minister mounted a stiff dictated defence of the toad, supporting a request from Mungomery to release the rest of the darling little toadlets he didn't have the heart to kill. That letter, written under Kerr's supervision, went to the Queensland premier then straight on to the prime minister:

> The entomological literature from the sugar world is unanimous in its opinion respecting the value of this animal, and not one valid criticism has been levelled at it. In Puerto Rico and Hawaii, it is in demand in both field and town.
>
> It is certain that the toads which have already been liberated could never be recovered, and the animals will continue to multiply. It is felt, therefore, that no objection could be raised against our proposal that permission be granted for the release of the toadlets which are produced at Meringa, in those areas in which liberations have already been made.[5]

Kerr knew of the toads swamping suburban Honolulu and there's no doubt the Puerto Ricans would have been stepping around them in San Juan too. The BSES was imposing its ugly invasive toad not just on the cane fields but wherever in Australia they would invade, and the staff knew it. So, there's industry-funded science for you.

Prime Minister Joseph Lyons rescinded the ban on 2 December 1935. Within a couple of years, the toads spread throughout Queensland's cane growing areas. In just over a decade, the cane toads were on the nose wherever they spread. Independent commentators were even then suggesting that the toad would prove a bigger menace than the rabbit. But even after fourteen years of evidence that the toads were worse than useless in the cane fields, the even worse as well as delusionary

Queensland government still defended them by insisting their benefits far outweighed their possible disadvantages.

With foresight a century ahead of his misguided, under-pressure contemporaries, Froggatt famously predicted that:

> All our ground fauna will become their prey, and all our curious, mostly harmless, and often useful ground insects, in forest and field, will vanish. The eggs and nestlings of all our ground nesting birds will be snapped up by these night-hunting marauders. All our frogs and lizards, most valuable insectivorous creatures, will be in danger of their lives.
>
> There is no limit to their westward range, and though originally natives of tropical regions will probably adapt themselves to our mountain ranges, and even reach the riverbanks and swamp lands of the interior ... this great toad, immune from enemies, omnivorous in its habits, and breeding all year round, may become as great a pest as the rabbit or cactus [prickly-pear].[6]

Mungomery wrote to his boss moaning that he thought it was pathetic that Froggatt displayed such incurable bias that 'the statements contained in his article are so crammed full of inaccuracies, as to render his criticism's quite worthless'. Mungomery gloated that Froggatt must have been disappointed that the toads were already at liberty and were now 'here to stay'.[7]

Boss Arthur Bell got in on the act and sent Froggatt a dumb letter asking what authority he had to cast doubt over the professionalism of his entomological staff. Even Froggatt's ex-mate Cyril Pemberton, who was drowning in cane toads with the rest of Honolulu, continued to sing the toad's manifold virtues despite an absence of scientific evidence, and said that even in the face of multitudes of toads squished on the roads every night, they weren't overrunning the place at all and that veggie and flower gardeners were especially grateful for them. He forgot to say how pleased the local cane farmers were with them.[8]

Walter Froggatt had no chance of saving Australia from the toad. He had the virulent opposition of a powerful, demanding industry, its puppet research body mesmerised by scientific heresy, the equally mesmerised CSIR, and the clueless and complicit Queensland and federal governments – all ranged in invincible error against him.

Twenty years later when the wretched toads were exceeding every one of Walter Froggatt's predictions by poisoning native and non-native animals, the cane grub problem was worse than it had ever been. By then Reg Mungomery was in Brisbane kicking cane toads off his home's welcome mat and heading the BSES division of entomology and plant pathology. In 1964, he became the assistant director of the Queensland BSES, whose experiment stations experimented on every cane field pest except the cane toads they insisted on inflicting on Australia. Later the BSES found that new potent pesticides were useful in killing off cane beetle grubs … and the Great Barrier Reef. But that's another story.

The fact sheet on cane toads published by the federal Department of the Environment, Water, Heritage and the Arts provides an insight into the toad's impact on the broader environment:

> The cane toad defends itself through poison and is
> poisonous, to varying degrees, during all its life stages.

Adult cane toads produce toxin from glands over their upper surface, but especially from bulging glands on their shoulders – these exude venom when the toad is provoked. While some birds and native predators have learned to avoid the poison glands of adult toads, other predators are more vulnerable and die rapidly after ingesting toads. Toads contain poisons that act on the heart and on the central nervous system. The poison is absorbed through body tissues such as those of the eyes, mouth and nose.[9]

Like all the smaller invasive species, the cane toad story is the same story on repeat no matter where you find them. Typical of the bio-invader, the density of the cane toad in Australia is far greater than its distribution in its native range of the southern USA and Central and South America. There are now possibly more than a billion of the ugly things hopping around Australia like they own the place, and with typical feral hide they continue to aggressively claim new territory armed with the tools like no other feral.[10]

Since their release in far north Queensland, cane toads have invaded all of mainland tropical and semi-tropical Australia, from the Coral Sea to the Indian Ocean. In February 2009, cane toads crossed the Northern Territory border into Western Australia. It took them just 74 years. Toads were introduced to the cane fields of the northern rivers region of New South Wales in 1965 and since then hopped their warty, poisonous way south to Port Macquarie on the New South Wales mid-north coast by 2003.

So efficient has the cane toad invasion been that science has made the disturbing discovery that toads at the invasion front are bigger, stronger, and able to cover more ground than your common garden-variety cane toad. However, that superior physical prowess comes at the cost of smaller testicles, large ones apparently being a hindrance for the travelling toad. For such a low to the ground amphibian needing to cover up to sixty kilometres a year that could be quite a burden. Luckily for the toads (and mercifully for everyone who has to handle or even just look at them) their testicles, which are the size of their kidneys, are stored internally. It's the toads in the centre of the distribution area, the relaxed playboys, that have testicles up to thirty per cent larger than the pioneering toads. These incredible testicular adaptations appear in New South Wales and Western Australian toads and are the great point of difference between state toad lines, and possibly confer bragging rights to Queensland toad enthusiasts who, in this sphere, don't have a great deal to brag about.

No feral deals in death and destruction quite like the cane toad. Foxes kill endemic native species by eating them. Rabbits kill endemic species by evicting them from their underground homes and decimating their food supply. Feral pigs trash every environment and devour any edible thing, but pound for pound pale into insignificance compared to the destructive powers of the cane toad. Cane toads have a worse image problem than the feral pig, because feral pigs aren't in everyone's backyard eating the cat food and poisoning the dog.

Toads eat anything they can fit in their mouths, killing native animals and domestic creatures such as honey bees. They out-compete native animals and evict the competition they can't devour, they poison anything that tries to eat them, and they spread diseases to our native amphibians and fish. Even in death they continue to kill native carrion-eating birds, reptiles and mammals, and little is known of the impact of the toxins washed from toad roadkill into our stormwater systems and waterways.

Hardier than a cockroach, they can survive the loss of up to fifty per cent of their body water and can survive temperatures ranging from 5°C to 40°C but need to rehydrate at least every second day. Of course, being an invasive species, cane toads are prolific breeders and have mating rituals devoid of delicacy. Males start bellowing for mates after the first summer storms and congregate after dark around shallow water to mount females as they arrive at the water's edge. The male grips the female in the armpits and she releases her eggs, which are fertilised externally by the male's sperm. Females lay 8000 to 35,000 eggs at a time and may produce two clutches a year, although only a small proportion of young survive to adulthood.[11]

Cane toads are active at night during the warmer months. Their appetite for all food includes pet food and household scraps, and they exploit the insect-attracting outdoor lights of suburbia, but it is this habit that brings them into deadly conflict with certain humans. Toads are impossible to eradicate by killing the adults but that has not stopped the nocturnal backyard warriors of Australia from trying. Though normally quite kind to small animals, many usually mild mannered Aussies have discovered that there is nothing like the cane toad to bring forth one's inner killer – teenaged boys being traditionally most susceptible to this alarming condition. Yet it is a condition that seems to have abated somewhat with the introduction of computer games which keep the addicted youth of Australia indoors glued to a screen blowing up computer-generated bad guys rather than outside enjoying the fresh air practising their golf swing with their dad's driver.

Still, besides toad-smeared wooden golf driver clubs, the traditional toad home-extermination toolkit ranges from slug guns, cricket bats, tomato stakes, to salt and poison. About everything works with varying success against the unfortunate individual toad, but with no effect on the greater creepy horde. There must be an easier way!

There is. Sort of. Collecting the jelly-like strings of cane toad eggs from waterways is a more effective but labour-intensive way of trying to limit their numbers. There has been all manner of fencing tried to prevent toad access to places too, but these cause more problems for native fauna than the toads.[12]

*

There was no excuse for the introduction of the cane toad. As cane toads are yet to achieve their full range, they are the great feral the plague of our day and Australia's most hated feral. Until a safe biological response is found to counter this disastrous biological controller the cane toad will continue to do as it pleases and overachieve on even Walter Froggatt's dire predictions. About the only crimes cane toads haven't committed are blackmail, kidnapping and arson, but give them time.

Yet Froggatt's lone voice in the wilderness echoes still. The Invasive Species Council honour those who have made a major contribution to protecting Australia's native plants and animals, ecosystems and people from dangerous new invasive species with the Froggatt Awards. And front and centre of that feral line-up of the usual suspects sits the cane toad.

# CHAPTER 21

# Ugly Times in the Rabbit Game

While the new century brought the disaster of the cane toad, the rabbit problem hadn't gone away, even if its their chief promoters had declined. By 1900, the Acclimatisation Society of Victoria, like the other state societies, had faded into irrelevance. It had long become an anachronism as Victoria moved towards federation with all her sister colonies.

Least affected by their feral releases, of course, were the city-dwellers. Yet they did have their gardens turned over by thrushes in search of the garden snails released with them, and no doubt blackbirds, starlings, sparrows and common mynas annually destroyed their fruit trees and veggie patches.

But that destruction was a small price to pay for what the society's 'scientific arm' Professor Frederick McCoy had called the 'varied, touching, joyous strains of those delightful reminders of our early home'. And it was all thanks to his energy that those touching joyous strains resound yet in cities and towns around Australia. Unfortunately, the good professor, his work here done, fell suddenly and seriously ill in April 1899, and a month later he acclimatised himself to the hereafter. The natural sciences would never see his like again, yet the fruits of his labours, and those of his colleagues are with us still.

At the time of the professor's passing, rabbits were in their billions, foxes in their millions, and accusing fingers pointed towards the Acclimatisation Society of Victoria for starting the rabbit plague. Frederick Race Godfrey, the society's aged president (first elected president in 1862), was not having a bar of it. So, girding his loins, he treated the press to a heroic dose of hypocrisy, stridently condemning the release of 'this terrible rodent', and stressing that the society was in no way connected with the private persons responsible.[1] And though he did not name the late Thomas Austin it was impossible not to know who he was referring to. While technically correct, it was mean-spirited to try to wash the stink of Thomas Austin's rabbits off the society's hands. When the heat was on, unlike even thieves, there was no honour among old acclimatisers.

\*

As the new century neared, Australian agriculture weakened by previous droughts could not avoid the greater devastation of another — the Federation Drought. Sheep perished in their millions, the country was dying, and still the rabbits multiplied. Though the drought would drag on, one day it would rain again and the rivers would run, and the green pick would emerge ... and the rabbits and the starving stock and other animals would eat it as soon as it could be got at. It should not have bothered to rain at all.

When the Federation Drought ended, the western division of New South Wales recovered as best it could, but under pastoralism's drastic influences there could be no going back to the lightly wooded country of the past. And still the rabbits increased. If nothing else, at least rabbits paid well. The unemployed and workers on minimal wages found a healthy and lucrative living trapping the endless supply of these pests. Despite the devastation all around, common people made fortunes while the once powerful squatters, their flocks and land decimated, waited for things to improve.

The rabbit industry had a profoundly positive effect on the lives of thousands of rural Australians. For over a hundred years, trappers were able to earn more money each week than in any other manual occupation. As one Narrabri rabbit trapper put it to Sydney's *Evening News* in 1909:

> I have been a labouring man for 30 years and could never make anything to speak of. This rabbiting is the best ticket I ever struck. I consider I have the life of a gentleman. I make from £4 to £5 a week all the year round. I am never short of a 'tenner', and I went down to the Burns–Squires and Burns–Johnson fights [staged in Sydney on 24 August 1908 and 26 December 1908]. The rabbits paid for these trips. Talk about exterminating them! I say preserve them – they are a godsend to many a poor man and his family.[2]

There was also nasty stuff published about the rabbiters. Without doubt, the lure of easy money and the opportunity to work for oneself attracted types that gave the profession a bad name. The allegations of rabbiters seeding areas with rabbits to keep themselves in work is also true, and while it was a stupid practice, it was an attempt to guarantee their working futures. But the article below, reproduced in full for effect, and published in the Sydney *Farmer and Settler* newspaper in 1909, gives an idea of the venom directed at the rabbiters by the pastoral industry. Take a deep breath and read on:

There can be no doubt in the minds of anyone long conversant with the rabbit trade that it is in the worst sense of the word 'A Parasitic Industry', for not only does it exist as a parasite on the land-holder large or small, but the necessity of its existence is that the rabbit which it is every landholders' interest to destroy, should be maintained in undiminished number on the land.

It is true that in the past and even now there are many who, looking to the nominal cheapness of allowing trappers on their land, still encourage them there; but as their knowledge of the actual working of the system is gained by hard experience this number is gradually becoming smaller, and the wider view of the injury that will eventually accrue to every man on the land from encouraging the building up of vested interests in a trade that owes its existence to a pest that is ruinous to him, is steadily gaining ground.

It is sad to see so many of our politicians, with little or no practical knowledge on the subject, encouraging this trade, because of the money it brings into the country and the labour it is supposed to create, where the real truth is that the losses caused by it are such that were the rabbits exterminated tomorrow, ten times the amount the trade brings here would be received at once in the added quantities of our staple products and a wages fund thus created that would find employment over and over again for those now employed in rabbit trapping – in an employment, too, in which they would add to the real wealth of the country.

Our crying need in Australia is for labour to develop our resources, and the man who works at that, whatever his position, is an asset to the country whose value cannot be calculated. As against this the rabbit trapper by the nature of his occupation, is a nomad, living at the expense of others, and if, as is often the case, he is married, his children in nine cases out of ten follow in his footsteps. Before long, these circumstances we shall have a large section of our people turned, though [sic] no particular fault of their own, but owing to the attraction that the unrestricted life of a trapper exercises on many minds, into a class that will yet be a menace to the state and to all that makes for its welfare and advancement.[3]

The squattocracy had found itself labour-less and it didn't like it. Their seasonal slaves found a lucrative way to make a buck and deserted the shearing sheds and sheep yards and crowbars and wire-strainers for rabbit traps. Suggesting that the rabbiters were developing into a menacing social sub-class was as churlish as it gets. The graziers conveniently forgot the menace wool's pioneers used to appropriate 'their' land. Granted, a great many woolgrowers were hard-working, honest people who had lately come into the industry, but it wouldn't have been them funding the nasty propaganda.

Still, there are at least two sides to every story. Gerald Kempe was an English immigrant who managed the huge Tolarno Station on the Darling River south of Menindee from 1885 to 1890, with over 100,000 sheep on the property. He was also a key figure in the importation of Rutherford collies from Scotland and the development of the Tully dog, the same breed as those that became known as the kelpie. He was a great working-dog man and diarist. He submitted an article to the *Observer* in Adelaide titled 'Rabbits on the Darling', relating to his involvement with the rabbit plague when managing Tolarno. Kempe wrote that the rabbit was responsible for the high losses of stock in 1888 and lowered for all time the stock-carrying capacity of New South Wales by ten million.

Tolarno's loss from 1885 to 1890 was 90,000 sheep and lambs, and an expenditure of £25,000 on the work of rabbit destruction. Before the rabbits, the shearing average was about 100,000 sheep and, at the time of his writing in 1916, Tolarno was unable to carry half that number. Kempe stated that the strong permanent grasses and edible shrubs were gone, the pastures stripped by rabbits that were even digging up and eating the seeds. The country, he wrote, changed into a moving dust heap before an ordinary drought was halfway through.

Kempe was a severe critic of the New South Wales *Rabbit Act*. In its short two years of life, it had cost Tolarno £25,000 in rabbit control initiatives, caused bush-labour troubles, and spread the pest. Two hundred rabbiters once worked Tolarno. Kempe considered them to be little more than an unproductive, unreliable, untrustworthy expense.

Overall, he had a poor opinion of rabbiters, as most sheep men did. He claimed that rabbiters were seeding other areas with pregnant does they had trapped. It sounds about right, and certainly explains the extremely rapid spread of the rabbit through the interior of eastern and central Australia. And it had obviously been going on for a long time.[4]

The Great War proved a boon for rabbiters. Demand for rabbit meat had never been higher, and by 1917 the canning factories were back on top and paying trappers a shilling a pair – triple what they were earning in the 1890s. Early in 1917, the federal government, acting on behalf of the British government, purchased large numbers of carcases for the army.

There was agitation to suspend all poisoning of rabbits in Australia so that the trappers could operate more efficiently and keep up with the heavy demand. The rabbit-control authorities stood their ground and poisoning continued. Many trappers were able to invest in property with their profits from the industry, and no one in Australia went hungry during the war years (nor during the Great Depression) with the endless supply of rabbit meat at hand. Though, by the 1950s, you'd have been lucky to find an Australian who would have been looking forward to tucking into their next feed of 'underground mutton'.

Many women followed their husbands into the bush and maintained camp while the old man worked his traps and handled the rabbits. Children also helped. One woman, Estelle Enos, was not going to have a bloke keep her away from the action and struck out on her own to become a rabbiter in her own right. She submitted an article to the *Australian Women's Mirror* in 1927 titled 'The Woman Rabbiter'. She thought, like other successful rabbiters, that it was a good wicket that other women should be happy to bat on:

> Although rabbiting is an industry supposedly worked by men, woman really plays quite a large part in it, and out here in Far Western N.S.W. Madame Rabbiter is by no means a rarity.

Trapping seems to be the most popular method of catching Bunny, and though to the uninitiated it may seem to be hard work for a woman, it is really no more trying than the majority of household tasks she is expected to do. The hardest part is carrying the traps over the shoulders, but providing she is sensible enough to take only a few at a time she will manage quite well.

There is not much art or brainwork required in setting the traps. By accompanying the menfolk a few times on the round of their traps a woman soon learns how and where to set them.

Certainly, most of the work is done at night, but it is not necessary for Madame Rabbiter to be out very late, for she generally goes only two rounds at night. The traps should be set before sundown and a round may be made at dusk, after which she comes home, has tea, and goes round again.

If the rabbits are being trapped for the skins she will kill them at once (a simple and instantaneous operation which she learns from the menfolk), but if they are wanted for the freezing works she carries them alive in a chaff-bag until she gets to her 'screen'. This is a line strung from tree to tree, or, maybe, a wire fence, where a screen is kept to cover the rabbits after they are dressed. Having dressed the bunnies, hung them up and covered them, she has a 'spell' of, say, half an hour and goes back over her trail of traps. Although it may not be long since she first passed, there is generally a good percentage of further catches. There is a second screen at the other end of the line of traps, and after dressing the additional catches she leaves them covered up till morning and goes home to bed.

In the morning Madame Rabbiter is up about six
o'clock and goes her round, dresses whatever bunnies she
catches and has them ready for the carter when he comes
along to take them to the freezing works. Then she goes
home to breakfast ...

Rabbit-trapping is a work that makes for physical
fitness, and when you see a woman out in the paddocks
swinging along in her breeches, leggings, man's hat and
shirt, you will always be impressed with her healthy-
looking complexion and springy stride.

Rabbiting, too, is non-class. There is on our land a half-
caste rabbiter with his wife and three children. The man
stays at home, cooks, and looks after the children while the
wife does the rabbiting.[5]

Whether Miss Enos's article inspired women to take up the
Lane's Ace rabbit trap and rabbiter's hoe and pocketknife is not
known. It certainly didn't appeal to a correspondent from New
South Wales using the pseudonym Sisera:

Estelle Enos certainly presents the occupation of rabbit-
trapping in an attractive light, but, speaking from my own
experience, the work is anything but pleasant. Trapping is
a particularly brutal form of capture; the sight of the
bunnies' torn and swollen legs is enough to nauseate any
woman. It is all very well to picture the lady-rabbiter
swinging along with her traps over her shoulder, but as one
who has tried it, I can't overlook the detail that her hands
are covered with blood and fur. Also, the odour of rabbits
is particularly permeating and sickening.

I am not squeamish; on more than one occasion I have

attended the victims of a ghastly accident without experiencing the sick feeling that accompanied me on the three rounds of trapping I accomplished. Nor do I hold a brief for rabbits; but for the furry little brutes my family would be wealthy to-day. The extermination of rabbits is one of Australia's greatest problems, but I question whether trapping them is a woman's job.[6]

By 1929, rabbits were big bucks, pardon that terrible pun. Twenty thousand rabbiters worked full-time trapping for carcases or skins. Thousands were employed in freezing works located in rural towns and capital cities: grading, sorting, packing, skinning and transporting carcases by the tens of millions. Thousands were employed in the fur industry and selling rabbit meat directly to the public through street stalls and shops, making felt hats out of the rabbit skin.

Australians ate an estimated 27 million rabbits each year during the 1940s.[7] Australian soldiers in the Second World War marched into battle wearing slouch hats made of rabbit fur-felt – ten rabbits per hat, and Australia produced 5,500,000 hats during the war. That's a lot of rabbits, but still not enough to appreciably thin their ranks. Akubra and other popular hat brands proved the mainstay of the rabbit industry and the skin trade remained dominant until the early 1950s when everything changed. Because there was still a large, well-funded bloc looking for ways to do away with the rabbit forever. The wool industry was at the forefront of funding research into the fight against the rabbit and the cure was tantalisingly close.

# CHAPTER 22

# Searching for the
# Magic Rabbit Cure

While other ferals used the late-nineteenth and early-twentieth centuries to consolidate and expand their populations and ranges, the rabbit didn't let the grass grow under its feet ... or anywhere else. One bleak rabbit-sick decade followed another, and still the rabbit gained ground. Men poisoned and gassed and trapped millions of them every year. They ripped up warrens and burned fallen cover, and everyone owned a .22 rifle, the bullets of which accounted for millions more dead, because rabbits were in everyone's sights. Netting fences formed endless grids across the pastoral lands, preventing the movement of every terrestrial creature except the rabbit and the fox. Everyone hated the rabbit except those dependent on them for food and livelihood.

The desperate New South Wales government, in trying to find an effective response to the rabbit plague, had established the Royal Commission of Inquiry into Schemes for Extermination of Rabbits in Australasia in 1887. More commonly called the Intercolonial Rabbit Commission, it had offered a £25,000 prize for a 'cure' (for want of a better term) to the rabbit problem. While there's nothing like a little incentive – and the prize attracted a few credible applications –

the public appeal for help proved to be little more than an irresistible ratbag magnet.

The idiotic respondents had three things in common. They all wanted the twenty-five grand, none of them had ever seen a rabbit before, and all thought they'd astonish the commission with ground-breaking ideas like fences, poisons, natural enemies, traps, electricity, destruction of burrows, cutting off food and water, and even hunting them.

Biological-control suggestions included polecats, skunks, minks, civets, lynxes, jackals, coyotes, meerkats, ferrets, stoats, weasels, mongooses and giant South African driver ants.[1]

Meanwhile, at Tintinallogy Station, about midway between Wilcannia and Menindee on the Darling, rabbits were wasting away from an apparent disease. The disease spread to Ivanhoe and Wilcannia and 'in a short time there was not a rabbit to be seen at either place'.[2]

The apparent disease sparked the interest of Dr Herbert Butcher, who was a student of Louis Pasteur and lived on Tintinallogy. Was this a naturally occurring blight that could decimate the rabbits? Dr Butcher hoped so. He was a man of his own considerable means and did not have to practice medicine to make a living. He fenced off a 500-acre bend in the river and claimed he introduced the condition to the rabbits within, but rabbits all around the district were dying from the disease anyway. The afflicted rabbits displayed bulging, weepy eyes and noses, harsh upright fur, loss of power in the hindquarters, emaciation and death around twenty-one days after they first showed symptoms. Locals dubbed it Tintinallogy disease.

To cut a long story short, the Intercolonial Rabbit Commission examined Tintinallogy disease and found it was no disease, but probably a form of a widespread single-celled parasite, which 'assumed the aspect of an epizootic [temporary disease]'. The government lost interest in Tintinallogy disease, but the graziers of the western division of New South Wales didn't. They were paying Dr Butcher up to £50 for his crook rabbits, but eventually the condition fizzled out and that was that. No £25,000 for Dr Butcher.

Herbert Butcher died on 24 March 1893 at the young age of thirty-eight. His obituary saltily claimed that the failure of his Tintinallogy disease to spread had more to do with 'the indifference of the Government of the day' than inherent inadequacies in the condition's transmission viability.[3]

Dr Butcher wasn't the first medico to try to find a biological answer to the rabbit. In 1874, Anthony Willows, the New South Wales Veterinary Officer, began searching for a disease aimed at rabbit eradication. Willows inoculated a healthy doe with tuberculosis from the lung of a diseased heifer. He mated her with a healthy buck, and she gave birth to seven TB-infected young that all died within a fortnight. The doe died a fortnight later and the buck six weeks after her, both parents infected with TB. Willows found the disease deadly to rabbits but extremely hard to make virulently contagious. The TB experiment looked like it was going nowhere.

In 1884, Willows travelled to Tasmania to investigate an outbreak of tuberculosis in the livers of rabbits on Ellenthorpe Estate. He found that graziers all over the island colony were buying Ellenthorpe's diseased rabbits to release among their warrens. The TB outbreak at Ellenthorpe came, went, and had no lasting effect on rabbit numbers.[4]

Professor Archibald Watson of the University of Adelaide had travelled to France to visit Louis Pasteur, the renowned microbiologist and benefactor of pasteurised milk moustaches the world over, and they had kept in contact. Watson imported scabby rabbits from Germany, to the horror of the wool industry, which had just overcome a major sheep-scab infestation in Australia. The rabbit scab flopped, but it set Pasteur's eyes on the prize. Using chicken cholera, he had decimated a colony of rabbits that infested a French champagnery. He thought that, if done right, the chicken cholera would be just the ticket to sort out the Australian rabbits. He contacted the New South Wales government and, having received approval, sent over two capable scientific underlings to show the Intercolonial Rabbit Commission how to beat the rabbits, and collect the twenty-five big ones, francs preferred.

The commission wasn't so keen to have diseases potentially harmful to humans like cholera being set loose, no matter how bad the rabbits were. Members of both the commission and the New South Wales government were frosty towards the two Pasteur scientists from the beginning. The government eventually found them workspace on Rodd Island, a small island in Iron Cove in the Parramatta River, Sydney. Unfortunately, while the chicken cholera killed rabbits alright, it wasn't particularly contagious. Monsieur Pasteur's scientists went back to France in a great huff, the great man did not win the £25,000 prize, and he complained that the New South Wales government had treated him shabbily.

One could never accuse the French of not having a go, though. In 1888, Professor Charles Édouard Brown-Séquard, a French-Mauritian physiologist and neurologist, claimed human breath killed rabbits. *The Bulletin* reported:

Professor Brown-Sequard has recently been making experiments to determine whether the human breath was capable of producing any poisonous effects. From the condensed watery vapor of the expired air he obtained a poisonous liquid, which, when injected into the skin of rabbits, produced almost immediate death. He ascertained that this was an alkaloid, and not a microbe. The rabbits thus injected died without convulsions, the heart and large blood vessels being engorged with blood. Brown-Sequard considers it fully proved that the expired air, both of man and animals, contains a volatile poisonous principle which is much more deleterious than carbonic acid.[5]

Professor Brown-Sequard's death-breath was probably more repellent to his at-arm's-distance fellow researchers, family and friends than it was a danger to the rabbit plague in Australia. *Non!*

A New Zealander named Coleman Phillips found a common bladder fluke in rabbits and hurried over to show the Rabbit Commission. His wonder-disease was just a big yawn. It had been in Australia all the while and took four months to kill an infected rabbit, and the Commission dismissed him and his claim. But Phillips was persistent if nothing else. He called himself 'the apostle of the natural method'[6] and unfortunately, other prominent and influential people, like the Premier of New South Wales and the Linnean Society, were silly enough to take him seriously.

Phillips had a grand but simple rabbit eradication plan for the grazier to follow. It would rid them of rabbits forever. Step 1: The grazier was to gather about him as many dogs as he could – two hundred would be good. Step 2: The landholder would feed his two hundred dogs a diet that consisted only of rabbits infected with tapeworms. Step 3: When the infected dogs carried massive tapeworms and the segments were evident in the faeces, they should be dosed with areca nut, a virulent laxative, and taken out into the paddocks. Step 4: The netting fences were to be dropped so as not to impede the dogs' 'movements', or the grazier's because … Step 5: The grazier and any bystanders were to walk away quickly, even run, most preferably upwind, and let nature take its noisome course. Hopefully, the dogs would get about their business and wouldn't follow the grazier and/or bystanders. Step 6: The rabbits would eat the infected grass and they'd all die.

Phillips's puppy purge-a-thon never really won the hearts and minds of the graziers. Or their dogs. Funny that. Phillips moved on and espoused other ratbag theories, enthralling and exciting the gullibly influential folks who still gave him airtime, but eventually you've got to put up, and Phillips couldn't.

Despite plenty throwing their hats in the ring, nobody won the £25,000. The Intercolonial Rabbit Commission eventually established that a biological agent was the only method with any chance of working. However, even without the promise of a twenty-five-large pay day, the rabbit issue so consumed the nation that plenty of self-made rabbit messiahs emerged from the woodwork. The one most endowed with invincible self-belief, apparently limitless funding and persistence was one William Rodier.

Rodier owned a property of 26,000 hectares, fifty kilometres west of Cobar, named Tambua. He was mad, but energetic – a good grazier and an amateur biologist and scientist.

Rodier believed that trapping killed more bucks than does because traps were often set on buck-heaps, or dunghills – the places where the bucks defecated. He also claimed that the method of the poison cart, ploughing a furrow and seeding it with poisoned pollard, also killed more bucks than does. His belief was that killing the bucks caused overpopulation. The cure, he said, was to get rid of most females and the bucks would harass the remaining does to death and kill all the young. Simple.

In *They All Ran Wild*, author Eric Rolls learned about Rodier's fanaticism the hard way:

> Many of Rodier's papers are in the Mitchell Library. I expected it to be an amusing experience to go through them. It was for ten minutes until the extent of his belief became clear; then it was sickening. He had the conviction of a fanatic and the stamina of a martyr. He advertised in newspapers; he printed handbills and elaborate cartoons – many of them in colour – at his own expense and distributed them all over the world; he published booklets complete with photographs; he lectured; he wrote to President Hoover to tell him how to get rid of rats and sparrows; he issued challenges of £500 to £100 to anyone who could prove him wrong; and, in spite of the fact that his own results disproved his theory, he maintained his stand for over forty years until he died in the 1930s.[7]

Rodier caught his rabbits using a device of his own invention. It was a mesh cylinder with a one-way spring-loaded and weight-activated door that let rabbits in but not out. Placed at the mouths of burrows it was bulky, but clever. So were a lot of Rodier's practical devices, but they belonged to an age long past when people had a couple of hectares to manage, not 40,000. Still, Rodier placed large, illustrated and expensive advertisements for it in the *Sydney Stock and Station Journal*, which naturally gave it a glowing review:

> The Tambua rabbit trap has been in use for some time by the inventor and others and has proved to be a very great success. It catches the rabbits alive and has been specially designed by Mr Rodier for this purpose, in order to carry out his method of rabbit extermination by killing the does and liberating the bucks, so as to eventually bring about polyandrous instead of the polygamous conditions under which he maintains they increase so rapidly.[8]

Just seven years after the graziers of Cobar tried to get government backing for a barrier fence, the rabbits had turned their region into a devastated wasteland, despite 1891 being a good year for rain. Just one property remained in good nick: Tambua, William Rodier's patch. It was jokingly known around Cobar as 'the buck farm' because of Rodier's theory, but Rodier was the only grazier around Cobar laughing.

Tambua was carrying more stock than ever and had plenty of feed. It appeared that Rodier's theory was working, but Rodier employed several men and took unceasing and unrelenting war to the rabbits. Tambua was wire-netted and had all manner of highly effective trapping systems in place that killed thousands of rabbits a day. Rodier reduced the rabbit problem to a matter of landholder apathy and laziness. It is hard to argue against that, but not every grazier had Rodier's resources or energy. He showed that it was possible to eliminate rabbits off a property, but it must have cost him a fortune and he must have had time for little else.

With a fanatical zeal, he persecuted the Tambua rabbits out of existence. Almost. The truth is, he may as well have killed all the bucks he caught instead of taking off half an ear for easy future identification and releasing them. He would have killed twice as many rabbits in the first instance. What was the point of not killing bucks that had nothing to breed with? Seems to make sense to just get rid of all of them. But Rodier wasn't about sense. He was about William Rodier.

Yet, for a while, he was taken seriously by the New South Wales government, and although he was too late to collect the Rabbit Commission's prize, for a short while his methods were approved as legal eradication methods, though that 'approval' was without any scientific testing or support.[9] It was another example of the obvious lack of will of the New South Wales government to do anything concrete about the rabbits. Once science began to evaluate Rodier's theories, they flopped. In the end the foot soldiers put their faith in poison or traps and .22 rifles, but even then, nothing would slow down the rabbits, or Rodier.

Fast-forward to 1918, and Rodier was still trying to convert and indoctrinate apathetic Australia to his rabbit extermination cult. He puffed out his chest and challenged everyone in the universe with £100 to spare to prove him wrong:

> To all whom it may concern throughout the universe. Let
> 'em all come. I, William Rodier, hereby make the
> statement that the plan known as the Rodier method for
> the extermination of rabbits throughout Australia is the
> best that can be brought forward for that purpose. I use the

word best as that comprises everything, such as effectiveness, practicability, freedom from disease, and other drawbacks, simplicity, cheapness, etc., etc., and I am prepared to support my plan with £500 as against any other plan that may be brought forward by anybody throughout the Universe, and supported by the sum of £100. Adequate terms and conditions, extending over a term of years, to be arranged. This challenge to remain open till the end of the present year, 1918.

In the event of more than one acceptance, a sweepstakes to be arranged. Any person knowing any better plan of rabbit destruction, than the above, has now a chance of saying so and backing their opinion, if not, for ever after hold their peace, and don't ridicule or throw cold water on the only practical scheme to cope with a national calamity, and one they probably know very little about. I venture to make the statement that there is not anyone throughout the universe who knows of a better plan of rabbit destruction, and who has sufficient belief in his scheme to support it with £100. The money need not be found till the end of this year.[10]

The great irony is that Rodier was only tub-thumping because Australia still hadn't found an antidote to the rabbit plague. But an Italian biologist had, twenty-two years earlier. Fifty-four long years after making it to Australia and negotiating a frustrating journey full of rejection, bureaucratic obstacles, wrong turns, and dead ends, his discovery would finally reclaim Australia from the rabbit. For a while.

\*

In 1895, the Uruguayan government appointed eminent Italian biologist Giuseppe Sanarelli to establish the Institute of Hygiene in Montevideo. Dr Sanarelli imported rabbits from Europe to form the basis of the institute's laboratory stock. The institute kept its rabbits in an outdoor facility but the following year, 1896, they were all killed by a highly contagious and lethal mystery disease. Sanarelli named this new rabbit disease 'myxoma virus'. It turned out to cause a minor condition in its natural host, the South American rabbit known as the tapeti or Brazilian cottontail.

Dr Sanarelli found that myxoma virus transmitted by mosquitoes had an exceedingly high mortality rate in the European rabbit. The deadly condition was characterised by multiple lesions and tumours of the skin and conjunctivitis, but mozzie-bitten tapeti only developed a small lesion at the bite site. That same mozzie bite on a European rabbit would kill it.

Australia's rabbit plague was big news all around the world. Even Dr Sanarelli knew about it. He published his investigation into this new virus, but it didn't attract any scientific interest in Australia.[11]

# CHAPTER 23

# Dame Jean Macnamara Champions Myxoma Virus

In 1925, the New South Wales government commissioned David Stead, a highly respected Sydney-born naturalist and zoologist, with investigating the status of the rabbit menace in New South Wales and to make recommendations as to its eradication. Stead was a thorough man and took two years to conduct his investigation. The lack of official records regarding the methods of rabbit control tried by the former colony astounded Stead. His report was 745 pages long and full of inaccuracies because, due to the dearth of records, he took certain officials at their word. Regardless, he produced twenty-two pragmatic recommendations that might have saved the government millions.

David Stead was aware of the myxoma virus and wrote that 'it would seem to be well worthwhile to experiment with the disease'. While he recommended a hutch-rearing rabbit industry be subsidised and supported to offset the loss of the wild rabbit industry, he also recommended, in short, that the rabbit be exterminated. That was the last thing the New South Wales government wanted to hear – vested interests had ensured that the government's attitude to rabbits had changed dramatically since the days of the Intercolonial Rabbit Commission.

Eric Rolls in *They All Ran Wild* wrote that, 'parliament treated the report with expediency and contempt. Both sides of the House moved to stop its publication. One party favoured the rabbiters, the other the dealers and exporters of skins and carcases. Both sides wished to nurture the Pasture Protection Boards. The rabbits flourished with parliamentary sanction.'

There were plenty of opportunities for colonial, state and federal governments to take serious war to the rabbits. Yet, as we have seen and will see, Australia's leaders sat on their hands until bullied and humiliated into doing something. And in the meantime, the rabbits continued to do what rabbits do.

\*

It was never going to be pretty. If anything could eliminate the billions of rabbits destroying Australia, it would have to break every convention of the altruistic desire of city-dwellers for every rabbit to experience the impossible 'quick, painless end'. It doesn't get much uglier than myxomatosis, and the pending end of the plague meant the inevitable death of the rabbit trade. Those dependent on the rabbit and those removed from the ugly realities of rabbit-related life vigorously opposed the development and release of myxomatosis. What both sides of the pro-rabbit argument failed to count on was the tenacity of a remarkable woman determined to reclaim Australia's natural heritage.

In 1919, the Commonwealth Institute of Science and Industry (CISI) published a small article in their official journal to the effect that Dr Henrique de Beaurepaire Aragão of the

Institute Oswaldo Cruz at Rio de Janeiro, Brazil, thought that a disease he was working with, called rabbit myxoma virus, might be the thing Australia was searching for. Dr Aragão said the disease only affected rabbits, was common around Rio de Janeiro, and when in epidemic proportions has a mortality rate of 90 to 100 per cent.

That small article came about because Dr Anton Breinl, director of the Institute of Tropical Medicine at Townsville, and Mr FH Taylor, the CISI entomologist, had received correspondence from Dr Aragão alerting them to the virus. Neither man received encouragement to investigate the rabbit myxoma virus. The CISI stymied the proposal because 'the trade in rabbits both fresh and frozen, either for local food or for export, has grown to be one of great importance, and popular sentiment here is opposed to the extermination of the rabbit using some virulent organism'.[1] They obviously didn't ask the man on the land for his opinion.

True, the rabbit business was booming, but booming at the expense of the environment and agriculture in general. That the CISI, a scientific organisation, was able to summarily scupper any further investigation into a remedy for the rabbit plague that was destroying the continent not only beggars belief, but demonstrates gross indifference, if not incompetence.

So the rabbit was still ruling the roost in 1924 when Dr Herbert Seddon, director of veterinary research for the New South Wales Department of Agriculture, wrote to Dr Aragão in Brazil and asked him to send over the rabbit myxoma virus. It took over two years to land a viable virus in Sydney and while they eventually jumped that hurdle, the researchers were prohibited from running field trials, which basically torpedoed any chance of trialling the virus in the only place it naturally worked. A Mr HC White continued with experiments at the Veterinary Research Station at Glenfield, New South Wales, but the researchers there were unaware that insects maximised transmission of the virus and their so-so results failed to fire any further excitement or commitment.

The development of myxomatosis may well have ended there – such was the languid attitude of Australia's scientific leadership – if not for the indomitable conviction and energy of Dr Jean Macnamara, a chain-smoking Melbourne paediatrician, who was studying poliomyelitis at the Rockefeller Institute of Medical Research in New York in 1933. She was at the forefront of the fight against polio in Australia and as part of her research she visited Dr Richard Shope, a world authority on animal virology, at the US Department of Animal and Plant Pathology. Dr Shope was at that time studying a disease related to myxomatosis: Shope's fibroma.

As part of his investigations, Dr Shope was looking at the cross-immunity of his disease with myxomatosis as a means of protecting domestic farmed rabbits in California. Dr Macnamara was unaware of Dr Aragão's work with myxomatosis in Brazil or Dr Seddon's in New South Wales. But being a country girl, she was extremely aware of the devastation caused to her homeland by rabbits.[2]

Dr Shope's work inspired her to embark on a course of action that would pit her against members of the scientific community, who did not believe myxomatosis would work in Australia. And while her faith in the virus and her energy in pushing for further research finally resulted in myxomatosis toppling the rabbit in Australia, Dr Macnamara, later Dame

Macnamara, had to overcome obstacle after obstacle, and she wasn't always overly sweet about how she got the job done.

First, she obtained a couple of phials of myxomatosis from Dr Shope and had them sent to her dear friend, and later husband, Dr J Ivan Connor, Acting Director of the Walter and Eliza Hall Institute in Melbourne. The protocols required Dr Connor to inform the Commonwealth Director-General of Health and, typical of the pig-headed, uncooperative attitude of the Australian public service of the time, the director-general's agents intercepted the phials at the dock and destroyed them in front of Dr Connor, who had arrived to collect them. Charming. Another opportunity lost.

Undeterred, Dr Jean sent a detailed memo on myxomatosis to her friend (and former prime minister) Stanley Bruce, who was then Australia's High Commissioner in London. It was a good move and circumvented the stodgy opposition in Australia. Stanley Bruce arranged for the eminent scientist Sir Charles Martin to investigate myxomatosis further in Britain, where quarantine (and arrogant stupidity) was not such a scientific roadblock as it was in Australia.

Dr Jean travelled to Manchester, cattle class, in a Canadian cattle boat and met with Sir Charles. After discussion, he agreed to commence research into myxomatosis at Cambridge University in 1933 on behalf of the Australian Council for Scientific and Industrial Research (CSIR). He specified that the disease must:

- be sufficiently infectious to spread throughout the population;
- have such virulence that few animals recover to build up gradually a resistant race;

- maintain its virulence when passing from one animal to another by natural means so the epizootic will not 'peter out';
- be specifically dangerous to the animal it is desired to exterminate and harmless for domestic and other useful animals;
- not be too troublesome to propagate, keep in active condition, and apply in practice.

After three years' work, in 1936, Sir Charles announced that 'a good strain of virus satisfied those precise requirements in a circumscribed area'. But he had grave reservations about its ability to spread effectively. 'The range of infectivity does not seem to be great nor do the cages recently inhabited by sick animals retain the infection for long.'

Based on his assurances that myxomatosis was safe to experiment with again in Australia, Dr Lionel Bull of the CSIR Division of Animal Health began working with a virulent form of the virus designated 'Strain B'. Like Sir Charles, Dr Bull commenced with infectivity tests in the laboratory. And like Sir Charles, Dr Bull did not fully understand the need for insects to properly transmit the virus.

When it came time for field testing, the rabbit industry kicked up such a fuss that state governments were reluctant to provide testing grounds for fear of upsetting the local rabbiters and processors. Eventually the South Australian government made Wardang Island in Spencer Gulf, South Australia, and dry country north-east of Peterborough, available. However, field testing in dry country – where the rabbit problem was worst – failed, or at best returned poor results, and at one stage an over-abundance of foxes wrecked their research.

Dr Aragão's advice from Brazil was that 'the rainy season is best'. The Australian scientists either forgot it or ignored it. Rainy season was mosquito season and at that time mozzies were myxo's best hope, but with no insect vector to spread the disease in dry old South Australia, the experiments were doomed to failure. The CSIR lost interest and shifted blame onto state authorities. The phial-smashing office of the Director-General of Health, helpful as ever, refused to allow the state authorities access to the virus, perhaps concerned the virus might escape captivity and kill millions of rabbits.

Myxomatosis research ceased in 1943. The war in Europe, North Africa and the Pacific rightfully took precedence over every other domestic issue Australia was dealing with at the time. After the war in 1948, the CSIR morphed into the CSIRO, with Ian Clunies-Ross at the helm. He established a specialist group, the Wildlife Survey Section, to deal with fauna and animal pest issues and appointed Francis Ratcliffe the leader. All the while Dame Jean Macnamara was standing back, impatiently tapping her foot, rolling her eyes, watching.

Francis Ratcliffe knew his business and was familiar with the work done with the myxoma virus. He was sceptical about the chances of its success and he publicly said so. Dame Jean begged to differ and suggested the CSIRO restart the research with greater vigour, but in rabbit country with higher rainfall. It seems highly unlikely that Dame Jean knew the importance of mosquito-friendly conditions in the transmission of myxomatosis, but in the course of things she was quite right. Either way, her criticism and constant high-level coercion caused field trials to recommence again in May 1950 along the Murray River.

The results once again were disappointing. 'Myxo', as it became known, killed rabbits, but the natural transmission left much to be desired because it seemed impossible to spread effectively. In September, the team started more trials around Corowa and Albury. Once again, nothing.

It was while the research team were home over Christmas that they received a call from the owner of a property at Balldale, north-east of Corowa in New South Wales. His property was one of the release sites. He rang to say that he had sick rabbits all over the place. And then the floodgates opened.

By the end of December 1950, the disease had spread to the Lachlan, Murrumbidgee and Darling rivers. Rabbits were infected in their thousands and farmers were collecting dying and dead rabbits to infect their own properties with the virus. They need not have worried. By mid-1951 the virus had spread over an area of southern Australia measuring 1600 kilometres north to south and 1760 kilometres east to west.[3]

For over ninety years, the rabbit had hopped around with an air of invincibility. Not anymore. They died in their millions, the stench in places unbearable, with mortalities ranging between ninety and ninety-nine per cent. Francis Ratcliffe wrote that it was 'a biological fluke, a spectacular epizootic ... almost without parallel in the history of infections.'[4]

With appallingly coincidental timing, an outbreak of human encephalitis appeared at Shepparton and Mildura in the Murray Valley. The public and the press hit the panic button and fingered myxomatosis. It wasn't until prominent scientists Ian Clunies-Ross, Sir Frank Macfarlane Burnet and Professor Frank Fenner inoculated themselves with the myxomatosis virus and showed no ill-effects that community concerns abated.

By 1953, myxomatosis had spread to everywhere in eastern Australia. It took longer to establish itself in Western Australia and Tasmania, but the 1950s was the decade when the rabbit appeared to be down and out. Not exterminated – not by a long country mile – but as vulnerable as it ever would be. A concerted, organised program of warren fumigation, warren destruction and poisoning could have wiped out the rabbit when the opportunity was best. It would have been heavy in fiscal commitment, time, effort and manpower, but cheaper than the perpetual warfare that is still ongoing.

What did the federal and state and territory governments do when they had the chance? Aside from hotchpotch attempts at aiding transmission via infected rabbits ... nothing. And the graziers? Aside from replacing rabbits with sheep ... nothing. It was our best opportunity missed, and one we're still paying for.

Myxomatosis had knocked the rabbit on the head, and down it went, apparently finished. Wool couldn't hide its glee. And why wouldn't it be pleased? In 1950, it was estimated that rabbits were eating the same amount of fodder as 40,000,000 sheep and costing graziers and farmers at least £50,000,000 in pasture deterioration and soil erosion, and in fencing, netting, poisoning, fumigating, trapping and other control measures.

Agriculture and wool were providing serious funding for rabbit research, but the job wasn't anywhere near done and, like every good horror story, the villain everyone thought dead lived yet. It took a little while, but the rabbit would develop resistance to myxomatosis, which is what happens with every viral epidemic. Eventually the rabbit would recover – never in such extraordinary numbers, but numbers enough to remain a serious environmental problem.

Scientists continued their work in trying to improve transmission through improved insect vectors. Mozzies were only effective when there was water lying about in pools in which they laid their eggs. This necessity confined the effectiveness of mosquitoes to areas of high rainfall, which isn't most of Australia. In hilly terrain and the dry interior, where favourable conditions didn't exist, mozzie-borne myxo wasn't so effective. The CSIRO needed a better insect vector if myxo was going to remain a force for rabbit destruction.

Francis Ratcliffe had long thought the European rabbit flea would be the ideal insect vector, but in 1955, none other than the rabbit plague's apparent best mate and guardian, the director-general of health, refused Ratcliffe's request to import it. Frustrated interest groups succeeded in making enough noise to have the ban overturned, and flea importation and breeding began soon after.

The myxo-carrying European flea certainly ravaged the rabbit. In some areas rabbit mortality was as high as eighty-four per cent in the period from 1975 to 1981. As encouraging as these figures are, there were shortcomings to using the European flea as a myxo vector. It had the same requirement for rainfall – over 200mm (8 inches) – as the mosquito. A better vector for the job existed in the Spanish rabbit flea, which gained approval for use in 1993. Either way, Señor flea was too late to prevent an increase in myxo-resistant rabbits, which by 1995 had multiplied to an estimated 300 million.

The myxo epizootic has copped the blame for the demise of the rabbit industry, and fair enough, too. But it also coincided with a change of the times and Aussie palates. After eating rabbit and not much else during the Depression and war years, Australians were over the rabbit. By the late 1950s, rabbit was a Volkswagen product at a Mercedes Benz price. In 1953, the Victorian Fur Skin Buyers Association protested that myxomatosis had practically wiped out the export trade in rabbit fur – comments received with mirthful disregard by the wool exporters.

With healthy rabbits harder to source, the wild rabbit industry folded for good in the 1960s, when domestic producers in Europe and China, and poultry growers in Australia, effectively ended the demand for Australia's wild myxomatosis-tainted rabbits.

Like every other viral eruption, myxomatosis has lost much of its virulence as rabbits developed resistance to it. In areas of higher rainfall, particularly in years of good rainfall, myxo still reappears and kills off enough rabbits to continue to make a worthwhile contribution to the war against Australia's biggest pest. But by the 1990s, Australia needed a new bio-controller.

# CHAPTER 24

# Rabbit Haemorrhagic Disease [Calicivirus]

**W**hile everyone in Australia was congratulating themselves on a job well done, a whole new generation of rabbits rose again. The myxo–resistant survivors bred up and got back to doing what their forebears had spent over a hundred years doing. Yet, just when it seemed that myxomatosis had lost much of its effectiveness, a new disease made its timely appearance. But its release into the wild rabbit population did not go as planned.

In 1984, a deadly new virus, first called calicivirus, but now known as rabbit haemorrhagic disease (RHD), started killing commercially bred Angora rabbits in Jiangsu Province in China. The rabbits had recently come from Germany and, in less than a year, 140 million domestic rabbits in China were dead over an area of 5 million hectares. The Chinese tried to blame the Germans but there is no evidence at all of the disease appearing in Germany before it appeared in China. Exported Chinese rabbit skins spread the disease to neighbouring Korea and to Italy by 1986. From Italy, it took less than a year to spread throughout Europe including Spain, the natural home of the European wild rabbit.[1]

While RHD was terrible news for countries that had significant domestic rabbit industries, it sounded like it could make itself useful in Australia. Scientists were continually looking for better insect vectors that might reinvigorate myxomatosis, particularly one suited to the dry interior where the disease was much less potent. So it was that Australian biologist Professor Brian Cooke was in Spain at the time of the RHD outbreak, investigating a species of rabbit flea that might have been useful in giving myxomatosis another push-start. He was able to report back to the CSIRO on RHD, and a joint working party was eventually set up to assess the pros and cons of releasing it in Australia.

While the rest of the world laboured to create vaccines to protect rabbits from RHD, Australia was doing the opposite. Death by RHD is much quicker and kinder than myxomatosis. Infected rabbits show little or no signs of abnormality until a few hours before their death, when they cease most activity and sit or lie quietly. There are few if any signs of pain or discomfort. Death usually occurs between two and four days after infection.

In September 1991, the CSIRO Australian Animal Health Laboratory imported a Czech Republic strain of RHD to its microbiologically secure facility at Geelong, Victoria. Testing on a wide range of domestic, wild and native animals proved that no species other than the rabbit appeared to be susceptible to RHD.

Testing confirmed other points. It appeared that Australian rabbits had never experienced a pathogen like RHD before, but also that young rabbits (less than eight weeks old) were less likely to suffer illness or death through RHD.

After establishing agreed quarantine protocols, Wardang Island off the Yorke Peninsula, the previous site for the myxomatosis trials, was selected as the site of the RHD field trials. Inside two large pens of fifty hectares with rabbit-proof fences were seven smaller double-fenced pens containing an artificial warren and ten rabbits. After ripping up a 300-metre-wide buffer strip around the testing area, completely clearing it of rabbits, the field trials were ready to begin.

On 23 March 1995, scientists inoculated two rabbits in a pen of ten with RHD. After three weeks there was no evidence of the transmission of the disease to the other eight rabbits. Again, on 27 April, two more pairs in separate pens received RHD injections. One pair spread the disease to the others in their pen, but there was no transmission from the other pair.

A third trial on 20 June returned similar results, but a rabbit in a nearby pen died of RHD. The warrens were destroyed and fumigated, and the trials suspended. No further cases of RHD appeared on the island. Mid-September's trial used the same experimental design and once again transmission was poor, with only two in-contact rabbits infected in the same pen. Two days later, the disease appeared in a sentinel pen. Again, the trials ceased, and the warrens and rabbits were destroyed.

A week later, a rabbit outside the quarantine area contracted RHD. Four more caught RHD two days later. Then, on 12 October, RHD mysteriously appeared at Point Pearce on the mainland opposite. Within days, rabbits at Yunta (360 kilometres away to the north-east) were dead from RHD.

RHD was off and running, but how had it escaped Wardang Island? Earlier in the century when Wardang hosted the myxo trials, the lack of insect vectors inhibited the spread of the virus. Things had changed by 1995, and Brian Cooke noticed an abundance of bush flies on the island. But how could flies carrying the disease appear 360 kilometres away in Yunta?

The probable answer lay in an enormous updraught over the region, which picked up infected bush flies, carried them to the north-east and dumped them on the waiting rabbits. RHD was out, and so was the word. Newspapers ran dramatic headlines like 'KILLER VIRUS ON THE LOOSE', and 'DEADLY VIRUS ESCAPES', putting Australia into a state of self-inflicted dread that Brian Coman, the author of *Tooth and Nail*, called 'virophobia'.[2]

Only a year before, equine morbillivirus pneumonia – an often-fatal viral respiratory infection in horses caused by Hendra virus – had appeared in Brisbane and killed one person and fourteen horses. The awful ebola virus in Africa had everyone worried, and movies such as *Outbreak* and *The Plague* were getting everyone, including the jittery federal government, nervous about the RHD outbreak. And then the wild rumours and stupid theories started doing the rounds: farmers had smuggled RHD out of Wardang Island and released it on their properties ... renegade scientists with a rabbit agenda had smuggled infected rabbits off Wardang and released them ... the CSIRO engaged in a conspiracy to release RHD.

The disquiet in Australia received an unwelcome injection when two American virologists, Dr Alvin Smith and Dr David Matson, experts in human caliciviruses, but completely ignorant of RHD, issued a joint press release that suggested Australian scientists were 'playing with dynamite'. They cautioned, incorrectly, that RHD might jump to other species and even infect humans.

The CSIRO objected to the ill-informed and provocative press release and countered by refuting the claims in a dismissive press release of their own, which only inflamed Smith and Matson more. They retaliated by sending a letter to the Biological Control Authority in Australia and cc'd the prime minister. They dobbed on the CSIRO for being antagonistic and engaging in personal attacks. No matter that they stuck their ill-informed noses into Australia's business, and no matter that they were wrong, that RHD had been known for over forty years and had never jumped species in Asia or Europe, and no matter that the CSIRO Australian Animal Health Laboratory had conducted extensive testing into RHD, infecting a wide range of other species with a negative result. Smith and Matson had their noses out of joint because no one had consulted them before the CSIRO imported RHD.

Back on the ground in Australia, RHD was spreading throughout the rabbit population like myxomatosis had forty-five years earlier. The spread was rapid and at times patchy, but it was estimated that RHD eliminated up to ninety-five per cent of the rabbit population in the areas to which it spread. And coinciding with the reduction of rabbits was an amazing regeneration of the bush.

Hopeful farmers were sourcing RHD-infected or dead rabbits and transporting them to their properties to infect their own rabbits. By mid-January 1996, RHD was right through South Australia's rabbit country and approaching Broken Hill in New South Wales. The joke getting about was, 'How fast does RHD spread? A hundred kilometres per hour on bitumen roads and sixty on gravel.'[3]

In 1996, the Biological Control Authority declared rabbits a target organism and legitimised RHD as an agent organism. RHD gained registration for field use and the first deliberate inoculations of wild rabbits in the field began that spring.

A spring release gave variable results in young rabbits because of the high resistance to RHD in the young and spring is baby bunny time.

Unlike myxomatosis, RHD worked best in the dry interior and not so well in high rainfall areas. Still, for a decade or so it did its job and no species jumping ever occurred, vindicating the CSIRO's insistence that it would pose no threat to Australia.

But, just like myxomatosis, the efficacy of the rabbit haemorrhagic disease virus waned over time as rabbits developed immunity. The CSIRO is ever vigilant in monitoring and adapting to the status of the RHD viruses active in Australia and around the world, and it has recently had some success with a new Korean variant of RHD, commonly known as K5, released widely throughout Australia in 2017.

The war against the rabbit continues. It is an enemy that will never know total defeat, but the dark days of continental plague are just an ugly memory as Australia's scientific community leads the charge in reclaiming Australia from the cute little monster.

# PART FOUR

# The Extremes of Feral Animal Management

I t is understating things to say that, during the nineteenth and early-twentieth centuries, Australians weren't all that environmentally sensitive. During the rabbit plague, rural Australia was one big killing field. Men, women and even children killed rabbits and other animals for a job, for sport or for survival. Killing animals, sometimes by the thousands, was just a fact of life.

Environmentalism was in short supply in colonial wool-mad Australia. Throughout my research I tried to find just one green squatter, but I came up empty-handed no matter how many rusty mountains of toxic sheep dip drums I looked behind. Efficient stock management is based on the no-brainer principle of containment and control. Fenceless pastoralism caused many of our feral livestock travails, but Australia's biggest bio-blunders were the acclimatised pest plagues.

We can sometimes dismiss acclimatisation as a well-intentioned error in judgement when Australians had little or no understanding of the vulnerability of our ecosystems. Applied to the nineteenth century, perhaps we can forgive those men of privilege and wealth. But the same cannot apply to the twentieth century, when even scientists imported and released what will arguably become our worst acclimatised pest.

No matter what era or circumstances, the acclimatisers had (and still have) a couple of things in common: not one of them ever considered the consequences of opening the carry box or hessian bag and shaking out its travel-weary contents. And none ever faced prosecution or even censure, and even their obituaries fail to make any mention of their environmental crimes.

Considering the fruits of acclimatisation's labours are still out there destroying our homeland, costing us millions a year, it's a fair cop that the attitudes and practices and trumpeted accomplishments of acclimatisation's arch-influencers should be critically appraised.

It is regrettable that reclaiming Australia from the ferals is impossible without a great deal of killing. Bio-weapons that work 'behind the scenes' take a lot of heat out of extermination programs, and over the last four decades there has been an increasing emphasis on humane destruction of vertebrate pests. The painless, humane end for every pest animal is a noble ideal, but out in the paddock, economy and expediency are invariably the priority, which has created its own battlelines among the millennial generation and younger. While weary farmers seek to protect their pastoral lands from an introduced threat, others seek alternative solutions with low-tech livestock and things like immunocontraceptives. Where Australia will land, and whether it will ever truly recover from the onslaught of introduced species, only time will tell.

# CHAPTER 25

# The Sandstone Island and Other Atrocities

Early battles over animal welfare were not between well-meaning city folk and those in the country who have to face the realities of life under the thumb of introduced species, but were instead between the acclimatisers who released game animals for their exclusive hunting pleasure and sporting poachers who saw those same introduced species as an easy meal.

In the nineteenth century, while the Acclimatisation Society of Victoria had graciously released British songbirds for everyone listen to – Australian songbirds being too boring – their releases of game animals and gamebirds were strictly the preserve of the society's sporting members and their invited guests. Yet sometimes things went awry.

When Thomas Austin's rabbits escaped and invaded the surrounding country, he couldn't prevent anyone shooting them – until the government agreed to legislate against their killing, resulting in the ironic persecution of a man fined £10 for shooting one of William Robertson's rabbits mere years before Robertson was paying a battalion of men to kill the descendants of those same rabbits. Robertson should have made reparations to the man he had charged.

The Acclimatisation Society did its best to release its imported gamebirds into secret havens accessible only to members. But the society's unwritten but clearly implied 'No Pheasants for Peasants' edict was always going to get a workout when the great unwashed discovered where the society had released (read: stashed) its exotic game. And soon they did, on Sandstone Island situated off the western shore of Western Port, the large bay east of Port Phillip and Melbourne. Surprisingly, Western Port didn't get its name from someone with absolutely no comprehension of the four cardinal directions. Rather, the name came from George Bass, the Royal Navy surgeon and explorer, who named it so in 1798 because it was the westernmost extent of his exploration of the southern coast of what was then New South Wales.

Thrice in 1862, the perfidious enemies of acclimatisation had made covert expeditions by small boat from nearby Hastings or Bittern, and thrice did these lowbrows shoot up the Californian quail the society had released there. And typical of the criminal class, these brazen assaults occurred each time Mr Rogers, the society's hired gamekeeper, had gone for a Tosca. Poor old Mr Rogers. For five years he had been lovingly breeding and rearing those birds so that everyone (in the Acclimatisation Society of Victoria) could experience the joy of shooting them.

Californian quail qualified as pheasants under the society's 'No Pheasants for Peasants' edict and Mr Rogers had also kindly donated some of them to landed society members so they could breed them up and shoot them on their own patches. But now there were none left for anyone (in the Acclimatisation Society of Victoria) to shoot because common criminals – worse, *uninvited* common criminals – had slaughtered the lot in the most despicable, unsporting circumstances conceivable: an unsanctioned hunt enjoyed by non-members. What the deuce!

And no, dear reader, just as you suspect, the tentacles of evil did not end there. The Acclimatisation Society had selected Sandstone Island not only as a suitable spot to breed and blast Californian quail, but also a wonderful place in which to liberate various English songbirds. These, under Mr Rogers' care, had bred freely. The Acclimatisation Society members shooting there loved hearing their melodious songs, which raised one's patriotic devotion to Queen and country. But now, it seemed a great number of them fell to those very same hooligans desiring their four and twenty blackbirds to bake in a pie. Or perhaps the birds had just decided to take their leave of Mr Rogers and noisy, dangerous Sandstone Island and make the short half-mile flight over to the safe, quiet mainland to avoid the fowling piece-toting society members. It didn't matter; the interlopers copped the blame.

A furious society member, probably Acting President Dr Thomas Black, wrote an indignant letter to the society's propaganda machine, Edward Wilson's *Argus*, about these outrages under the alias of 'Canary'. Canary thought it was a pity that the society could not make the names of the offenders public and let the outraged horde (read: the other prohibited peasants) take care of them on the society's behalf, because, he obviously believed, that's what the outraged peasants, armed with their pitchforks and firebrands, would do on behalf of their betters. Perhaps the reality – that the mystery shooters broke no laws, not even trespass, as the Island was not owned or even leased by the society – tempered his calls for the severest summary punishments.

Canary kept singing. He confirmed that it was acclimatisation's great and noble goal:

> [To] stock our rivers with the choicest fish procurable in
> Europe, to convert our sandy plains into rabbit warrens, and
> to make our fern brakes populous with hares; to naturalize
> the roe and fallow deer, the springbok, the eland, and the
> antelope, the partridge, partridge-quail, and pheasant, and
> to lay all parts of the world under contribution for the
> purpose of enriching our poultry yards, improving our
> forest timber, beautifying our gardens, and augmenting the
> produce of our orchards and vineyards, are surely purposes
> which demand encouragement, and ought not to be
> frustrated by the malice, thoughtlessness, selfishness, or
> stupidity of any small section of the community.[1]

Unfortunately for Australia, acclimatisation achieved some of those goals. A few decades on and its sandy plains were indeed just one big rabbit warren. Tick. The hare and deer had successfully acclimatised and done their bit to destroy Australia. Tick. But the eland, springbok and antelope did not even get a guernsey. Fortunately too for Australia, every attempt to acclimatise gamebirds failed. Sometimes the native or introduced predators cleaned them up, and sometimes 'armed criminals' (read: non-members) found them and decided to enjoy some sport, like the Sandstone Island atrocity.

But our inflamed correspondent revealed that 'a gentleman' complained to him that several pheasants, which he had brought out and liberated, were all criminally shot. The gentleman in question was William Lyall, another wealthy grazier who also had property at Western Port.

Unsurprisingly, Lyall was a member of the Acclimatisation Society of Victoria and a member of Victoria's Legislative Assembly. He had also been quite successful in acclimatising hares. And for a while he was doing alright with pheasants – until a government survey team working nearby saw some of them and promptly shot, plucked, cleaned and cooked them. One of the party innocently told Mr Lyall that they had found a new, good-eating Australian bird that looked much like a proper pheasant. Mr Lyall flew into an impassioned rage and demanded to see the feathers of the birds, determined to prosecute the persons responsible. The surveyors found lyrebird feathers and showed Lyall these instead. This only enraged Mr Lyall who declared 'the insult of these killings was made worse by the perpetrators having the audacity to plead ignorance of what bird they were when the mischief was done!'[2]

Canary was on a roll. He further complained that a shop in Collins Street, Melbourne, had for sale a nest containing three English blackbirds, unfledged. What the double-deuce? The nest had obviously been the ill-gotten gain of an unknown but unconscionable scoundrel. Canary then asked, 'who was worse: the receiver of the pillaged nest or the thief who had stolen it from the public, for whose benefit the progenitors of these birds had been imported from home?' There were enough difficulties and dangers managing acclimatisation, he sniffed, without having it 'unnecessarily endangered and retarded for the selfish gratification of people who ought to know better.'[3] So, pack that in your meerschaum pipe and smoke it.

With such public bleating, the Sandstone Island massacre became public. Unfortunately (for Acclimatisation Society members), it created an unsavoury notion among the masses that the society's liberations were fair game for the benefit of everyone. As word got about regarding the society's releases of gamebirds, the unwelcome horde began shooting them. Pheasant, peafowl, partridge, Californian quail and Guinea fowl were all considered fair game by anyone who found them anywhere. So, under their 'No Pheasants for Peasants' policy, the Society began to make more distant and more secretive releases and eventually, in the mid-1880s, they bought 260 hectares near Gembrook, sixty kilometres east of Melbourne, on which to release their birds.

The gamebirds initially prospered at Gembrook but by then Thomas Austin's rabbits had spread into Gippsland and were eating all the vegetation. The society turned loose foxes and cats to kill the rabbits, but these preferred the gamebirds wreaked total havoc on them. The society then decided to poison the rabbits, but the remaining gamebirds ate the poisoned pollard laid for the rabbits and destroyed themselves instead. Which left the cats and foxes to predate on the remaining native fauna and the 'No Pheasants for Peasants' Policy in irreparable tatters.[4]

Meanwhile, Canary's acclimatising colleagues continued along on their merry way to 'stock our rivers with the choicest fish procurable in Europe'. Four years after Her Majesty declined to convert a man-of-war vessel into 'a herring boat' for Thomas Wilson's salmon importations, another found a merchant vessel fast enough to get them to Australia alive. In April 1864, a fly-fishing acclimatiser named James Youl managed to ship live brown trout ova to Australia from Britain. After previous unsuccessful attempts, the *Norfolk* docked at Railway Pier in Melbourne with 90,000 salmon ova and 2700 brown trout ova aboard, packed between layers of moss, inside 164 wooden boxes and stored in the icehouse of the ship. The journey had taken eighty-four days.

A little over two weeks after arriving in Melbourne, all but eleven boxes of the salmon ova went to Tasmania, where a hatchery was being set up on a tributary of the Derwent River at Plenty, and the first Australian trout hatched on 4 May. The hatchery retained some as brood stock, but successfully stocked local rivers with trout and salmon in the following years in Ballarat and Geelong, whose acclimatisation societies in turn distributed the Loch Leven strain of brown trout from New Zealand stock to Victoria, Tasmania and New South Wales. The remaining eleven boxes of salmon ova from the *Norfolk* stayed in Melbourne at the Victorian Ice Company, where the first Victorian salmon hatched on 5 May.

The Acclimatisation Society oversaw the release of Atlantic salmon into various Tasmanian rivers and the fish began to run to sea and back into the rivers of their origin to breed, as they are supposed to do. This thrilled the society, but their joy was short-lived when, in another episode almost as outrageous as the Sandstone Island massacre, they learned that the enemies of acclimatisation netted 'their' salmon rivers. This of course meant that persons in no way connected to the society could benefit from the salmon. Well, that would never do! They wrote to the Tasmania police commissioner and demanded that the wallopers police the river mouths and apprehend the offenders. The commissioner, who obviously had bigger fish to fry, informed the displeased society that, on the scale of things, these perpetrators were small fry and that the colony's police were not employed to function as gamekeepers.[5]

Love 'em or hate 'em, trout – arguably Australia's greatest sportfish – are fair dinkum ferals. They support a massive recreational angling industry in south-eastern New South Wales and Victoria, and in Tasmania where they make a significant contribution to the island state's economy. But, like all aggressive implants, trout have bullied their way to success at the expense of Australian native fish and aquatic animals.

However, as Australia's pests have repeatedly shown, you don't need to be big to be awful. Tiny eastern gambusia or mosquito fish are yet another aquatic species imported into our waterways – this time for pest control rather than sport. Originally native to south-eastern USA, they were imported by City of Sydney Council health inspector William Vogwell in 1926. He thought they'd be just the ticket to clean up mosquitoes, and released imported gambusia in New South Wales waters. When will we learn?

Mr Vogwell believed what he read about their reputation for mosquito control. Sucked in – it was all false. A council worker showing such initiative should, on the surface of it, be a great thing. However, after the gambusia proliferated and spread throughout temperate Australia, their ability to control mosquito larvae was revealed to be no greater than that of the small native fish that they displaced. Gambusia are now common in New South Wales waters and throughout Victorian, Queensland, Western Australian and South Australian waterways. Like tiny toothless piranhas, gambusia are a terrible little fish in Australia and have affected fish species in Australia directly through competition and predation. They prey upon native fish and amphibian eggs and are known to be responsible for the serious decline of native species.

CHAPTER 26

# Viruses Are the New Control Species

For all their impact on native inhabitants, salmon, trout and gambusia are far from the most damaging aquatic species introduced into Australia. Of those, it would be hard to conjure up a more hideous bio invader than the carp. A truly awful fish, they had often found their way into the hitherto happy Australian waterways on many occasions through the actions of acclimatisers, but did not become widespread until a release of 'Boolara' strain carp from a fish farm into the Murray River near Mildura in 1964.

The spread of carp throughout the Murray–Darling Basin coincided with widespread flooding in the early 1970s, but fishermen using carp as live bait for Murray cod assisted their spread throughout the system. Carp are now the most dominant freshwater species in south-eastern Australia. For decades it looked like carp were here to stay, but the CSIRO had other ideas.

Carp are ecological generalists that live in a wide range of habitats in Australia and overseas. They typically inhabit mid-latitude, low-altitude, slow-flowing rivers as far downstream as tidal freshwaters, and even enter estuaries. They also live in standing waters ranging from small billabongs and ephemeral wetlands to large lakes and reservoirs. In New South Wales, carp are rare at altitudes above 500 metres. They are less common in clear, cool, swift-flowing streams. These limits keep them from the high altitude trout streams favoured by the more endearing salmonoid ferals.

Where carp really thrive is in poor water-quality environments with low oxygen concentrations, turbid water and moderate salinities like the inland rivers of the Murray–Darling system. And being dyed-in-the-wool ferals, they are almost indestructible and, of course, have higher tolerances to toxicants than many other species.

The numbers of carp in our rivers is mind-boggling but, depending on the season, their numbers fluctuate. The 'National Carp Control Plan Progress Report' of December 2019 estimated Australia's carp biomass at 368,357 tonnes in May 2011. In May 2018, the carp biomass was 205,744 tonnes. Predictions for 2024 indicate carp biomass could be as low as 167,960 in a dry cycle or as high as 858,696 tonnes in a flood cycle.

Even when the carp biomass is as low as 100 kilograms per hectare, they are still able to cause significant environmental damage. You'd think carp are a problem because they prey on other fish, but they are more like dirty vacuums, feeding from the bottom by drawing in mouthfuls of sediment, consuming the edibles such as the tiny zooplankton they mostly live on, and expelling inedible matter, clogging the water with suspended sediment, causing reduced visibility, increased turbidity, and reduced oxygen. This mode of feeding is all about the carp and disastrous for the species in the unlucky ecosystems they have invaded, particularly for bottom-nesting species such as the eel-tailed catfish, whose numbers have drastically declined since the carp invaded.

Carp also have the feral advantage over their outnumbered native competitors by spawning at lower water temperatures than most native fish and before many species, which gives their offspring an unfair advantage in feeding and growth opportunities. The bad news is that densities of 200 to 400 kilograms of carp per hectare are common through the middle and lower reaches of Australia's major southern river systems. The good news is that the CSIRO has a plan for them.

Cyprinid herpes virus is a viral disease that is highly contagious to the common carp. Like myxomatosis in rabbits, carp herpes virus promises to be the breakthrough needed to win the war against carp. The virus has been proven harmless to all other fish species, humans and animals, but it causes kidney failure in carp, attacks their skin and kills them after about seven days.[1] The CSIRO study indicates that the virus could reduce carp populations by an average of forty to sixty per cent, which would effectively drop their density below ecological damage thresholds in many areas. The CSIRO believe that level of biomass suppression should last at least five to ten years or even longer, after which it may lose its effectiveness and the carp may begin to build in numbers again.

Fishing holidays in the outback were once one of the great attractions of the eastern interior. Land degradation, the degradation of the Murray–Darling system and carp have destroyed the west for many people, particularly the residents of the river communities. Getting rid of the carp will go a long way – but not all the way – to reclaiming another great piece of our vandalised heritage. It won't be a moment too soon, and few people will shed a tear for the loss.

*

It appears that science may also be on track to develop a similar bio-controller for the cane toad. Scientists have revealed three viruses found embedded in the cane toad's DNA that have the potential to eliminate the species, according to findings published in *GigaScience* journal in September 2018.[2]

Scientific teams from the University of New South Wales, the University of Sydney, Deakin University, Melbourne, and scientific facilities in Portugal and Brazil have unlocked the toad's genetics. A virus based on this knowledge could lead to a cull of the estimated 200 million cane toad population, which now occupies more than 120 million hectares across the top half of Australia.

Virologist and project leader Peter White, a professor in microbiology and molecular biology at the University of New South Wales, said laboratory viruses could turn the tables on the pest: 'Once you know the genome, you know the blueprint of the animal. When you know the exact amino acid sequence of every protein in its body, how the enzymes work, you've got the deeds to the house.'[3]

Any virus developed in the laboratory would need to pass field-testing before a full-scale release to ensure there could be no impacts on other native animals. First it was the rabbit with myxomatosis and RHD, now the carp faces extermination and, with a little scientific ingenuity, the terrible toad may be facing the end as well. One wonders what the Queensland State of Origin rugby league team thinks of that!

*

Science has repeatedly shown that, if provided with adequate support, it is more than capable of developing effective feral control strategies. The viral decimation of the rabbit and the carp herpes virus are clear proof that science leads the way. Our best hope of controlling or eliminating ferals lies with the new generation of frontline scientists gunning for them, armed with the latest weaponry of environmental, biological and technical sciences.

Tech-savvy field workers are now utilising camera traps, drones and a host of other techno-aids to gather once-impossible-to-obtain data and intelligence on secretive ferals. By using this new technology, the actual behaviours and habits of feral predators such as wild dogs become better understood by the people charged with dealing with them or identifying threats. Know thy enemy. It's a huge psychological and tactical advance and advantage.

Over the past few years governments and industry have invested millions into research and development of new tools and technologies, as well as for strategic landscape management to tackle pest animal problems. Rabbits still threaten over three hundred species of plants and animals, and cost Australia more than $209 million annually, despite ongoing manual and biological rabbit control measures. The rabbit cannot get another chance to overrun the country again. There are too many of them as it is.

For the rural sector, Australia's mammalian predator pest species cost the beef industry up to $220 million per year, and losses to the wool industry are at around $100 million per year. Underlying these costs is the huge number of lamb, sheep, calves, cattle and goat deaths and maulings that impact each producer's bottom-line and livelihood. Not to mention the heart-wrenching impost placed on primary producers, who must deal daily with the realities of wild dog and fox predation on their stock.[4]

The broader community can also assist in Australia's war against the ferals in various ways, but lending science a hand has become a crucial component of pest-animal management. Citizen science – the participation of members of the public in scientific endeavours – has become increasingly prominent in contributing to ecological research. The ability to engage a potentially large team of widely dispersed observers has created exceptional opportunities for data collection. The rise of citizen-science programs has also been enabled by the development of internet-based data-entry technologies that allow citizen scientists to submit location-based data electronically.

In addition to enabling broad scale data collection, citizen-science programs have the benefit of increasing positive engagement by the public with scientific research. Rabbit-control researchers now routinely use citizen-science data to model the distributions, abundance and species richness of plants and animals.

The new Korean variant of RHD known as K5 received approval as a registered rabbit biocontrol agent in April 2016. K5 was selected for release as it is still effective in the cool, high-rainfall areas of Australia, whereas the original RHD strain worked best in hot, dry areas.

To maximise the potential impact of this new strain on rabbit populations, the plan for the K5 virus called for its release in various locations, distributed widely over the known range of rabbits in Australia. To help achieve this, in March 2017, a citizen-science program was established to encourage participation in the release and the use of best practice follow-up control. It was also intended to take advantage of the citizen science to capture data on the impact of K5 on rabbit populations across the country.[5]

Citizen science has always been a part of the fabric of Australian pastoralism. The man or woman on the land understands their country and what is happening on it. Observation is a key part of farming, and farmers know and understand the daily and seasonal comings and goings of not just their stock but of native and non-native animals. It makes perfect sense to exploit this local intelligence and recruit the frontline workers to the cause. Farmers have long understood the efficacy of bio-controls and were quick to seed their properties with myxo- and RHD-infected rabbits or carcases.

In the post-COVID world we share, the power of viruses is pretty apparent to all of us. Used in the right way, potent viruses can work *for* us and not against us. The viral road will be the only effective way to win Australia back from the ecological disasters that affect the countryside and our waterways. The issue for feral animals that have domestic counterparts will be establishing protection measures for the domestic versions through vaccination or perhaps exclusion and isolation.

# CHAPTER 27

# The New Feral Dog Plague

Types other than the dingo type don't succeed in the Australian wild. Eventually the domestic ferals hybridise with the dingo, or the dingo hybrid population and the domestic build inevitably gives way to the dingoes' much stronger genes. Untypical colouration is the first physical sign of dingo hybridisation. It is common now to see hybrids with the dingo build but domestic dog colouration and markings such as brindles and white with patches, called white parti-coloured.

There has been some speculation that dingoes are naturally found in colouring other than tan with white points, black and tan, and black. One should be cautious accepting such theories when none of the diaries or journals of pioneers, explorers or pastoralists have ever noted dingoes in any colour than the foregoing. The colours now being ascribed to dingoes are the colours displayed by the popular breeds that have historically turned feral and mixed with dingoes: brindle with or without white, white parti-colours and sables.

So how does this hybridisation affect the dingo? In eastern Australia, except for Fraser Island, there probably remains no pure dingoes at large at all. They are all mixed-blood feral dogs, or 'wild dogs' as they are generically known. The hybrids pose a genetic threat to the unique identity of the Australian dingo, which faces a bleak future on mainland Australia. Sanctuaries that maintain pure stock are key to the species' survival.

Feral dogs are bold and enterprising and prey on whatever animals they can most easily kill. Reptiles, amphibians and mammals. Wild, domestic stock or pets. It does not matter to the dog if it is easy. The impact on biodiversity is profound. Wild dogs are opportunistic predators and will prey on everything from goannas to birds to koalas. In one study, scientists tracked more than 400 koalas fitted with electronic collars over two years. Around 130 were dead, killed due to injuries from wild dogs.

Left to manage their own affairs, dogs are an incredibly lazy creature and will always take the easiest choice. Feral dogs do not mind living near humans because their chief survival strategy is to exploit the easy-to-access resources of human production – sheep and other stock, and refuse – and they cost us tens of millions every year in stock losses and other damage.

Once it was working dogs that were most likely to turn feral, but times have changed. Feral dogs are appearing where once they were unknown. This pattern follows the new ranges of feral pigs. Lost or abandoned pigging dogs of the heavy mastiff, wolfhound, pointer, and bull breed types make up the general modern wild dog.

Losing or dumping dogs in the bush is an act of incredible irresponsibility. The feral pigging dog problem is directly related to the illegal transportation and release of feral pigs in areas closer to settled areas. If there were two awful feral creatures that do not need a helping hand it's the pig and the dog. Both are nothing but trouble.

Dogs not kept under effective control on hobby farms and rural acreages also regularly contribute to the feral dog problem.

These dogs attack easy-to-kill stock such as sheep kept on neighbouring farms. About two-thirds of Australia's primary producers regularly experience wild dog problems on their properties with a third describing their problems as severe.

Domestic pet dogs have also caused immeasurable damage to Australian fauna over two hundred and something years. The bandicoots and blue-tongue lizards and other small creatures that inhabit backyards and remnant and surrounding bushland have always been preyed upon by dogs large and small. And a dog doesn't have to be living as a fully wild dog to have a similar impact on livestock and fauna. Urban ferals come in all shapes, sizes and lifestyles. Effective control of domestic pets is now more important than at any previous time in Australia.

CHAPTER 28

# Ethical Dilemmas in Feral Animal Control

O nce, people didn't care how a pest died as long as it was gone. Poisoning, leg-hold trapping, exclusion from water and even clubbing were once acceptable means of vermin destruction. No one shed a tear for the animals so destroyed because everyone was over the pests, particularly the rabbit, and Australia was a hard place back then.

But as Australians urbanised and enjoyed a higher quality of life, they raised serious concerns about the humaneness of pest-extermination methods and strategies. Myxomatosis was the classic case. The media of the day showed images and footage of severely infected rabbits, which raised the ire of mostly city-based folks who did not approve of such methods. Outlawed too were the unpadded gin or leg-hold traps that unquestionably caused injury, stress and general trauma to their victims.

This has led to an increasing emphasis on humane destruction of pests, in particular vertebrate ones. A discussion paper, 'A National Approach towards Humane Vertebrate Pest Control', arising from the proceedings of the Humane Vertebrate Pest Control Working Group in August 2004 in Melbourne described humane pest-control methods as 'one where the animal experiences no pain, suffering or distress. In the case of lethal control, humane killing is defined as an immediate and irreversible loss of consciousness followed by cardiac or respiratory arrest and the ultimate loss of brain function.'

Other than legitimate recreational hunters or teenage ghouls with golf drivers teeing off on cane toads, most people take no pleasure in destroying pests, which are incapable of 'good' or 'bad' and are really doing no more than conducting their daily economy. Feral-pest eradication is just a bigger version of putting down cockroach baits, swatting a mozzie, or spraying a blowie. And most of us are capable of that.

As much as the ethicists desire a totally stress-free, painless end for pest animals, the reality is that you can't make an omelette without breaking a few eggs. It's a dirty job, but someone must do it. And when feral pests threaten someone's livelihood, the last thing they are worried about is that the pest they are about to kill might not enjoy a stress-free end. That said, the chief objective of pest destruction should be the quickest and most painless possible end that does not degrade the humanity of those conducting the work.

The other reality is that for most people involved in vertebrate pest extermination, out of sight is out of mind. Destroying a rabbit warren with a bulldozer that drags ripping tines through it causes the rabbits below some level of distress. But the operator sees none of that and remains indifferent. If the operator had to destroy the rabbits by hand, perhaps that indifference might wane.

That is why poisoning was so popular. People only rarely saw the slow, painful death of their target, and when they did it was usually because their own dog had taken the bait. Lots of folk changed their opinions of strychnine after seeing it kill their dogs. Thousands of great working and pet dogs died because of that terrible poison.

Sodium fluoroacetate or 1080 (ten–eighty) was the preferred poison during the late–twentieth century. Aerial baiting, especially for dingoes and feral dogs, has become the most cost- and labour-efficient method of targeting those creatures in rugged, inaccessible country. Still, there are animal-welfare issues that make the use of 1080 ethically questionable, and science continues to search for a more humane alternative.

In the 1990s, scientists based at the Victorian Institute of Animal Science demonstrated that a compound known as 4'-aminopropiophenone (*para*-aminopropiophenone or PAPP) was a rapid acting and humane means of feral cat and fox control.

In simple terms, PAPP kills by preventing the blood from carrying oxygen, which quickly leads to painless coma and death. Researchers also discovered that the delivery of PAPP in feral cat baits within a specialised capsule could limit the exposure of non-target animals to PAPP even if they consumed the bait. This became a significant feature of a feral cat bait that became known as 'Curiosity'.

The Curiosity bait for feral cats has been a long-term $5.9 million project to develop a humane, broad-scale toxic bait to control feral cats in conservation areas. The Curiosity bait comprises a small meat-based sausage containing a small hard plastic pellet encapsulating a humane toxin. Cats do not have molar teeth and tend to chew their food less so they may swallow portions of the sausage including the pellet. Most Australian native animals nibble and chew their food and are likely to reject the pellet. The pellet is designed to dissolve in the cat's stomach and deliver a rapid dose of the toxin.[1]

\*

While the high-end of science has been forging ahead with biological advances in the feral wars, the low-end science of guarding animals has found a cost-effective way of providing protection to stock from predators like feral dogs and foxes.

Foxes are the easier predator to keep at bay with a guardian animal. The fox is a small, naturally shy and cautious creature that hunts alone. Feral dogs, on the other hand, can be quite large, are bold and enterprising, and hunt in packs.

Guardian dogs are native to Europe and Asia. Some of the breeds available in Australia are the great pyrenees from France, the komondor from Hungary, the akbash dog and the Anatolian shepherd from Turkey, the maremma sheepdog from Italy, and the similar Hungarian kuvasz. All of these are large – the great pyrenees being one of the heaviest of all dogs. They are mostly sheep-white or fawn-coloured with dark muzzles.

There's a lot of work in guardian dogs, but used in the right place and correctly raised, trained and managed they provide excellent protection for livestock. Sourcing well-bred guardians and supporting them with unvarying routine and commitment is the key, and on smaller holdings in rougher country where large canine predators make life hell for small stock, guardian dogs can provide the best possible protection.

Llamas also make excellent protectors against fox predation. Alpacas aren't bad either, but the llama's wool-free head and large unobstructed ears, coupled with its imposing height, make them handy companions for all kinds of small livestock.

The humble donkey also makes a determined guardian and is capable of offering stiffer resistance to feral dogs. Gelding and mare donkeys work best when born and raised with the flock they are to guard, as long as they don't develop a trust or friendship with dogs.

Of course, llamas, alpacas and donkeys provide the best protection for their companion flocks when kept in cleared, level paddocks, where they have a better chance of detecting predators when they are still a long way off. Foxes and dogs attacked by llamas and donkeys are usually reluctant to cop another kicking and look elsewhere for a feed.

# Conclusion

We are slowly clawing Australia back from the grasp of ferals, but the war rages still. Science now has us on the front foot and, for the first time in decades entrenched feral species are facing threatened futures.

The disparate feral eradication programs of the past had no hope of ever alleviating the broader problems because, like wartime intelligence failures, all the agencies involved were not talking or sharing information, much less acting in concert. A coordinated national approach to all feral animal management is critical if we are to eventually succeed. And now the right hand finally knows what the left hand is doing. That's the basis of the Australian Pest Animal Strategy and the national feral animal offensive.[1]

It all sounds great in theory, and here's hoping it works, because piecemeal programs only fix localised issues, but invasive species directly and indirectly impact every Australian.[2]

Supporting that national strategy are federal and state and territory biosecurity laws. Ignorance is no longer an excuse to threaten Australia by introducing or maintaining invasive species of any kind. Under Australia's federal and state biosecurity acts, people must have a basic level of knowledge about the biosecurity risks they might take in their normal work and recreational activities.[3]

The new threats to Australia's biosecurity are the foreign pet species smuggled into Australia. The foreign species most often illegally imported are reptiles, including corn snakes; boas such as constrictors, rainbow and rosy boas; veiled chameleons; Californian kingsnakes; leopard geckos; and red-eared sliders and Horsfield's tortoises. The Australian Quarantine and Inspection Service is leading the fight against these and other dangerous importations.[4]

Australia has many ferals who have, like the dingo before them, become so embedded within the Australian ecosystem that one could see a path towards their naturalisation. The northern palm squirrel made itself at home in Perth, Western Australia, in the late-nineteenth century. It has been in residence at the Perth Zoo since 1898. Native to northern India, where it lives around houses and causes damage to fruit and vegetable crops, the squirrel was an 'enhancement' to the zoo's park, and kiddies could keep them if they could catch them. Good luck with that, kids. Although the squirrel remained confined to the zoo grounds for years, they dispersed to an area of about 3000 hectares outside the zoo grounds. They are a bit of a nuisance, but other people find them endearing, though they continue, as they did in India, to raid fruit trees and gardens and cause considerable damage to houses they find attractive.

Perth seems to be the home of unusual ferals. First the mongoose, then the palm squirrel, now the rainbow lorikeet. True. It is one of the world's most recognisable, beautiful, and noisy birds, but it is a feral in south-west Western Australia. Rainbow Lorikeets are native to south and east Indonesia, New Guinea, the Solomon Islands, Vanuatu, New Caledonia and parts of Australia – proving that even Australian natives can go feral in places they don't belong. There are two varieties of lorikeets: green-collared and red-collared. The red-collared variety occurs naturally in the Kimberley in the north-west of Western Australia and is endemic throughout the Top End of the Northern Territory east to the gulf country of Queensland. The more common green-collared variety is home east from there to Cape York and round the entire eastern portion of the continent, all the way around to the Eyre Peninsula in South Australia. While they are usually associated with coastal regions, they do venture some way inland across all their natural range.

Rainbows are a popular aviary and pet bird, and hand-raised they make gregarious companions. But being nectar and fruit eaters, they have messy, watery excretions delivered with water-pistol-like velocity. A lot of them become too destructive, noisy and messy for their people, who eventually let them go to fend for themselves. In their natural range, released or escaped birds join the wild locals. But outside their natural range, releasing them makes them a genuine invasive species. Ferals.

The Perth lorikeets now number around 15,000, grown from an initial population of around ten birds that were either deliberately released or had escaped from aviaries around 1968.

Rainbow lorikeets are no shrinking violets. They are swift flyers, form huge flocks, and are noisy and aggressive. Like any other avian feral species, they're too much bird for the endemic natives, and they outcompete native bird and arboreal mammal species for food and nest sites. In Perth and the Swan Valley rainbow lorikeets damage commercial and domestic fruit crops, foul outdoor areas and vehicles with droppings, and cause noise problems.

Modelling conducted by the New South Wales Department of Environment and Conservation suggests that their numbers could be brought down to as low as 1000 birds over a period of about seven years, but that they could never be truly eliminated.[5]

Nature has very good reasons why it has ordered all species to remain in defined areas. It has much to do with balance and sustainability. As soon as those distribution boundaries are breached, there's trouble, native species or not. And it's the rule-breakers who always seem to be on the front foot.

\*

Is it unreasonable to expect complete victory in the feral wars? The real issue caused by the introduction of foreign species is that they overpopulate. Small, confined populations like the trout — confined to cold water rivers and lakes — do only limited damage. Australia can live with that, and that might be the best we can hope for. Of course, with species that do have a defined, localised population, such as Asiatic buffalo and banteng cattle, or island-based ferals, it is possible to exterminate entire populations. The eradication of mice, rats, and rabbits from Macquarie Island is a good example.[6]

The feral rabbits, dogs, pigs, cats, foxes and cane toads need to go. But as for the rest of them, the Australian ecosystem will adapt to living with controlled numbers of the introduced herbivorous mammalian species; likewise with the introduced birds of our cities and towns. Feral population minimisation is the most realistic expectation. Most of our feral species are here to stay and given a few thousand years might one day be considered locals like the dingo.

In a future Australia mostly free of feral animals, what would become of the feral dependencies – the rural communities, regions and even states that rely on hunting and fishing tourism based on the value of feral animals? How would the Snowy Mountains region of New South Wales react to a plan to remove trout from their lakes and waterways? What would Tasmania, so dependent on trout fishers, do if the trout disappeared?

The Snowy and Tasmania are also destinations for hunters seeking feral deer. Those feral species bring in visitors to these regions seasonally. The same issues apply to regions that rely on income generated from feral pigs, goats, buffalo, banteng cattle, camels and donkey commercial and recreational hunting. Feral goats in the red mulga country of the interior are now proving to be a significant resource for embattled graziers.

Just as happened with the rabbit, Australians adapted to the feral situation they found themselves in. There's good money, even economies, in ferals now. It is a difficult situation when the environmental damage plays a secondary role to emerging game meat or recreational economies, and one needing some level of sustainable compromise. A farmer who supplements his income by charging a fee for hunters to hunt feral animals is not going to manually eliminate his income or support bio-controllers that will leave him poorer. Even the rabbit does its bit to support the recreational hunting economy. Much of the pain of having to share the land with ferals diminishes by finding some form of value in them. However, while even the carp has found value as a source of liquid fertiliser, the cane toad so far defies any form of meaningful commercial exploitation.

Value-adding ferals varies from species to species. The livestock ferals can be left to proliferate, and then mustered or trapped then sent off live (except pigs) to abattoirs or even shipped to foreign live markets. It's the preservation of free-ranging feral species that damage their local environment that creates a moral dilemma for farmers and environment managers. What is the priority? Removing the ferals or the livelihood of the farmer?

Australia's feral woes began when control of the land passed from the environmentally cooperative stewardship of Indigenous Australians to the bull-at-the-gate management of a remorseless new order determined to 'civilise' the bush. During the early days of colonial Australia, when the native predators remained largely unmolested, the smaller to medium-sized terrestrial ferals stood no chance of establishing viable populations.

All that changed when the dingo was eliminated to make way for sheep, and the quolls, and a great many large reptiles and birds of prey went with them. Millions of acres of woodland were cleared, and the land was overstocked with millions upon millions of hungry, thirsty, hard-hoofed ungulates that placed an impossible burden on the fragile environment. This is how the pastoral foundation of modern Australia was built. The consequence in the eastern interior was environmental degradation and dysfunction, the land overrun by foreign species.

When the feral floodgates opened, they stayed open. Environmental disaster seen and unseen became the norm. Livestock, domestic and feral, became the large, widespread herbivore; rabbits the small. Foxes and cats became the widespread carnivores, and no one blinked an eye. Native fauna was eliminated or persecuted. But it was all in the name of progress … and then in the name of sport. All this was committed by people with no evil intent, but rather blind – or at the very least, indifferent – to the catastrophic destruction unfolding before them.

While we've had plenty of time to contemplate the wisdom of releasing any foreign-animal species in Australia, hindsight is an exact science, and it is easy to be critical of the mistakes of the past. Conversely, it is only fair to concede that the wool and other agricultural pioneers and men like the Thomases Austin and Chirnside could not conceive the damage their livestock and rabbits and foxes would eventually cause. None of them ever set out to destroy the land.

It appears that as we now move into the third decade of the twenty-first century, the greatest dangers to Australia are the complacency that views feral infestations as 'someone else's problem' and consigns the feral plagues of the past to ancient history. Every feral problem, past or future, is every Australian's problem, because ferals never sleep and those who forget our feral history are condemned to repeat it. It bears remembering that no feral infestation has ever been totally eradicated, so based on past experience, once ferals become established in Australia they are here to stay.

We can never take a backward step in the fight to protect what we have and reclaim our natural heritage.

# Endnotes

A note on sources: Many of the historical newspaper articles cited below were circulated widely among publications. The source article quoted might not be to the original publication but to a reprint in another publication located on the Trove resource at the National Library of Australia trove.nla.gov.au/

### Introduction

1   *Mammal loss in Australia.* John CZ Woinarski, Andrew A Burbidge, Peter L Harrison. Proceedings of the National Academy of Sciences Apr 2015, 112 (15) 4531-4540; DOI: 10.1073/pnas.1417301112.

### Australia's First Feral

1   *Tasmanian Tiger No Match for Dingo.* University of New South Wales. ScienceDaily. ScienceDaily, 12 September 2007, www.sciencedaily.com/releases/2007/09/070905095352.htm. These conclusions are based on sophisticated computer simulations revealing bite forces and stress patterns applying to dingo and thylacine skull specimens. The simulations illustrate mechanical stresses and strains applying to the skull, jaw, teeth and cranial muscles of both animals across a range of biting, tearing and shaking motions that simulate the impact of controlling and killing a struggling prey.

### Part One – Phillip's Ferals

1   www.firstfleetfellowship.org.au/library/first-fleetlist-livestock-provisions-plants-seeds/

### Chapter 1 – Cattle Head for Greener Pastures

1   John Hunter, *An Historical Journal of the Transactions at Port Jackson and Norfolk Island.*

2   David Collins, *An Account of the English Colony of NSW,* Vol 1.

3   Hunter, op cit.

4   *The Voyage of Governor Phillip to Botany Bay with an Account of the Establishment of the Colonies of Port Jackson and Norfolk Island,* Various Contributors, London Printed for John Stockdale, Piccadilly, 1789.

5   Ibid.

6     Collins, op cit.

7     Ibid.

8     *Sydney Gazette and New South Wales Advertiser*, Sunday 3 July 1803.

9     Ibid, Saturday 7 December 1816.

10    *Methodist*, Sydney, Saturday 30 September 1893, p 9.

11    Tom McKnight, *Friendly Vermin: A Survey of Feral Livestock in Australia*, University of California Press, 1976.

12    *Sydney Morning Herald*, Thursday 11 April 1957.

13    Bert Howard, *Australian Origins and Heritage Files*, NSW, 2017.

## Chapter 2 – Brumby's Hawkesbury Horses

1     Samuel Sidney et al, *Gallops and Gossips in the Bush of Australia*, London, 1854.

2     AW Campbell, 'Brumby, James (1771–1838)', *Australian Dictionary of Biography*, National Centre of Biography, Australian National University, 1966.

3     *Illustrated Australian News for Home Readers*, Melbourne, Friday 27 September 1867.

4     *Riverina Recorder*, Wednesday 10 November 1897.

5     *Albury Banner and Wodonga Express*, NSW, Friday 15 November 1901.

6     *Snowy River Mail*, Orbost, Victoria, Thursday 18 January 1912.

7     *Queensland Times*, Wednesday 6 July 1927.

8     *Yass Courier*, Monday 25 February 1929.

9     *Mudgee Guardian and North-Western Representative*, Monday 5 January 1948.

## Chapter 3 – Goats Take Over Sydney Town

1     Fiona Carruthers, *The Horse in Australia*, Random House, Sydney, 2008.

2     Henry Lamond, *Walkabout*, Vol 16(1), Sunday 1 January 1950.

3     *Sydney Stock and Station Journal*, Tuesday 6 September 1921.

4     *Glen Innes Examiner*, NSW, Saturday 20 January 1945. For more information on Goat Town see *Newcastle Sun*, Saturday 17 January 1931.

5     *Sydney Mail*, Wednesday 28 July 1937.

6     *Barrier Miner*, Broken Hill, NSW, Wednesday 1 September 1948.

## Chapter 4 – Pigs Dig their Snouts into the Environmental Trough

1     *Walkabout*, Vol 9(12), Friday 1 October 1943.

2     www.allancunninghambotanist1839.com/index.php/allan-cunninghams-botanical-journals

3     Collins, op cit.

4    *Queensland Country*, Thursday 15 June 1950.

5    *Mercury*, Hobart, Tuesday 9 July 1918.

6    *Warialda Standard and Northern Districts' Advertiser*, NSW, Monday 11 February 1924.

7    *Observer*, Adelaide, Saturday 30 March 1907.

8    *Journal*, Adelaide, Thursday 21 August 1913.

9    *Daily Telegraph*, Sydney, Saturday 20 June 1914.

10   *Murray Pioneer and Australian River Record*, Renmark, Friday 18 January 1929.

11   *Dubbo Dispatch and Wellington Independent*, Tuesday 18 June 1918.

12   *Daily Examiner*, Grafton, NSW, Monday 16 January 1939.

13   *Morning Bulletin*, Rockhampton, Friday 19 November 1948.

### Chapter 5 – Feral Dogs Rule

1    Collins, op cit.

2    Australia, Parliament, Joint Library Committee and Frederick Watson, 'Proclamation of Governor Philip Gidley King, Tuesday, 17 February, 1801', *Historical Records of Australia: Series 1 – Governors' Despatches to and from England*, Vol 3, 1801–1802 (Library Committee of the Commonwealth Parliament, 1915) p 50.

3    *Sydney Gazette and New South Wales Advertiser*, Sunday 7 June 1807.

### Chapter 6 – No Place for Scabby Sheep

1    *People's Advocate and New South Wales Vindicator*, Sydney, Saturday 9 December 1848.

2    *Maitland Mercury and Hunter River General Advertiser*, NSW, Saturday 13 January 1849.

3    *Bell's Life in Sydney and Sporting Reviewer*, Saturday 26 March 1853.

4    *Bathurst Free Press and Mining Journal*, Saturday 28 May 1853.

5    *People's Advocate and New South Wales Vindicator*, Sydney, Saturday 12 June 1852.

6    *Sydney Morning Herald*, Tuesday 2 June 1885.

7    *South Australian Advertiser*, 4 July 1879.

8    Ibid, 22 July 1878.

### Chapter 7 – Camels and Donkeys Open the Interior

1    *Perth Gazette and Western Australian Journal*, Saturday 5 December 1835.

2    *Sydney Morning Herald*, Tuesday 8 August 1871.

3    *Ibid.*

4   *Sydney Mail*, Wednesday 19 December 1934.

5   Burke and Wills Web Digital Archive, JA Horrocks's last letter, 1846, www.burkeandwills.net.au/Camels

6   Burke and Wills Web Digital Archive, www.burkeandwills.net.au/Brief_History/Chapter_02.htm

7   Governor Richard MacDonnell to Charles Sturt, 10 August 185, quoted in Mrs Napier Sturt's *Life of Charles Sturt,* 1899.

8   Burke and Wills Web Digital Archive, www.burkeandwills.net.au/Royal_Society/Exploration_Committee/Exploration_Committee

9   Burke and Wills Web Digital Archive, www.burkeandwills.net.au

10  Burke and Wills Web Digital Archive, www.burkeandwills.net.au/Camels/index.htm

11  Ibid.

12  From a manuscript of a lecture by Sir Thomas Elder, 1879, Rare Books & Special Collections.

13  www.adelaide.edu.au/library/special/stories/elder/camels/

## Chapter 8 - Motor Vehicles Supersede Camels and Donkeys

1   *Victorian Express*, Geraldton, WA, Friday 10 March 1893.

2   *Sydney Mail*, Wednesday 6 January 1937.

3   *Jack's Enlisted*, Ernestine Hill, *Walkabout*, issue 4, 1943.

4   *Age*, Melbourne, Saturday 18 September 1954.

## Chapter 9 – Acclimatisation Societies and the Feral Free-for-all

1   *Courier*, Brisbane, Friday 18 October 1861, from the *Yeoman and Australian Acclimatiser.*

2   www.biodiversitylibrary.org/page/55205811?utm_medium=social%20media&utm_source=blogger&utm_campaign=Book%20of%20the%20Month&utm_content=Museums%20Victoria#page/8/mode/1up; and for all quotes in this chapter from the annual meetings of the Acclimatisation Society of Victoria.

3   *Cornwall Chronicle*, Launceston, Wednesday 13 November 1867.

4   www.feralscan.org.au/deerscan/

5   *Argus,* Melbourne, Monday 17 February 1908.

6   *Benalla Standard*, Friday 19 February 1909.

7   *Farmer's Journal and Gardener's Chronicle*, Melbourne, Saturday 6 September 1862.

8   Ibid.

## Chapter 10 – Thomas Austin and the Rabbits of Barwon Park

1    *Argus,* Melbourne, Thursday 1 January 1857.

2    Ibid, Saturday 31 May 1862.

3    *Star*, Ballarat, Friday 22 April 1864.

4    trove.nla.gov.au/work/34308181, Acclimatisation Society's dinner: held at Scott's Hotel, Collins Street West, on Wednesday 6 July 1864.

5    Ibid.

## Chapter 11 – Royal Rabbit Routs and the Stately Shooter Shot

1    Eric Rolls, *They All Ran Wild*, Angus & Robertson, Sydney, 1969, p 24.

2    www.biodiversitylibrary.org/bibliography/141530#/summary

3    *Mercury*, Hobart, Monday 8 March 1869.

4    *Horsham Times*, Friday 10 March 1939.

5    *Geelong Advertiser*, Friday 28 October 1870.

6    *Argus*, Melbourne, Monday 18 December 1871.

7    *Australasian*, Melbourne, Saturday 23 December 1871.

8    PL Brown, 'Austin, Thomas (1815-1817)', *Australian Dictionary of Biography*, National Centre of Biography, Australian National University, adb.anu.edu.au/biography/austin-thomas-1521

9    *Geelong Advertiser*, 2 January 1843, 29 June 1843, 30 June 1843, 30 December 1871, 23 August 1889; Paul H De Serville, 'Austin, Elizabeth Phillips (1821–1910)', *Australian Dictionary of Biography*, National Centre of Biography, *Australian National University*, adb.anu.edu.au/biography/austin-elizabeth-phillips-1522/

10   www.austin.org.au

## Chapter 12 – Barwon Park's Rabbits Conquer Victoria

1    agriculture.vic.gov.au/agriculture/pests-diseases-and-weeds/pest-animals/a-z-of-pest-animals/european-rabbit/about-european-rabbit

2    Ibid.

3    Rolls, op cit, p 21.

4    Ibid, p 28.

5    Ibid, p 119.

6    W Eather and D Cottle, 'The Rabbit Industry in South-East Australia, 1870–1970', 2015.

7    *Telegraph*, Brisbane, Saturday 9 November 1878.

8    Eather and Cottle, op cit.

9    Ibid.

### Chapter 13 – Victoria's Rabbits Breach Colony Lines

1   Rolls, op cit, pp 38 and 55. Unless otherwise indicated, this chapter relies on Rolls.

2   *South Australian Parliamentary Papers,* 137: 1879.

3   *South Australian Advertiser,* Thursday 12 April 1877.

4   E Stodart and I Parer, *Colonisation of Australia by the Rabbit,* CSIRO Publishing, 1988

5   Rolls, op cit, p 53.

6   Phillips, K. Zenger, B. Richardson, 'Are Sydney Rabbits Different?', Centre for Biostructural and Biomolecular Research, University of Western Sydney, Hawkesbury Campus, //meridian.allenpress.com/australian-zoologist/article/32/1/49/134568/Are-Sydney-rabbits-different

7   *Portland Guardian,* Victoria, Thursday 14 June 1883.

8   Rolls, op cit, p 57.

9   *Freeman's Journal,* Sydney, Saturday 27 October 1883.

10  *Weekly Times,* Melbourne, Saturday 24 November 1883.

11  *Hillston News,* Saturday 19 May 1883.

12  *Goulburn Herald,* NSW, Thursday 7 February 1884.

13  *Register,* Adelaide, Saturday 8 July 1916.

14  *Sydney Morning Herald,* Friday 2 October 1885.

15  RJ Murchison and Robert Barr, *The Rabbit Plague in Australia and a Scheme for Its Suppression,* George Robertson & Company, Melbourne, 1887.

16  *Sydney Morning Herald,* Saturday 3 October 1885.

17  Ibid, Monday 5 October 1885.

18  Ibid, Wednesday, 7 October 1885.

19  CB Schedvin, 'Rabbits and Industrial Development: Lysaght Brothers & Co Pty Ltd, 1884–1929,' *Australian Economic History Review* (1970), Vol 10, pp 27–55.

20  Ibid.

21  Rolls, op cit, p 156.

22  *Sydney Morning Herald,* Tuesday 22 June 1886.

23  Rolls, op cit, p 142.

### Chapter 14 – Thomas Chirnside and the Foxes of Werribee Park

1   *Sydney Gazette and New South Wales Advertiser,* Saturday 26 December 1835.

2   Ibid, Saturday 16 April 1836.

3    *Argus*, Melbourne, Monday 24 September 1860.

4    *Rockhampton Bulletin and Central Queensland Advertiser*, Wednesday 10 June 1863.

5    *Courier*, Brisbane, Friday 19 June 1863.

6    J Ann Hone, 'Chirnside, Thomas (1815–1887)', *Australian Dictionary of Biography*, National Centre of Biography, Australian National University, adb.anu.edu.au/biography/chirnside-thomas-3203/text4815

7    www.dpi.nsw.gov.au/biosecurity/vertebrate-pests/pest-animals-in-nsw/foxes/fox-biology

8    *Argus,* Melbourne, Saturday 8 August 1885.

9    *Weekly Times*, Melbourne, Saturday 12 September 1885.

10   *Argus*, Melbourne, Thursday 9 September 1886.

11   Ibid, Friday 4 October 1889.

12   www.parliament.vic.gov.au/images/stories/historical_hansard/VicHansard_18890409_18890619.pdf

13   Ian Abbott, 'The Importation, Release, Establishment, Spread, and Early Impact on Prey Animals of the Red Fox Vulpes vulpes in Victoria and Adjoining Parts of South-eastern Australia', meridian.allenpress.com/australian-zoologist/article/35/3/463/135337/The-importation-release-establishment-spread-and; *South Australian Parliamentary Debates, Legislative Council,* 30 October 1889, p 1378; AD Handyside, *South Australian Parliamentary Debates*, 22 October 1889, column 1288.

14   Abbott, ibid; *Australasian,* Melbourne, Saturday 4 June 1904.

15   *Land*, Sydney, Friday 31 March 1911.

16   Ibid, Sydney, Friday 9 January 1914.

17   *Sunday Times*, Perth, Sunday 11 January 1914.

18   *Western Mail*, Perth, Friday 8 June 1917.

19   Abbott, op cit; Rolls, op cit.

## Chapter 15 – Alpacas, Buffalo, Banteng and Ostriches

1    Helen Cowie, 'Charles Ledger (1818-1905)', The Hispanic-Anglosphere: transnational networks, global communities (late 18th to early 20th centuries), https://hispanic-anglosphere.com/individuals/charles-ledger-1818-1905

2    *Sydney Morning Herald,* Wednesday 14 April 1875.

## Part Three – The Federation Plagues

1    www.daf.qld.gov.au/__data/assets/pdf_file/0014/55301/prickly-pear-story.pdf

## Chapter 16 – The Destruction of Western New South Wales

1    Daniel Lunney, 'Royal Commission of 1901 on the Western Lands of New South Wales – an Ecologist's Summary', meridian.allenpress.com/rzsnsw-other-books/book/616/chapter/12052465/Royal-Commission-of-1901-on-the-western-lands-of; unless noted, evidence to the commission is sourced to this.

2    www.parliament.tas.gov.au/tpl/PPWeb/1875/LC1875pp25.pdf

3    *Sydney Mail and New South Wales Advertiser*, Saturday 21 April 1877.

4    Lunney, op cit.

## Chapter 17 – The Rat, Mouse and Cat Plagues

1    Hunter, op cit.

2    firstfleetfellowship.org.au/library/first-fleetlist-livestock-provisions-plants-seeds/

3    Collins, op cit.

4    Ibid.

5    Ibid.

6    Julianne Farrell, 'Mouse Plagues – When, Where and Why', Department of Natural Resources and Environment, Queensland, 1999, storedgrain.com.au/wp-content/uploads/2013/06/24.pdf

7    Information on cat dispersal relies on John CZ Woinarski et al, *Cats in Australia, Companion and Killer*, CSIRO Publishing, 2019.

## Chapter 18 – The Prickly Pear's Green Hell

1    Arthur Phillip, *The Voyage of Governor Phillip to Botany Bay*, John Stockdale, Piccadilly, 1789.

2    Alan P Dodd, *The Biological Campaign against Prickly-Pear*, Government Printer, Brisbane, 1940.

3    Ibid, p 86.

4    Rolls, op cit.

5    *Gympie Times and Mary River Mining Gazette*, 17 July 1915, storedgrain.com.au/wp-content/uploads/2013/06/24.pdf

## Chapter 19 – The Great Cane Toad Con Job

1    The most detailed story of the cane toad disaster is by Nigel Turvey, *Cane Toads: A Tale of Sugar, Politics and Flawed Science*, Sydney University Press, 2013. The following chapters rely on Dr Turvey's account unless otherwise indicated.

2    Ibid, pp 107-109.

3    www.qhatlas.com.au/introducing-cane-toad

4    Ibid; Turvey, op cit, p 109.

5    Turvey, ibid, p 129.

6    Ibid, p 133.

## Chapter 20 – Walter Froggatt Tackles the Toad

1    Quoted in Luke Keogh, 'Introducing the Cane Toad', Queensland Historical Atlas, www.qhatlas.com.au/introducing-cane-toad

2    Turvey, op cit.

3    Ibid, p 147.

4    Ibid.

5    Ibid, p 150.

6    Ibid, pp 152–153.

7    Ibid, p 153.

8    Ibid, p 154.

9    www.environment.gov.au/biodiversity/invasive-species/publications/factsheet-cane-toad-bufo-marinus

10   David Dall, 'A Catastrophe of Cane Toads', *Outlooks on Pest Management* (2011) 22.

11   www.dpi.nsw.gov.au/biosecurity/vertebrate-pests/nia/key-new-incursions-species/new-incursions/cane-toad

12   www.invasivespeciesinitiative.com/cane-toad

## Chapter 21 – Ugly Times in the Rabbit Game

1    Rolls, op cit, p 338.

2    *Evening News*, Sydney, Friday 26 February 1909.

3    *Farmer and Settler*, Sydney, Friday 30 April 1909.

4    *Observer*, Adelaide, Saturday 1 July 1916.

5    *Australian Woman's Mirror*, Vol 3(8), 18 January 1927.

6    Ibid, Vol 3(10), 1 March 1927.

7    Eather and Cottle, op cit.

## Chapter 22 – Searching for the Magic Rabbit Cure

1    Rolls, op cit, p 149.

2    Ibid, p 60.

3    *South Australian Register*, Adelaide, Saturday 25 March 1893; and ibid p 258 for details about Herbert Butcher.

4    Rolls, op cit, p 203.

5    *Bulletin*, Vol 9, No 436, 9 June 1888.

6     Rolls, op cit, p 212.

7     Ibid, p 214.

8     *Sydney Stock and Station Journal*, Friday 28 March 1902.

9     Rolls, op cit, p 218.

10    William Rodier, 'The Rabbit Pest in Australia', 1918, self-published, nla. gov.au/nla.obj-2567957687/view?partId=nla.obj-2567982735#page/n0/ mode/1up

11    B Spiesschaert et al, 'The Current Status and Future Directions of Myxoma Virus, a Master in Immune Evasion' (2011). *Vet Res* 42(1), p 76.

### Chapter 23 – Dame Jean Macnamara Champions Myxoma Virus

1     Rolls, op cit, p 223; this chapter relies on Rolls's account, unless otherwise indicated.

2     Ibid, p 224.

3     Brain Coman, *Tooth and Nail: The Story of the Rabbit in Australia*, Text Publishing, 1999.

4     Rolls, op cit, p 235.

### Chapter 24 – Rabbit Haemorrhagic Disease (Calicivirus)

1     J Abrantes et al, 'Rabbit Haemorrhagic Disease (RHD) and Rabbit Haemorrhagic Disease Virus (RHDV): a review' (2012), *Vet Res* 43(1), p 12.

2     For more information on the rabbit haemorrhagic disease, one of the best accounts of the events surrounding its arrival is Brian Coman, op cit; information in this chapter draws on this account.

3     Abrantes, op cit.

### Chapter 25 – The Sandstone Island and Other Atrocities

1     *Argus*, Melbourne, Monday 24 September 1860.

2     Rolls, op cit, p 315.

3     *Argus,* Melbourne, Wednesday 14 May 1862.

4     Rolls, op cit, p 315.

5     *Annual Report of the Acclimatisation Society of Victoria*, 1864. www. biodiversitylibrary.org

### Chapter 26 – Viruses Are the New Control Species

1     David W Cerny, 'Australia to Spend over $11mn to Eradicate Carp by Releasing Herpes Virus into Rivers', 1 May 2016.

2     Richard J Edwards et al, 'Draft Genome Assembly of the Invasive Cane Toad, *Rhinella marina*', *GigaScience*, Vol 7(9), September 2018.

3     Ibid.

4    www.pestsmart.org.au/wp-content/uploads/2010/03/Social-impacts-
     FINAL-report.pdf

5    www.csiro.au, *Rabbit Biocontrol Case Study*, October 2017.

**Chapter 27 – Ethical Dilemmas in Feral Animal Control**

1    CA Marks et al, 'Fox control using a para-aminopropiophenone
     formulation with the M-44 ejector' (2004) *Animal Welfare* 13(4).

**Conclusion**

1    www.environment.gov.au/biodiversity/invasive-species/publications/
     brochure-australian-pest-animal-strategy

2    www.agriculture.gov.au/sites/default/files/sitecollectiondocuments/pests-
     diseases-weeds/consultation/apas-final.pdf

3    www.dpi.nsw.gov.au/fishing/aquatic/freshwater-pests/species/gambusia

4    pestsmart.org.au/wp-content/uploads/sites/3/2020/06/Incursions_2011.pdf

# Acknowledgements

You're only ever as good as your last game. After the warm response to *The Dogs that Made Australia*, I ventured into this story with an appreciable, but not unreasonable, weight of self-imposed expectation to produce an entertaining overview of the story of Australia's not-so-favourite animals.

Thanks to Trove, the National Library's fantastic online research portal, there's plenty of easily accessible historical material to support a foray into Australia's feral travails. Accordingly, the research and construction of a workable manuscript was one thing. Developing that raw product into a polished interesting book was quite another.

My publisher, Mary Rennie, my editor, Shannon Kelly, and HarperCollins senior editor Lachlan McLaine seek no recognition for their inestimable contributions to this project. Yet all have been a pleasure to work with and I wish to acknowledge their dedication, professionalism, and Job-like patience. I also wish to thank Darren Holt for another fantastic and entertaining cover, and my agent, Virginia Lloyd, for her advice and guidance.

Some blokes have all the luck. My wonderful partner, Kirsty, has selflessly provided me all the space and time I needed to research, write and edit this story. *The Ferals that Ate Australia* would not have been possible without Kirsty's forbearance, incredible sense of humour, wise counsel, and generosity. I hope this acknowledgment and the book's dedication adequately express my gratitude to her.